Dedicated to

My Treasured Mother & Father

Who Always Believed In Me

With Thanks To God

Acknowledgements

To my kind and loving father, Irv, the ultimate professor, and proof-reader in my life.

To my wonderful and brilliant mother, Marcia, the world's most under-appreciated diplomat, it's no wonder everyone loves you.

My brother, Mikey, for the most excellent cover design.

Willie Wagner and Wagner Printing (*Since 1853*) *Printers to the Universe*, is what I call them. Remember our breakfast club (before the movie).

To Lucero, gracias por tu adorable ayuda. Te amo mucho!

Barbara Glasser for her sage advice.

To Kat for being the first to address me as "Oh Great Guru."

To Madeline's, Uncommon Ground, and all the other Coffee shops in America for the endless supply of electricity.

To Mia for being my best friend.

David Konikoff, my loving friend and nephew from my past life.

Lloyd Eisenberg, thanks for everything. By the way, I like this better than digging ditches.

Thanks, Sue, for all your patience, assistance, and encouragement.

Thanks also to Lisa Belkov, Carol Able, Mark Kruger, Laura Parker.

And, not least, to my very own dream team, Nina Graybill, Andy Glatt, Terri Cohen, and *especially* my good friend, Tara Yelman.

Lastly thanks to all the authors, poets, wise women, and wise men without whose quotes there could be no compilation.

Table Of Contents

Friend ~

If you discover that a part of this book would benefit someone you know — please pass it on. If you know of someone who would benefit from the ideas in this book, but can't afford one — write me with the story and I'll see what I can do. To order more copies see page 429.

Jordan S. Metzger

Note To The Reader

The journey to discover a simple path to truth and enlightenment, was at first overwhelming. My intuition told me that it must exist, for Elias Canetti was keenly correct in saying:

'The great writers of aphorisms read as if they had all known each other well.'

These great writers also knew about the meaning of life. As a result <u>Lightning Fast Enlightenment</u> fell together in an even more illuminating way than I had originally envisioned. *Not only had the writers all known each other well, but I suspect they'd roomed together.*

As the great Masters speak there is an overwhelming collective consciousness, an uncanny agreement as to what is truth. We see, as never before, the relation between disparate philosophies throughout the world and over time. The people and ideas expressed herein lived all around the planet and had diverse places in the annals of history. Still, the dialogue created by this book is fluent across time and space, and pays no heed to artificial lines drawn by religion or race. <u>Lightning Fast Enlightenment</u> proves that what these exceptionally astute people wrote, or said, can be boiled down to intensely concentrated universal truths.

The grouping and juxtaposition of the passages reinforces their wisdom. One great thinker supports and adds to the views of the next. However, there is always an exception, and this one was best identified by George Santayana:

'Almost every wise saying has an opposite one, no less wise, to balance it.'

While this dynamism sometimes serves to skew meaning, or cultivate conflict, it can also add humor and insights previously unimaginable.

Yes, some quotes talk to each other —
And some quotes argue with each other —
But in <u>Lightning Fast Enlightenment</u>, they all lead to truth.

Jordan Seth Metzger
September 18, 1998

xi

Ten years' searching in the deep forest
Today great laughter at the edge of the lake.

Soen

The clearest way into the Universe is through a forest wilderness.

John Muir

Chapter One

The Ravine

What made me leave the cabin that night, I'll probably never know. All I remember is the strange impulse to go for an evening walk in the thick, late summer air. Usually I don't leave the cabin so late, but that evening I felt compelled to explore the path... the one that overlooks Azure Mountain Lake. I sensed an immediacy and, overwhelmed by this feeling, for some reason I can't explain, I went out...

It was incredibly humid. There I was out on a mountain path in the middle of the night, walking through a warm cloud. The mist rested on the ferns, so heavily that it squeezed them until they exuded a fragrance. I felt a little light–headed, so I stopped to catch my breath, leaning against a thin pine tree.

Then I saw this thing shimmering in the distance; its astoundingly vibrant electric blue was a striking contrast against the green nighttime forest. It hovered at about eye level, and was brilliantly illuminated, yet the color was so strangely mellow it didn't hurt my eyes. I had the ludicrous thought that maybe someone beamed down an iridescent, vibrating blue butterfly from another planet — an immensely vivid, concentrated form of dense blue energy. I had to follow it. I started running after it. I started running after it in such a hurry, that I forgot about the waterfall ravine.

I slipped. I'll never forget that plummeting sensation and the stars spinning... oddly unafraid I plunged toward the light, for a split second I thought of the passages I'd recently read about near–death experiences. It seemed an eternity before I hit the water. I must have been carried by the current, because I washed up by the edge of the lake, and awoke there under a white pine.

At first, even with the bright moonlight, everything appeared like a grainy photograph. I tried to focus, but couldn't. Then that blue light flashed across my eyes and things became sharply clear. There was a campfire crackling at the side of the translucent mountain lake. A sense of déjà vu told me I'd been in this place before, but tonight it had a more mystical, almost supernatural facade. It may have been the same place, but I saw things differently. The cool lake glimmered, a thousand crystals in the moonlight.

"What is going on here?" I wondered out loud, shaking my head side to side slowly. I nearly jumped back up the ravine when a heavy, bass voice just inches from the back of my head answered, "Welcome."

I turned quickly, to find myself staring at a startlingly statuesque man. The clear, bright whites of his eyes, incandescent against the backdrop of his deep ebony skin, were a stunning, almost ominous contrast to the moonlit night. His presence, while powerful, was polite; there was a strict firmness, but like my grandfather pretending to be angry, his eyes were laughing. The way he spoke too, seemingly hinted at a laugh or a mischievous smile ready to spontaneously beam. He possessed the aura and calmness of an ancient master of Aikido or Tai Chi, with movements projecting classically ancient wisdom and energy, blended with contemporary charisma. He wore old–style long and flowing robes, but looked more like he'd stepped back from the future. One thing for sure, he had nothing to prove.

Beyond him was a mass of objects that were still blurred. They were white and seemed to be made of sparkling, almost buzzing, light energy. He sat casually next to me, watching as I tried to make out what they were.

Then I saw it. In his hand was the blue light! "Hold this sapphire and you'll see them as they looked when they were last on earth." He passed the blue stone carefully in front of my eyes then handed it to me. The gem was glowing and warm. I felt a soft tranquil vibration as I held it, as if it had a small, flickering candle flame inside.

There they all were. I was looking at the throng of objects, but now I was holding the sapphire and they weren't objects. They were men and women, famous men and women! Famous, *dearly–departed*, men and women; so many illustrious and renowned people, I thought for a minute that I was dreaming... or dead. Per chance I'd passed

2

through the thinly veiled door from whence we all came. All these great people, many of whom were presumed to have passed on centuries ago — hadn't. I figured I must be dead too. I mean, it did seem like I had fallen for a really long time, and here I was surrounded by people who were long since pushing up daisies.

The Herculean guy turned to me, he seemed to be reading my thoughts, "They may be dead, but their energy lives on," he said, referring to the esteemed assembly. "Your energy will live on too someday, here that's common knowledge. Those you see around you who still live on earth... their presence is here by way of a deep dream; they will awake forgetting it ever happened. I invited them all here for tonight's Enlightening. They call me *Jah*, it's short for Eli*jah*. The Indians who lived on these very grounds before us would have called me your 'spirit helper.' "

I'd heard that in tradition the prophet Elijah lived on through eternity, incarnated into every generation; but if this were him, he wasn't what I'd pictured your average prophet to look like. "You can still see these people in their earthly form," Jah continued, "but to each other they are just intense, impassioned energy — shimmering lasers of light."

"Oh," I said, still without a hint as to *what* he was talking about, "but what am *I* doing here?"

"You are *supposed* to be here; that fall down the ravine was no coincidence: there is no such thing as coincidence. Everything comes about for a reason," Jah told me softly. "After eons and eons, if your soul has been attracted to an entity for some reason, it's your next step."

"Where am I?" I pondered aloud.

"Wherever you go, there you are, beyond that you do not need to know now." He read my mind and quickly added, "You're not dead though."

I was so glad to hear that, I didn't ask any more questions.

He took me aside and told me he'd been watching over me for a long while... I was lucky to still be here, given some of the dim–witted things I'd done. He said we'd known each other for some ages, on one plane or another. I understood, more through intuition than words, that he'd been my guardian angel since the beginning, helping me through hard times and meeting me in dreams or meditations to guide me. He had brought me here and this was my chance to repay

3

the favors. I felt a bit ashamed for wondering what I'd have to do and how much work it might be.

He continued to read my mind and instantly responded, "It's nothing big, simply be my messenger; write down what goes on here tonight and reveal it to those who are receptive, open–minded, and trustworthy enough to contemplate these Universal secrets," he appeared pleased, almost excited. *"The secret key has been placed in your hands."* I'd always been searching for truth, and then one day, the Truth found me.

I wasn't sure where or how, but it was true; I had definitely met him before. Maybe Jah just represented the ideal in us all, what we'll be when we live up to our potential. Legs crossed, sitting like a guru, he quietly turned to me saying kindly, "If you are ready, we will begin." With my slight nod he arose instantaneously; the sound of his robes crisply snapping immediately induced a hush over the entire group. He, too, was noiseless for a time, surveying the crowd and looking as content as a father whose baby had just uttered her first words, and they were 'dada'. To me the air was thick with the silence. Time seemed to move in slow motion as everyone looked up to Jah with reverence, ravenous for revelation. I felt comfortable and cozy now, like nothing bad could ever happen to me. As Jah gazed out benevolently at the assembly, the light and happiness of love radiated. He smiled, and from his lips the words flowed flawlessly.

"Finally the day has come. We have all been looking forward to this for a long time. What we say tonight will be transcribed for history so we'll go by subject, each beginning with a short address or tale. Intuition will help us achieve fluent conversation, and thus each statement will relate to the one before... You'll know when it's your turn."

"I, as you all know, am Jah, your conductor, and host for the evening!" He let a zany, uninhibited, song–like, laugh escape and fully outstretched his arms, gesturing to the crowd, "You have all said words worth repeating. <u>Congratulations</u>! Now... Let the symphony of wisdom begin!"

Returning to where I sat with the others, Jah folded down into a lotus position. He turned to me and held up a crystal goblet, in it some water. "Is the glass half empty or half full?" he asked.

4

My response was quick... "I'll be an optimist," I said, "it's half full."

"Ahh! It is, but it isn't," Jah smiled brightly. "True it is half full of water, but the other half is also full... of air. They both give you life, but *you* live in a trance, and take them both for granted."

"Appreciating and savoring every instant of life's adventure, becoming good at its game and having fun at it — it's all in the mind." Jah stopped talking, but there was no break in the rhythm or in the spirit. As if cued, the others began to join in.

~~~*~~~

William Shakespeare: There is nothing either good or bad, but thinking makes it so...

Earle Ferris: There's nothing neither good nor bad that can't be made more so.

Epictetus: There is nothing good or evil save in the will.

Mme. de La Fayette: If one thinks that one is happy, that is enough to be happy.

François de La Rochefoucauld: A person is never as happy or as unhappy as he thinks he is.

Charles C. Colton: There is the difference between happiness and wisdom: he that thinks himself the happiest man, really is so; but he that thinks himself the wisest, is generally the greatest fool.

Timothy Dwight: The happiest person is the person who thinks the most interesting thoughts.

Sir Philip Sidney: They are never alone that are accompanied with noble thoughts.

June Callwood:	No one is born happy.
Erich Fromm:	Happiness is not a gift of the gods.
Elbert Hubbard:	Happiness is a habit — cultivate it.
June Callwood:	It is an achievement brought about by inner productiveness.
Unknown:	Nothing more is needed to make a man unhappy than to believe he is.
A Fortune Cookie:	Your happiness is intertwined with your outlook on life.
Long Chenpa:	Since everything is an illusion, with some more perfect than others — with no relationship to good or bad, being or not–being, one might as well laugh from beginning to end.
Henry Ward Beecher:	The world's battlefields are in the heart.

Michel Eyquem de Montaigne:
A man is not hurt so much by what happens, as by his opinion of what happens.

Marcus Aurelius: If you are distressed by anything external, the pain is not due to the thing itself, but to your estimate of it; and thus you have the power to revoke it at any minute.

Jah:	As I lie in bed about to fall asleep one night, my dripping bathtub inspired the following speculation: There are three types of people who listen to dripping water. The first, annoyed not a little by the beating of the dripping water, remains in a state of insomnia for the entire night. The second, noticing the water, is bothered a bit, but soon ignores it, falling asleep; however the thought lingers of another chore to attend to in the morning. As the water drips, the third person, instead of experiencing annoyance on its account, perceives how steadily smooth the soothing dripping water can be, and thanks to its rhythmic tranquility, drifts off to the soundest slumber ever.
Epictetus:	It is not what happens to you, but how you react to it that matters.
Harold Azine:	Happiness... Is a matter of choice — *your* choice for yourself.
Unknown:	Every person has a choice — he can love the world's beauty and be happy, or he can hate its ugliness and be miserable.
Sister Mary Tricky:	If you really want to be happy, nobody can stop you.
François de La Rochefoucauld:	The happiness or unhappiness of men depends no less upon their dispositions than on their fortunes.
Aesop:	He that is discontented in one place will seldom be content in another.

Sir Roger L'Estrange:	It is not the place nor the condition, but the mind alone that can make anyone happy or miserable.
Abraham Lincoln:	Most folks are as happy as they make up their minds to be.
John Milton:	The mind is its own place, and in itself Can make a heaven of Hell, a hell of Heaven.
John Lilly:	In the province of the mind, what one believes to be true either is true or becomes true.
The Talmud:	There are those who are rich in the mind; there are those who are poor in the mind.
Louisa M. Alcott:	I had a pleasant time with my mind, for it was happy.
Duke Ellington:	What do you do with your beautiful, young, freckled mind?
Virginia Woolf:	I enjoy almost everything.
Helen Keller:	I have found life so beautiful.
William Lyon Phelps:	The happiest person is the person who thinks the most interesting thoughts, and we grow happier as we grow older.

Robert Louis Stevenson:

The world is so full of a number of things;
I'm sure we should all be as happy as
kings.

David Miller:
We have the power to make ourselves perfectly miserable or radiantly happy. It depends entirely on our thoughts. If we choose thoughts of health, life, good cheer, hope, love, and joy, happiness is ours.

Long Chenpa:
Since vision and commitment to vision have nothing to do with complacency or fear, one might as well be joyous.

~~~*~~~

Morris Wolfe:
It is easier and less costly to change the way people think about reality than it is to change reality.

Ralph Waldo Emerson: Life consists of what a man is thinking of all day.

Wilhelm Von Humboldt:
I am more and more convinced that our happiness or our unhappiness depends far more on the way we meet the events of life than on the nature of those events themselves.

Dale Carnegie:
Everybody in the world is seeking happiness and there is one sure way to find it. That is by controlling your thoughts. Happiness does not depend on outward conditions. It isn't what you have or who you are or where you are or what you are doing that makes you happy or unhappy. It is what you think about it.

Sir William Bragg:
The important thing in science is not so much to obtain new facts as to discover new ways of thinking about them.

Julius Rosenwald:	When you have a lemon, make a lemonade.
Italian Proverb:	Since the house is on fire let us warm ourselves.
George Bernard Shaw:	The only way to avoid being miserable is not to have enough leisure to wonder whether you are happy or not.
Jacopo Sannazaro:	Man is only miserable so far as he thinks himself so.
Henry David Thoreau:	Man is the artificer of his own happiness.
Ludwig Wittgenstein:	The world of those who are happy is different from those who are not.

Book of Proverbs 15:15:

The miserable man is unhappy every day; but the cheerful man enjoys a constant feast.

A Bumper Sticker:	All I want is a little more than I'll ever get.
Spanish Proverb:	Since we cannot get what we like, let us like what we can get.
Eddie Rickenbacker:	If you have all the fresh water you want to drink and all the food you want to eat, you ought never to complain about anything.
W. C. Fields:	Once, during Prohibition, I was forced to live on nothing but food and water.
Aldous Huxley:	Most human beings have an almost infinite capacity for taking things for granted.
Kentucky Saying:	My feet are cold, one says, and the legless man replies: "So are mine. So are mine."

Henry Kirke White:	"I never complained of my condition but once," said an old man, "When my feet were bare, and I had no money to buy shoes; I met a man without feet and became contented."
Jah:	If you're bald you never have to worry about having a bad hair day.
Bud Lutz:	I cried for the man with no hair, until I met the man with no head.
Charles de Montesquieu:	If only we wanted to be happy it would be easy; but we want to be happier than other people, which is almost always difficult, since we think them happier than they are.
Eric Bogosian:	I spend a lot of time thinking what it would be like to be other people.
Cary Grant:	Everybody wants to be Cary Grant, even *I want to be Cary Grant.*
Jay McInerney:	Marilyn Monroe probably wished she was Marilyn Monroe.
Maria Callas:	I would like to be Maria, but there is La Callas who demands that I carry myself with her dignity.
Jah:	Others often don't have all that you think they do.
Ralph Waldo Emerson:	Ah, if the rich were rich as the poor fancy riches!

Proverbs 13:7:	One man pretends to be rich and has nothing; Another professes to be poor and has much wealth.
Sir Boyle Roche:	Many thousands of them were destitute of even the goods they possessed.
Mike Todd:	I've never been poor, only broke. Being poor is a frame of mind. Being broke is only a temporary situation.
David Miller:	Even with very little money, we are rich if we are cheerful, but poor and miserable indeed is the morose, gloomy, sad, melancholy person, regardless of how much money he may own.
Jean Paul Getty:	Remember, a billion dollars isn't worth what it used to be.
Samuel Goldwyn:	He's living beyond his means, but he can afford it.

Senator Everett McKinley Dirksen:
A billion here, a billion there, and pretty soon you're talking about real money.

| Yogi Berra: | A nickel ain't worth a dime any more. |
| Samuel Johnson: | The habit of looking on the bright side of every event is worth more than a thousand pound a year. |

Oliver Wendell Holmes:

... happiness, I'm sure from having known many successful men, cannot be won simply by being counsel for great corporations and having a income of fifty–thousand dollars.

Balguy:

Contentment is a pearl of great price, and whoever procures it at the expense of ten thousand desires makes a wise and a happy purchase.

Robert Herrick:

Learn this of me, where e'r thy lot doth fall;
  Short lot, or not, to be content with all.

Schopenhauer:

We seldom think of what we have but always of what we lack.

F. Johnson:

If we fasten our attention on what we have, rather than on what we lack, a very little wealth is sufficient.

"The Beverly Hillbillies"

Jed Clampett:

Pearl, what d'ya think? Think I oughta move?

Cousin Pearl:

Jed, how can ya even ask? Look around ya. You're eight miles from yore nearest neighbor. Yore overrun with skunks, possums, coyotes, bobcats. You use kerosene lamps fer light and you cook on a wood stove summer and winter. Yore drinkin' homemade moonshine and washin' with homemade lye soap. And yore bathroom is fifty feet from the house and you ask "Should I move?"

Jed Clampett:

I reckon yore right. A man'd be a dang fool to leave all this!

Seneca:	... which may serve to show us, that it is the mind, and not the sum, that makes any person rich... No one can be poor that has enough, nor rich, that covets more than he has.
Marcus Aurelius:	Let not your mind run on what you lack as much as on what you have already. Of the things you have, select the best; and then reflect how eagerly they would have been sought if you did not have them.
Benjamin Disraeli:	Never take anything for granted.
G. K. Chesterton:	The way to love anything is to realize that it might be lost.
Roger de Bussy–Rabutin:	

Roger de Bussy–Rabutin:

> When we can't have what we love
> we must love what we have.

Proverbs 17:1:	Better a dry crust with peace, Than a house full of feasting with strife.
Chinese Proverb:	Peace in a thatched hut — that is happiness.
C. S. Lewis:	The sun looks down on nothing half so good as a household laughing together over a meal.
Thomas Fuller:	Better fare hard with good people than feast it with bad.
Robert G. Ingersoll:	A palace without affection is a poor hovel, and the meanest hut with love in it is a palace for the soul.

14

Abd–er–Rahman III of Spain:

I have now reigned about fifty years in victory or peace, beloved by my subjects, dreaded by my enemies, and respected by my allies. Riches and honors, power and pleasure, have waited on my call, nor does any earthly blessing appear to have been wanting to my felicity. In this situation I have diligently numbered the days of pure and genuine happiness which have fallen to my lot: they amount to fourteen.

Napoleon:

I have never known six happy days in my life.

Seneca:

If you have what seems to you to be insufficient, then you will be miserable even if you possess the world.

Charles Caleb Colton:

True contentment depends not on what we have; a tub was large enough for Diogenes, but a world was too little for Alexander.

Frederic Leighton:

Great is he who enjoys his earthenware as if it were plate, and not less great is the man to whom all his plate is no more than earthenware.

François de La Rochefoucauld:

Happiness is in the taste, and not in the things themselves. It is by having what we like that we are made happy, not by having what others think desirable.

Arthur Zimmerman:

He who wants little always has enough.

Jewish Proverb:

What a man wants, he does not have; what he has, he does not prize.

Epictetus:	He is a wise man who does not grieve for the things which he has not, but rejoices for those which he has.
Ogden Nash:	People who have what they want are very fond of telling people who haven't what they want that they really don't want it.
George Bernard Shaw:	As long as I have a want, I have a reason for living. Satisfaction is death.
Charles Lamb:	My motto is, "Contented with little, yet wishing for more."
Rabbi Hyman Schachtel:	
	Happiness is not having what you want, but wanting what you have.
Ken S. Keyes, Jr.:	To be upset over what you don't have is to waste what you do have.
Albert Camus:	If there is a sin against life, it consists... in hoping for another life and in eluding the implacable grandeur of this life.
Epicurus:	Do not spoil what you have by desiring what you have not; but remember that what you now have was once among the things you only hoped for.
Marlon Brando:	It's the hardest thing in the world to accept a little success and leave it that way.
Unknown:	Success is getting what you want; happiness is wanting what you get.
Oscar Wilde:	In this world there are only two tragedies. One is not getting what one wants, and the other is getting it.

| W. D. Hoard: | Happiness doesn't depend on what we have, but it does depend on how we feel towards what we have. We can be happy with little and miserable with much. |

~~~*~~~

| Channing Pollock: | Happiness is a waystation between too little and too much. |

| Unknown: | If you can't have the best of everything, make the best of what you have. |

| Steven Wright: | You can't have everything, where would you put it? |

| Maurice Sendak: | There must be more to life than having everything! |

Robert Louis Stevenson:

Make the most of the best and the least of the worst.

Antoine de Saint–Exupéry:

The men where you live raise five thousand roses in the same garden — and they do not find in it what they are looking for. And yet what they are looking for could be found in one single rose.

| Baba Ram Dass: | If I see one dilemma with Western man, it's that he can't accept how beautiful he is. He can't accept that he is pure light, that he's pure love, that he's pure consciousness, that he's divine. |

| Socrates: | Contentment is natural wealth, luxury is artificial poverty. |

Titus Maccius Plautus:	If you are but content, you have enough to live upon with comfort.
Earl Wilson:	Nature does her best to teach us. The more we overeat, the harder she makes it for us to get close to the table.
David Miller:	... wherever there is an abundance of wealth, of supplies, of food, there the desire, the enjoyment and the appetite are less abundant... But the desire, the appetite and the appreciation increase where there is the smallest amount of material possessions. Two things are necessary for the enjoyment of life: (1) the material means and (2) the desire, the appetite. One is just as important as the other. We observe that whenever a person has a steady plentiful supply of tasty food, his appetite for it diminishes... On the other hand, whenever the food is scarce, then as a rule there is no limit to the appetite, the desire, and the enjoyment. It would appear that nature has provided a safety valve, a governor, so that no one can get away with more than is allotted to him.
Giles:	If the poor man cannot always get meat, the rich man cannot always digest it.
Logan Pearsall Smith:	That's what this section is about. There are two things to aim at in life: first, to get what you want; and after that, to enjoy it. Only the wisest of mankind achieve the second.
William Cobbett:	It is not the greatness of a man's means that makes him independent, so much as the smallness of his wants.

18

Socrates:	Those who want the fewest things are nearest to the gods.
Henry David Thoreau:	A man is rich in proportion to the number of things which he can afford to let alone.
Eric Hoffer:	Man is a luxury–loving animal. His greatest exertions are made in pursuit not of necessities but of superfluities.
Igor Fedorovich Stravinsky:	
	If everything would be permitted to me, I would feel lost in this abyss of freedom.
Louis Gabriel Ambroise de Boland:	
	To demand nothing and complain of no one is an excellent recipe for happiness.
Kathleen Halter:	I kept saying to myself over and over, "Now listen, as long as you can walk and feed yourself and are free from intense pain, you ought to be the happiest person in the world."
A British Veteran:	There are two things that I shall always remember. The first is the sound of men's voices in the sea at night, when you can't stop to pick them up... and the other is the sound of people's voices complaining in the shops at home.

"Calvin and Hobbes"
Bill Watterson

Calvin: Some people complain all the time! They complain about the least little thing! If something bugs them, they never let go of it! They just go on and on, long after any one else is interested! It's just complain, complain, complain! People who gripe all the time really drive me nuts! You'd think they'd change the subject after a while, but they never do! They just keep griping until you start to wonder, "What's wrong with this idiot?" But they go on complaining and repeating what they've already said!

Hobbes: Maybe they're not very self–aware.

Calvin: Boy, that's *another* thing that gets on my nerves!

Jewish Proverbs: When life isn't the way you like it, like it the way it is.
When things are not as you like, like them as they are.
What can't be avoided can be welcomed.

Gabrielle "Coco" Chanel:
I invented my life by taking for granted that everything I did not like would have an opposite, which I would like.

~~~*~~~

Homer Phillips: One of the most difficult mountains for people to climb is the one they make out of a molehill.

Quentin Crisp: You should treat all disasters as if they were trivialities. But never treat a triviality as if it were a disaster.

Stuart Hughes:	No issue is so small that it can't be blown out of proportion.
Douglas Jerrold:	Some people are so fond of ill–luck that they run halfway to meet it.
Jewish Proverb:	From happiness to sorrow takes a moment; from sorrow to happiness takes years.
Arthur Zimmerman:	That happy state of mind, so rarely possessed, in which we can say, "I have enough," is the highest attainment of philosophy. Happiness consists, not in possessing much, but in being content with what we possess.
Plutarch:	"It is a great blessing to possess what one wishes," said one to an ancient philosopher. — "It is greater still," was the reply, "Not to desire what one does not possess."
Charles Dickens:	Reflect upon your present blessings, of which every man has many; not on your past misfortunes, of which all men have some.
Lucy Larcom:	I do not own an inch of land, But all I see is mine.
Elizabeth "Dibby" Clementine Gillies:	I can't hear and I can't see and I can't walk, but other than that I'm fine.
James Thurber:	Who flies afar from the sphere of sorrow is here today and here tomorrow.

Sara Teasdale:

Then like an old time orator
  Impressively he rose;
I make the most of all that comes
  And the least of all that goes.

~~~*~~~

Chapter Two

All Geniuses

I whispered to Jah, "I understand when you say everything we need to know to feel happy and enlightened is within us, but at times I find stuff like this difficult to accept. I can understand it intellectually, but living it is another story. How can we be positive that the answer to our quest is already within our soul? I'm not sure I can explain all this when I get back."

"Nonsense," Jah's deep voice retorted, "you'll do fine. Just tell everybody to look at children; sometimes we have neglected life's essence for so long that we have forgot *what* we have forgotten. The secret becomes progressively more elusive as the years pass. I myself was once so far lost that I didn't even realize there was something missing.

"Remember what Galileo once said? (I had no idea, but that didn't seem to bother Jah much):

> 'You cannot teach a man anything. You can only
> help him to find it among himself.'

"Everything we need lives in us now," Jah added emphatically. "It's a matter of chipping away at marble that has already been formed.

"As the brain matures, its filtering capacity amplifies. This helps us make our way in the material world; it's hard to stay on the road if you are in constant ecstasy over the beauty of each tree you pass. But often the filter takes over, it strains out more and more of the really substantial stuff; important things, like: It's not whether you win or lose... but how you play the game."

He persisted, "It pays at times to be less 'sophisticated' — to break down the barriers of our brain's filters. This can be done by playing with kids. When they play, kids aren't afraid someone will think they look childish. If they appear foolish to us, they don't care. Kids don't succumb to the same arbitrary societal norms to which we've somehow subscribed to become shackled. A child is enthralled by the moment; the everlasting here and now. Kids need no purpose in their endeavors. There is nowhere else they have to be, nothing pressing to be accomplished. The world, viewed with perpetually new eyes, is entertaining and enthralling. Watch a child laugh and smile as he chases a chipmunk. The secret is not far."

~~~*~~~

Palladas: Our Life's a stage, a playground; learn to play.

Vladimir Horowitz: You can't be serious 24 hours a day. You have to take half an hour or an hour a day to be childish.

Henry David Thoreau: Children, who play life, discern its true law and relations more clearly than men...

Basho: Look, children,
hail–stones!
Let's rush out!

Friedrich Nietzsche: In every real man a child is hidden that wants to play.

Friedrich Von Schiller: Man only plays when in the full meaning of the word he is a man, and he is only completely a man when he plays.

Heraclitus: Man is most nearly himself when he achieves the seriousness of a child at play.

Ralph Waldo Emerson: It is a happy talent to know how to play.

24

Madeleine L'Engle: In real play, which is real concentration, the child is not only outside time, he is outside *himself*. He has thrown himself completely into whatever it is that he is doing. A child playing a game, building a sand castle, painting a picture, is completely *in* what he is doing. His *self*–consciousness is gone; his consciousness is wholly focused outside himself.

~~~*~~~

"Wings of Desire"
Wim Wenders and Peter Handke:
    When the child was a child
      It had no opinions about anything.
    It had no habits.
      It sat crossed–legged, took off running, had a cowlick in its hair, and didn't make a face when photographed.

Alistair Reid: "Did you have a happy childhood?" is a false question. As a child I did not know what happiness was, and whether I was happy or not. I was too busy *being*.

G. K. Chesterton: The human race, to which so many of my readers belong, has been playing at children's games from the beginning, which is a nuisance for the few people who grow up.

Joseph Heller: When I grow up I want to be a little boy.

Bernie S. Siegel, M.D.:
    Being childlike is not childish.

Clifton Fadiman: Being a child is in itself a profession.

25

Abraham Sutzkever:	If you carry your childhood with you, you never become older.
Mark Twain:	My mother had a great deal of trouble with me, but I think she enjoyed it.
Isaac Bickerstaffe:	Young fellows will be young fellows.
Quentin Crewe:	The children despise their parents until the age of 40, when they suddenly become just like them — thus preserving the system.
Charles Wadsworth:	By the time a man realizes that maybe his father was right, he usually has a son who thinks he's wrong.
Mark Twain:	When I was a boy of fourteen, my father was so ignorant I could hardly stand to have the old man around. But when I got to be twenty–one, I was astonished at how much the old man had learned in seven years.

~~~*~~~

Mickey Rooney:	I was a fourteen year old boy for thirty years.
Shirley Temple:	When I was fourteen, I was the oldest I ever was... I've been getting younger ever since.
V. S. Pritchett:	I shall never be as old as I was between twenty and thirty.
Harry Blackstone, Jr.:	Nothing I do can't be done by a 10 year old... With 15 years of practice.

26

Satchel Paige:	How old would you be if you didn't know how old you was?
A Seventy–year–old man:	I do not feel old inside — I feel no great change. I'm simply appalled at how old my children are.
Jerry Garcia:	I still feel like a kid, I feel that anyone who looks like an adult is older than me.
110 Year Old Man Interviewed on CNN:	I feel *good*!
Tom Lehrer:	It's a sobering thought that when Mozart was my age, he had been dead for two years.
Casey Stengel:	A lot of people my age are dead at the present time.
Frank Bering:	Live your life and forget your age.
Mark Twain:	Age is a matter of the mind. If you don't mind, it doesn't matter.
Guatemalan Saying:	Everyone is the age of their heart.
Gertrude Stein:	We are always the same age inside.
Bernard Mannes Baruch:	To me, old age is always fifteen years older than I am.
Lillian Carter:	Sure, I'm for helping the elderly. I'm going to be old myself someday.
Tom Stoppard:	Age is a very high price to pay for maturity.

Maurice Chevalier:	Old age isn't so bad when you consider the alternative.
Robert Lucky:	Twenty–one, then senility sets in.
Margaret Thatcher:	I'd like to go on being thirty–five for a long time.
Lady Astor:	I refuse to admit I'm more than fifty–two even if that does make my sons illegitimate.
Lucille Ball:	The secret of staying young is to live hon estly, eat slowly, and lie about your age.
Leon Edel:	The answer to old age is to keep one's mind busy and to go on with one's life as if it were interminable. I always admire Chekhov for building a new house when he was dying of tuberculosis.
Norman Vincent Peale:	The longer I live the more I am convinced that neither age nor circumstance need to deprive us of energy and vitality.
André Maurois:	Growing old is no more than a bad habit which a busy person has no time to form.
Casey Stengel:	The trick is growing up without growing old.
Jah:	As a point of trivia, it's been proven that old dogs learn tricks faster than younger dogs, whether the tricks are old or new.
Plato:	It is always in season for old men to learn. He who is of a calm and happy nature will hardly feel the pressure of age.

Marcus Tullius Cicero:	Give me a young man in whom there is something of the old, and an old man in whom there is something of the young. Guided so, a man may grow old in body but never in mind.
Buddy Ebsen:	The one thing wrong with the younger generation is that I don't belong to it any more.
Pablo Picasso:	One starts to get young at the age of 60, and then its too late.
Irish Saying:	Oh to be seventy again! You're not as young as you used to be, but you're not as old as you're going to be.
Casey Stengel:	I'll never make the mistake of bein' seventy again!
Golda Meir:	Being seventy is not a sin.
George Burns:	People keep asking me how it feels to be ninety–five, and I tell them I feel just as good as I did when I was ninety–four.
"Newhart" George Utley:	If you make it to be one hundred, that fat weather guy will announce your name on TV.
"The Golden Girls" Rose Nyland:	My mother always used to say: "The older you get, the better you get — unless you're a banana."
George Burns:	You can't help getting older, but you don't have to get old.
Mae West:	You're never too old to become younger.

Zsa Zsa Gabor:	You're never too young to be younger.
Robert Frost:	A diplomatist is a man who always remembers a woman's birthday, but never remembers her age.
Icelandic Saying:	Everyone wants to live long, but no one wants to be called old.
Ashley Montague:	The idea is to die young as late as possible.
Oscar Wilde:	Those whom the gods love grow young.
Deuteronomy 34:7:	Moses was a hundred and twenty years old when he died; his eye was not dimmed, and his natural force had not abated.

~~~*~~~

James A. Garfield:	If wrinkles must be written upon our brows, let them not be written upon the heart. The spirit should not grow old.
Charles Dickens:	Cheerfulness and content are great beautifiers, and famous preservers of youthful looks.

William "Refrigerator" Perry:
　　　　　　Even when I was little, I was big.

Tom Robbins:	When they tell you to grow up, they mean stop growing.
Berkeley:	Our youth we can have but today; We may always find time to grow old.

Robert Louis Stevenson:
　　　　　　Youth is wholly experimental.

George Bernard Shaw: [Youth is] Far too good to be wasted on children.

Lord Asquith: Youth would be an ideal state if it came much later in life.

William Lyon Phelps: The belief that youth is the happiest time of life is founded on a fallacy.

William Hepworth Thompson: We are none of us infallible, not even the youngest.

French Proverb: Ask the young; they know everything.

James Matthew Barrie: I am not young enough to know everything.

Holbrook Jackson: No one is ever old enough to know better.

George Bernard Shaw: Even the youngest of us may be wrong sometimes.

Lord Chesterfield: Young men are apt to think themselves wise enough, as drunken men are apt to think themselves sober enough.

J. Robert Oppenheimer: There are children playing in the street who could solve some of my top problems in physics, because they have modes of sensory perception that I lost long ago.

Shunryu Suzuki: If your mind is empty, it is always ready for anything; it is open to everything. In the beginner's mind there are many possibilities, but in the expert's there are few.

Friedrich Wilhelm Nietzsche:
> Many a man fails to become a great thinker only because his memory is too good.

Hans Christian Andersen:
> "But the Emperor has nothing on at all!" cried a little child.

Kitaro Nishida:
> If my heart can become pure and simple like that of a child, I think there probably can be no greater happiness than this.

Confucius:
> A great man never loses the simplicity of a child.

Mencius:
> A great man is he who has not lost the heart of a child.

Antoine de Saint–Exupéry:
> It is only with the heart that one can see rightly; what is essential is invisible to the eye.

Soyen Shaku:
> Have the fearless attitude of a hero and the loving heart of a child.

Takuan:
> Zen is to have the heart and soul of a little child.

Meng–tzu:
> Great man retains child's mind.

Ruth Draper:
> Try to look at everything through the eyes of a child.

Vimalia McClure:
> Children, who are closer to their birth and thus to the experience of oneness, rightly reject hypocrisy.

Benjamin Hoff: Is it a mere coincidence that the Chinese suffix *tse*, which has come to mean "master," literally means *child*?

Diogenes: I threw my cup away when I saw a child drinking from his hands at the trough.

Antoine de Saint–Exupéry:
Grown–ups never understand anything for themselves, and it is tiresome for children to be always and forever explaining things to them.

Eric Hoffer: It is the malady of our age that the young are so busy teaching us that they have no time left to learn.

Paula Poundstone: Adults are always asking little kids what they want to be when they grow up — 'cause they're looking for ideas.

~~~*~~~

Rachel Carson: A child's world is fresh and new and beautiful, full of wonder and excitement. It is our misfortune that for most of us that clear–eyed vision, that true instinct for what is beautiful and awe–inspiring, is dimmed and even lost before we reach adulthood.

Luke 18:17: Whosoever shall not receive the kingdom of God as a little child shall in no wise enter therein.

Judith "Miss Manners" Martin:
We are all born charming, fresh, and spontaneous, and must be civilized before we are fit to participate in society.

Eric Berne:	We are born princes and the civilizing process makes us frogs.
Kermit The Frog:	It's not that easy bein' green.
Ray Kroc:	When you're green, you're growing. When you're ripe, you rot.
G. K. Chesterton:	Gullibility is the key to all adventures. The greenhorn is the ultimate victor in every thing; it is he that gets the most out of life.
Saul Bellow:	The child in me is delighted. The adult in me is skeptical.

Anton Pavlovich Chekhov:

In nature a repulsive caterpillar turns into a lovely butterfly. But with human beings it is the other way round: a lovely butterfly turns into a repulsive caterpillar.

Taisen Deshimaru:	From your first day at school you are cut off from life to make theories.
Alexandre Dumas:	How is it that little children are so intelligent and men so stupid, it must be education that does it.
Noel Coward:	I've over–educated myself in all the things I shouldn't have known.
"The Matchmaker" Mrs. Levi:	The very young are almost as smart as the very old,... it's in the middle that you get in all the trouble.
Aldous Huxley:	We are all geniuses up to the age of ten.

R. Buckminster Fuller: Everyone is born a genius, but the process of living de–geniuses them.

Pablo Picasso: Every child is an artist. The problem is how to remain an artist once he grows up.

George Bernard Shaw: Common sense is instinct. Enough of it is genius.

Ralph Waldo Emerson: Success is ... to win the respect of intelligent persons and the affection of children.

J. D. Salinger: Some of my best friends are children. In fact all of my best friends are children.

Addison Walker: It's not true that nice guys finish last. Nice guys are winners before the game even starts.

Grantland Rice: For when the One Great Scorer comes
  To write against your name,
He marks — not that you won or lost —
  But how you played the game.

~~~*~~~

Chapter Three

The Greatest
Thing In The World Is...

The night breeze brought a gift of spicy aromatic air from the fresh, fragrant crystal lake on whose shore we rested. Maybe I was in a trance, but I felt more alive than ever; somehow my time there seemed more real than even now. The light wind, mixed with the sweet humidity of the mountain forest summertime air, made my seat on the soft sandy shore as warm and comfortable as a kid listening to stories on grandma's lap. Jah, rising again from the calmness of his lotus position, must have been thinking of what had just been said; his head instinctively nodded as he smiled, then his clear voice rang out.

"Strolling his way to Congress every morning, during the depression of the 1930's, the late Representative Sol Bloom, from the Empire State of New York, always dropped a coin onto the sidewalks of Capitol Hill. If asked why, he'd laughingly reply, 'Somebody is sure to find it and be happy the rest of the day.' "

Jah's tone softened as he turned serious, "One must realize that what we do comes back to us, usually not today, sometimes tomorrow, perhaps in another lifetime — but it always comes back — measure for measure. This is one of the foremost principles of the universe, *the* major corollary to the Golden Rule. As assuredly as clapping two hands together sparks a vibration that can be heard as a sound, as positively as a pebble plunging into a pond perpetrates ripples, cause and effect does exist in this universe. Permitting pollution of the sea, albeit far from my home, will probably some day find me

37

with toxic fish on my table. Let's be accountable for what happens in this world. Remaining in view of the fact that we are all one, and that a good deed for someone else is indeed a good deed for us, pays more than ever envisioned.

"In the summer of 1949, Dr. Albert Schweitzer was met by a large contingent of friends and admirers in Grand Central Station. Suddenly he hurried off in another direction. When his bewildered companions finally caught up with him, they discovered that upon spotting an elderly woman lugging heavy suitcases, he had gone to assist her in carrying her bags to a cab.

"Next time you walk down the street, study the contrast in the people you meet. Some bright and lighthearted, others like frozen fish." Jah recounted, "There was a time when most of the people I passed looked more like the fish. I wondered: What's wrong with all these people? Suddenly I stopped and found myself gazing up at my own somber expression in a store window. I had a flash of cognition, and stood still, struck with the secret: ninety percent of the solemn looks I was getting, were my own reflection! Other people reflecting off of me like a mirror. Right then I decided I'd be a little more zany, easygoing, and a bit more off guard; we do live on a funny planet.

"These days, taking into account inflation, maybe it takes more than Congressman Bloom's coin to make someone glad for a whole day. Nonetheless you'd be awfully surprised at how golden it makes you, and those you encounter, feel when you merely dish out a 'Good Morning!' with a beaming grin." Jah scratched his chin looking deep in thought, as if remembering for a moment before he went on:

"It is told in the Talmud that a man known as Baruqa of Huza once had the honor to meet the Prophet Elijah in the marketplace. Baruqa asked, 'Is there anyone among all these people who will have a share in the World–to–Come?'

'There is none,' came Elijah's solemnly sad answer.

Later two men came to the market, and Elijah said to Baruqa, 'Those two will have a share in the World–to–Come!'

Baruqa was excited, he approached the newcomers to query as to their occupation. They answered,

'When we see someone who is sad, we cheer him up. When we see two people quarreling, we try to make peace between them.' "

Jah's smile radiated, and he added, "Here's an experiment to try: Walk down the street, beam at <u>everyone</u> you see, and say with a tone like you really mean it: *'Good morning!'* or *'How are you today.'* You can even fake it at first, some will wonder what you put in your tea... but who cares. Now, if they say 'Fine' or 'Okay,' reply with something like, 'That's fantastic!' At first you'll just be snickering under your breath, or maybe unable to hold back a laugh, but, that's just the idea; you can't *genuinely* laugh without lightening your mood.

"It worked on me one day," Jah told us. "I was on a motorcycle trip across a strange land called America, I entered the Stuart Florida Post Office with the intention of mailing an ordinary letter:

> An old black preacher came up to me just bursting with the light of happiness. Well, this fine gentleman saw me, a total stranger, and he just about couldn't hold back his enthusiasm.
>
> 'How y'all doin' today!' he said, turning his words into joviality with a southern accent.
>
> 'Good,' I said timidly, caught a bit off guard.
>
> 'Well that makes me feel good!' his smile was still beaming.
>
> 'You know what?' I returned.
>
> 'What?' he asked.
>
> 'In that case I feel great!'

"We spent the next half hour together. That old man, embodying the epitome of human society, will not soon be forgotten by me, and I'm sure he has a place in the World–to–Come."

~~~*~~~

Christopher Morley: Do every day, something no one else would be silly enough to do.

René Auberjonois:	Show me a guy who's afraid to look bad, and I'll show you a guy you can beat every time.
Sidney J. Harris:	The paradox in games is that most games are no fun unless you take them seriously; but when you take them seriously, they cease being games.
Yogi Berra:	The game is supposed to be fun. If you have a bad day, don't worry about it. You can't expect to get a hit every game.
Jim Bouton:	Have fun.
Bugs Bunny:	I don't ask questions, I just have fun.
George Yeo:	We have to pursue this subject of fun very seriously if we want to stay competitive in the twenty–first century.
Yogi Berra:	You can't win all the time. There are guys out there who are better than you.
"Pogo" Walt Kelly:	Don't take life so serious — it ain't no how permanent.
Yoko Ono:	I saw that nothing was permanent.
Herodotus:	If a man insisted always on being serious, and never allowed himself a bit of fun and relaxation, he would go mad or become unstable without knowing it.
Elbert Hubbard:	Do not take life so seriously; you will never get out of it alive.

Cynthia Heimel:	When in doubt, make a fool of yourself. There is a microscopically thin line between being brilliantly creative and acting like the most gigantic idiot on earth. So what the hell, leap.
Rudolf Nureev:	I'm forty years old. It's time to indulge, to be foolish if I wish.
Howard Ogden:	Don't take yourself too seriously. And don't be too serious about not taking your self too seriously.
Nicholas Murray Butler:	The one serious conviction that a man should have is that nothing should be taken too seriously.
Billy Wilder:	If there's one thing I hate more than not being taken seriously, it's being taken too seriously.
A Fortune Cookie:	It's a good thing that life is not as serious as it seems to the waiter.
Austrian Proverb:	The situation is hopeless, but not serious.
Gilbert Keith Chesterton:	Angels can fly because they take themselves lightly.
Ovid:	Burdens become light when cheerfully borne.
Nikita Khrushchev:	Life is short. Live it up.
Scottish Proverb:	Be happy while you're living for you're a long time dead.

~~~*~~~

Laurence Sterne:	Every time a man smiles, and much more when he laughs, it adds something to his fragment of life.
The Talmud:	He gives little who gives much with a frown; he gives much who gives a little with a smile.

Nixon Waterman:	Life's a mirror, if we smile
	    Smiles come back to greet us.
	If we're frowning all the while
	    Frowns forever meet us.

The Talmud:	Better is he who offers a smiling countenance then he who offers milk.
The Koran:	He deserves Paradise who makes his companions laugh.
Rabbi Shammai:	Receive all men with a cheerful countenance.
The Mishnah:	Like a water reflects a face, so does the heart of man.
Arthur Rubinstein:	I have found that if you love life, life will love you back.

Madeline S. Bridges:	For life is the mirror of king and slave,
	    'Tis just what we are and do;
	Then give to the world the best you have
	    And the best will come back to you.

Thomas Carlyle:	There is no greater every–day virtue than cheerfulness.

Charles Buxton:	You've not fulfilled every duty unless you have fulfilled that of being cheerful and pleasant.
Mark Twain:	The best way to cheer yourself up is to try to cheer somebody else up.
Dr. Karl Menninger:	Love cures people — both the ones who give it and the ones who receive it.
Elie Wiesel:	We have to go into the despair and go beyond it, by working and doing for somebody else, by using it for something else.
David Miller:	A noble character acquires happiness through the opportunity of making someone else happy. It is only that kind of kindness that will lead to happiness.

Robert Louis Stevenson:

A happy man or woman is a better thing to find than a five pound bank note. Their entrance to the room is as though another candle has been lighted.

Adlai Stevenson:	It is better to light one candle than to curse the darkness.
Unknown:	A candle loses nothing by lighting another candle.
Jah:	Yet it gains light, warmth, and companionship.
The Talmud:	A light for one is a light for a hundred.

Anne Frank:	Whoever is happy will make others happy too. He who has courage and faith will never perish in misery!
Josiah Gilbert Holland:	Joys divided are increased.
Mark Twain:	Grief can take care of itself; but to get the full value of a joy you must have somebody you divide it with.
Ralph Waldo Emerson:	So of cheerfulness, or a good temper, the more it is spent, the more remains.
Washington Irving:	How easy it is for one benevolent being to defuse pleasure around him.
John Bunyan:	A man there was, though some did count him mad, The more he cast away the more he had.
Old Epitaph:	What I gave, I have; what I spent, I had; what I kept, I lost.
Henry David Thoreau:	Goodness is the only investment that never fails.
DeWitt Wallace:	The dead carry with them to the grave in their clutched hands only that which they have given away.
Percy Ross:	He who gives while he lives Also knows where it goes.
Calvin Coolidge:	No person was ever honored for what he received. Honor has been the reward for what he gave.

| Dale Carnegie: | Do things for others and you'll find your self–consciousness evaporating like morning dew on a Missouri cornfield in July. |

~~~*~~~

| Lao–tzu: | The sage never tries to store things up. The more he does for others, the more he has. |

George Winslow Plummer:

... only use brings out or keeps up what we have. If we do not use our brains, they do not develop. If we do not use our muscles, they atrophy. If we do not use our house, it deteriorates... If we have wealth and do not use it for the common good, we either become useless misers or someone takes it from us. If we have talents and do not use them profitably, they diminish and are taken away... You can only keep by giving away, paradoxical as that may seem.

Harry Emerson Fosdick:

The Sea of Galilee and the Dead Sea are made of the same water. It flows down, clear and cool, from the heights of Hermon and the roots of the cedars of Lebanon. The Sea of Galilee makes beauty of it, for the Sea of Galilee has an outlet. It gets to give. It gathers in its riches that it may pour them out again to fertilize the Jordan plain. But the Dead Sea with the same water makes horror. For the Dead Sea has no outlet. It gets to keep.

Alan Watts: Buddha's doctrine: Man suffers because of his craving to possess and keep forever things which are essentially impermanent... This frustration of the desire to possess is the immediate cause of suffering.

André Gide: Complete possession is proved only by giving. All you are unable to give possesses you.

~~~*~~~

Lao–tzu: The sage takes care of all men and abandons no one.

Author Unknown:
Thru this toilsome world, Alas!
  Once and only once I pass;
If a kindness I may show,
  If a good deed I may do
To a suffering fellowman,
  Let me do it while I can.
No delay, for it is plain
  I shall not pass this way again.

John Wesley:
Do all the good you can,
  By all the means you can,
In all the ways you can,
  In all the places you can,
At all the times you can,
  To all the people you can,
As long as you ever can.

Ralph Waldo Emerson: You cannot do a kindness too soon, for you never know how soon it will be too late.

Jean Paul Richter: Do not wait for extraordinary circumstances to do good; try to use ordinary situations.

Martin Farquhar Tupper:
Despise not small things, either for evil or good, for a look may work thy ruin, or a word create thy wealth. A spark is a little thing, yet it may kindle the world.

Vietnamese Saying:
Never forget benefits done you, regardless how small.

Confucius:
Forget injuries, never forget kindness.

The Talmud:
He that gives should never remember, he that receives should never forget.

Albert Einstein:
I remind myself that my inner and outer life depend on the labor of other men, living and dead, and that I must exert myself in order to give the same measure as I have received.

William Wordsworth:
That best portion of a good man's life is his little, nameless, unremembered acts of kindness and of love.

Dr. Albert Schweitzer:
I don't know what your destiny will be, but one thing I do know; the only ones among you who will be truly happy will be those who have sought and found how to serve.

"The Mary Tyler Moore Show"
Mary Richards:
It's a lousy business we're in, Mr. Grant; I quit. I'm going to Africa to work with Schweitzer.
Lou Grant:
Mary, Albert Schweitzer is dead.
Mary Richards:
You see what I mean, Mr. Grant? It's a lousy, lousy world.

Alex Noble:	If I have been of service, if I have glimpsed more of the nature and essence of ultimate good, if I am inspired to reach wider horizons of thought and action, if I am at peace with myself, it has been a successful day.
Mother Teresa:	Unless life is lived for others, it is not worthwhile.
Erma Bombeck:	Know the difference between success and fame. Success is Mother Teresa. Fame is Madonna.
Gabrielle "Coco" Chanel:	How many cares one loses when one decides not to be something, but to be someone.

~~~*~~~

Unknown:	Too many people conduct their lives on the cafeteria plan: self–service only.
The Dalai Lama:	... our prime purpose in this life is to *help* others. And if you can't help them, at least don't hurt them.
Dr. Albert Schweitzer:	Whosoever is spared personal pain must feel himself called to help in diminishing the pain of others.
William Bulwer:	It is an inevitable law that a man cannot be happy if he does not live for something higher than his own happiness — He cannot live in or for himself. — Every desire he has links him with others.

Edwin Markham:	There is a destiny that makes us brothers:
	   None goes his way alone:
	All that we send into the lives of others
	   Comes back onto our own.

James Matthew Barrie:	Those who bring sunshine into the lives of others cannot keep it from themselves.
Lydia Maria Child:	Not having enough sunshine is what ails the world.
Steve Martin:	A day without sunshine is like night.
Addison:	What sunshine is to flowers, smiles are to humanity.
Chinese Proverb:	A bit of fragrance always clings to the hand that gives you roses.
Ralph Waldo Emerson:	Happiness is a perfume which you can't pour on someone without getting some on yourself.
Ralph Waldo Emerson:	It is one of the most beautiful compensations of this life that no man can sincerely try to help another without helping himself.
Jordan S. Metzger:	Our goal is not to be happy. Our goal is to bring happiness to others. That is the only way to be happy.
Benjamin Franklin:	When you are good to others, you are best to your self.
Zoroaster:	Doing good to others is not a duty. It is a joy, for it increases your own health and happiness.

Graffiti:	If we're all here to help others, what are the others here for?
W. H. Auden:	We are here on earth to do good to others. What the others are here for, I don't know.

~~~*~~~

The Midrash:	The poor does for the host more than the host for the poor.
Jewish Proverb:	The beggar does more good for the giver than the giver does for the beggar.
Dr. Karl A. Menninger:	Money–giving is a very good criterion of a person's mental health. Generous people are rarely mentally ill people.
Sam Levenson:	When it comes to giving, some people stop at nothing.
Psalm 37:	The righteous deal graciously and give.
Lillian Carter:	I don't know of anybody in my hometown who's destitute. I wouldn't let them be.
Ralph Waldo Emerson:	The only gift is a portion of thyself.
Kahlil Gibran:	You give but little when you give of your possessions. It is when you give of yourself that you truly give.
Unknown:	Not only is it more blessed to give than receive, it's deductible.
Philip Gibbs:	It's better to give than to lend, and it costs about the same.

Japanese Proverb: It's cheaper to buy than to receive a gift.

Taisen Deshimaru: To obtain satori, one must let go of the ego. To receive everything, one must open one's hands and give.

Henry Wadsworth Longfellow:
No man is so poor as to have nothing worth giving... Give what you have. To someone it may be better than you dare to think.

John Petit–Senn: We tire of those pleasures we take, but never of those we give.

~~~*~~~

E. W. Howe: What people say behind your back is your standing in the community.

Jordan S. Metzger: It is not good to be known unless you are known for good things.

Socrates: The way to gain a good reputation is to endeavor to be what you desire to appear.

1832 Farmer's Almanac:
When men speak ill of thee, live so as nobody will believe them.

Will Rogers: So live that you wouldn't be ashamed to sell the family parrot to the town gossip.

Mark Twain: Let us live so that when we come to die even the undertaker will be sorry.

Yogi Berra: Always go to other people's funerals, otherwise they won't come to yours.

Unknown:	Some cause happiness wherever they go; others whenever they go.
Red Skelton:	His death was the first time that Ed Wynn ever made anyone sad.
Homer:	He was a friend to man, and lived in a house by the side of the road.
Ralph Waldo Emerson:	The only way to have a friend is to be one.
Henry Ward Beecher:	No man is more cheated than the selfish man.
Thomas Jefferson:	... nobody will care for him who cares for nobody.
Addison Mizner:	Misery loves company, but company does not reciprocate.
Russell Baker:	Misery no longer loves company. Nowadays it insists upon it.

Ella Wheeler Wilcox:	Laugh and the world laughs with you
	   Weep and you weep alone,
	For the sad old earth must borrow its mirth,
	   But has trouble enough of its own.

Ella Wheeler Wilcox:	Talk happiness. The world is sad enough Without your woe. No path is wholly rough.
Amish Saying:	Be friendly to all and a burden to no one.
Robert G. Ingersoll:	Love is the only priest. Ignorance is the only slavery. Happiness is the only good. The time to be happy is now. The place to be happy is here. The way to be happy is to make other people happy.

Eartha Kit:	There is no greater reward in life than love. The rewards are so tremendous. Even if you don't get love from the person you're giving it to you get it from somewhere else.
Dale Evans:	I'm so busy loving *everybody*, I don't have any time to hate *anybody*.
Martin Luther King, Sr.:	
	Nothing that a man does takes him lower than when he allows himself to fall so far as to hate anyone.
Bess Myerson:	You can't be beautiful and hate.
A Billboard:	Hate takes way too much energy.
Buddha:	Hatred does not cease by hatred at any time; hatred ceases by love; this is an old rule.
Leviticus 19:18:	Thou shalt love thy neighbor as thyself.
The Talmud:	Do not unto others what you do not wish others to do unto you.
George Bernard Shaw:	Do not unto others as you would that they should do unto you. Their tastes may not be the same.
Bulgarian Proverb:	Don't salt other people's food.
Confucius:	What you do not want done to yourself, do not do to others.

Isaac Watts:
> Be you to others kind and true,
> As you'd have others be to you,
> And neither do nor say to men
> Whate'er you would not take again.

Hillel:
> What is hateful to you, do not to your fellow man: that is the whole Law; all the rest is interpretation.

Buddha:
> If you become angry with me and I do not get insulted, then the anger falls back on you. You are then the only one who becomes unhappy, not me. All you have done is hurt yourself. If you want to stop hurting yourself, you must get rid of your anger and become loving instead. When you hate others, you yourself become unhappy. But when you love others, every one is happy.

Adlai Stevenson, II:
> You can tell the size of a man by the size of the thing that makes him mad.

Booker T. Washington:
> You can't hold a man down without staying down with him.

Unknown:
> Some men fail because they think you have to strangle the world to make it cough up.

Henry Ford:
> If there is any one secret to success, it lies in the ability to get the other person's point of view and see things from his angle as well as from your own.

~~~*~~~

Henry David Thoreau:
> There is no remedy for love but to love more.

Lily Tomlin:	If love is the answer, could you rephrase the question?
Unknown:	If there is anything better than to be loved, it is loving.
Ann Landers:	Love is the most precious thing in the world. Whatever figures in second place doesn't even come close.
Emmet Fox:	There is no ... gulf that enough love will not bridge.
Joseph F. Newton:	People are lonely because they build walls instead of bridges.
Stan Dale:	It is never too late to clean up an interaction.
Joseph Joubert:	Kindness consists in loving people more than they deserve.
James M. Barrie:	Always be a little kinder than necessary.

Ella Wheeler Wilcox:	So many Gods, so many creeds,
	    So many ways that wind and wind;
	While just the art of being kind
	    Is all this sad world needs.

G. Young:	The greatness of a man can nearly always be measured by his willingness to be kind.
John W. Gardner:	Some people strengthen the society just by being the kind of people they are.
Mother Theresa:	Kind words can be short and easy to speak, but their echoes are truly endless.

Aldous Huxley (last words):

Let us be kinder to one another.

The Talmud: The highest form of wisdom is kindness.

The Talmud: The final goal of wisdom is to turn to God and to do good works.

Isaiah 6:8: Here am I; send me.

Arthur C. Clarke: It may be that our role on this planet is not to worship God, but to create him.

Elizabeth Kübler–Ross:

Each time you heal a person, you also heal Mother Earth.   We are all interconnected.

Kabir: All know that the drop merges into the ocean, but few know that the ocean merges into the drop.

Antoine de Saint–Exupéry:

How could the drops of water know themselves to be a river? Yet the water flows on.

Stanislaw J. Lec: No snowflake in an avalanche ever feels responsible.

The Talmud: To help a fellow man may be to tip the scales [of God's reckoning] for the entire world.

Bayazid Al–Bistami: Forgetfulness of self is remembrance of God.

Dogen: To forget oneself is to be enlightened by everything in the world.

Robert Louis Stevenson:

> In every part and corner of our life, to lose oneself is to be a gainer, to forget oneself is to be happy.

Henry Miller:

> Until we lose ourselves there is no hope of finding ourselves.

Hillel:

> If I am not for myself, who is for me? And if I am only for myself what am I? And if not now — when?

Kalonymus Kalman Shapira:

> The greatest thing in the world is... to do somebody else a favor.

Benjamin Franklin:

> If you want to make a friend, let someone do you a favor.

Mohammed:

> A good deed, is one that brings a smile of joy to the face of another.

Ralph Waldo Emerson:

> To know even only one life has breathed easier because you have lived...

George Eliot:

> What do we live for, if it is not to make life less difficult to each other.

Hubert Horatio Humphrey:

> Life's unfairness is not irrevocable; we can help balance the scales for others, if not always for ourselves.

The Talmud:

> He who destroys but a single life is as if he had destroyed the whole world. He who saves but a single life is as if he had saved the whole world.

Herbert Spencer:	No one can be perfectly happy till all are happy.
Robert Browning:	Make us happy and you make us good.
Matthew 5:41:	Who ever shall compel you to go a mile, go with him two.

~~~*~~~

Chapter Four

It's Your Face

At 50, everyone has the face he deserves.
George Orwell

Nature gives you the face you have at twenty; it is
up to you to merit the face you have at fifty.
Gabrielle "Coco" Chanel

The mask, given time, comes to be the face itself.
Marguerite Yourcenar

"**I**'ve given this some heavy thought," started Jah, "I mean, I've
got to see my mug everywhere I go.
"Then I read this by Kenneth Goode:

'No matter how much madder it may make you,
get out of bed forcing a smile. You may not smile
because you are cheerful; but if you will force yourself to smile, you'll end up laughing. You will be
cheerful because you smile. Repeated experiments
prove that when man assumes the facial expression
of a given mental mood — any given mood — then
that mental mood itself will follow.'

"How true this is. Life is short and we only live a few times," the
moonlight acted as a spotlight illuminating Jah's face, his smile

59

widened even as he talked. "Loosening your face, radiating your smile not just through your mouth, but in motions and movements, then projecting it through your eyes... the clearest windows to the soul."

~~~*~~~

Dale Carnegie:
Act as if you were already happy and that will tend to make you happy.

Martha Graham:
The gesture is the thing truly expressive of the individual — as we think, so we will act.

Jewish Proverb:
The bitterest misfortune can be concealed with a smile.

François de La Rochefoucauld:
There are certain tears which often deceive ourselves, after having deceived others.

Lydia Maria Child:
Half the battle is gained if you never allow yourself to say anything gloomy.

110 Year Old Man
Interviewed on CNN:
I feel *good*!

~~~*~~~

Tiny Tim:
Keep walking and keep smiling.

Leigh Hunt:
The groundwork to all happiness is health.

George Winslow Plummer:
Good health, since it depends almost entirely on one's own actions, without reference to the thoughts or desires of others, is one of the easiest achievements.

Shalom Aleichem: When the heart is full the eyes overflow.

Book of Proverbs 15:30:
                     Bright eyes gladden the heart;
                     Good news fatten the bones.

A Wise Fortune Cookie:
                     Age can never hope to win you while your
                     heart is young.

Book of Proverbs 17:22:
                     A merry heart doeth good like a medicine.

William Shakespeare: A light heart lives long.

Haliburton: Cheerfulness is health; its opposite,
                     melancholy, is disease.

Jewish Proverb: Melancholy creates nervous ailments;
                     cheerfulness cures them.

William James: The Lord may forgive us our sins, but the
                     nervous system never does.

Buddha: You will not be punished for your anger;
                     you will be punished by your anger.

Elie Wiesel: Our own insensitivity is already our
                     punishment.

Epictetus: In the long run, every man will pay the
                     penalty for his own misdeeds. The man
                     who remembers this will be angry with no
                     one, indignant with no one, revile no one,
                     blame no one, offend no one, hate no one.

Dr. Paul Pearsall:	Every thought you have is changed to neuropeptides. Every belief bleeds out into the body. Your belief becomes your biology.
Orison Swett Marden:	It has its effect on every cell in the body; it is uplifting, life–giving, efficiency–generating, happiness–making.
Orison Swett Marden:	An angry man is always full of poison.
Buddha:	Getting angry with someone else is like drinking poison and expecting the other person to die.
Joseph Krimsky, M.D.:	Hate and fear can poison the body as surely as any toxic chemicals.
Dr. O. F. Gober:	Fear causes worry. Worry makes you tense and nervous and affects the nerves of your stomach and actually changes the gastric juices of your stomach from normal to abnormal and often leads to stomach ulcers.
Dr. Joseph F. Montague:	You do not get stomach ulcers from what you eat. You get ulcers from what is eating you.
Satchel Paige:	If your stomach disputes you, lie down and pacify it with cool thoughts.

Dale Carnegie:

This day is too precious to be corroded by acid worries and vitriolic regrets. Keep your chin high and your thoughts sparkling, a mountain brook leaping in the spring sunshine. Seize this day. It will never come again.

~~~*~~~

Franz Alexander, M.D.:

The fact that the mind rules the body is, inspite of its neglect by biology and medicine, the most fundamental fact which we know about the process of life.

Walter Clement Alvarez, M.D.:

We little realize the number of human diseases that are begun or affected by worry.

Charles W. Mayo, M.D.:

Worry affects the circulation, the heart, the glands, the whole nervous system, and profoundly affects heart action.

Plato:

The greatest mistake physicians make is that they attempt to cure the body without attempting to cure the mind; yet the mind and body are one and should not be treated separately!

Zachary T. Bercovitz, M.D.:

Some patients I see are actually draining into their bodies the diseased thoughts of their minds.

David G. Myers:	... there no longer is any doubt that mind affects brain — that our appraisal of challenging situations affects our blood pressure, that chronic anger and resentment trigger the release of hormones that accelerate the buildup of deposits on the heart's vessels, that persistent psychological stress depresses the immune system, decreasing our resistance to various diseases.
Jah:	Researchers at the institute of Heart–Math have discovered that positive emotions like love, caring, and compassion are beneficial to the immune system. Conversely, hate, anger, and stress lower the system's ability to combat illness. During the experiment subjects who were induced into positive emotional states experienced an increase in their natural disease fighting antibody levels.
David Miller:	The best physicians take pains to cheer up their patients and to surround them with a bright, joyous, bracing, uplifting atmosphere, for they know that their patients' chances of recovery are thus greatly enhanced. Good cheer has brought many a sick person back to health.
Norman Cousins:	A hospital is no place for a person who is seriously ill.

~~~*~~~

Bernie S. Siegel, M.D.:

Feelings are chemical and can kill or cure.

Robert C. Peale, M.D.:

The best and most efficient pharmacy is within your own system.

Dr. Albert Schweitzer: We are at our best when we give the doctor who resides within each patient a chance to go to work.

W. H. Auden: Health is the state about which medicine has nothing to say.

Carl Jung: About one third of my patients are suffering from no clinically definable neurosis, but from the senselessness and emptiness of their lives.

George Melton: Of one thing I am certain, the body is not the measure of healing — peace is the measure.

Dr. Alexis Carrel: Those who keep the peace of their inner selves in the midst of the tumult of the modern city are immune from nervous diseases.

Bernie S. Siegel, M.D.:

It takes more distress and poison to kill someone who has peace of mind and loves life.

Maharishi Mahesh Yogi:

Life is bliss; no person need suffer any more.

Jordan S. Metzger: To meditate is to medicate.

Bernie S. Siegel, M.D.: Why do you need this disease?

Lucius Annaeus Seneca:
>To wish to be well is a part of becoming well.

<center>~~~*~~~</center>

Henry Ward Beecher: Mirth is God's medicine.

Jah: Laughter cleanses the system.

Sean O'Casey: Laughter is wine for the soul... the hilarious declaration made by man that life is worth living.

Norman Cousins: Laughter is inner jogging.

The Book Of Koheleth 30:22:
>Gladness of the heart is the life of a man, and joyfulness of a man prolongeth his days.

Mary Pettibone Poole: He who laughs, lasts.

Olga K. Jarvey: I am not so idiotic as to imagine that merely smiling can cure cancer. But I do believe that a cheerful mental attitude helps the body fight disease. At any rate, I experienced one of the miracle cures of cancer.

Jonas Salk: The best thing to do [for people worried about cancer–causing substances] is quit reading the newspaper.

Gilda Radner: I'm a comedienne, and even cancer couldn't stop me from seeing humor in what I went through.

Ella Wheeler Wilcox:	It is easy enough to be pleasant, 　When life flows by like a song, But the man worth while is one who will smile, 　When everything goes dead wrong. For the test of the heart is trouble, 　And it always comes with the years, And the smile that is worth the praises of earth 　Is the smile that shines through tears.
Joseph Addison:	Health and cheerfulness mutually beget each other.
Rabbi Jonah:	Let a man show a happy face to people, so that all men will be pleased with him.
Mark Twain:	Wrinkles should merely indicate where smiles have been.
Rabbi Ishmael:	Receive all men with cheerfulness.
Leo Buscaglia:	Do you know the wonder of walking into a room and having people happy because you're there. That's the greatest thing. Instead of an expression on their face: "Oh my God, there he is again," — a joyous smile appears because *you've* walked in.
Meiri:	Even if your heart does not rejoice when your fellow visits you, pretend to be cheerful when he arrives; let him think that your face lights up with joy at his coming.
A Fortune Cookie:	The secret to good friends is no secret to you.

Abigail Van Buren:	There are two kinds of people in the world — those who walk into a room and say, "There you are" — and those who say, "Here I am!"
George Carlin:	You know what I do? Every night I change the way I say goodbye. Whether I need to or not every month I start using a different phrase. People like that. They notice that little extra effort... Sometimes you can combine several ways to say goodbye that don't seem to go together, like: toodle–loo, go with God, and don't take any wooden nickels.
George Michael Cohan:	
	Always Leave Them Laughing When You Say Goodbye.

~~~*~~~

Thomas Hughes:	Blessed are they who have the gift of making friends, for it is one of God's best gifts. It involves many things, but above all, the power of going out of one's self, and appreciating whatever is noble and loving in another.
Sir John Lubbock:	Everyone must have felt that a cheerful friend is like a sunny day, which sheds its brightness on all around; and most of us can, as we choose, make of this world either a palace or a prison.
Frankenstein's Monster:	
	Friend... GOOD.
Dr. Irwin Sarason:	Good friends are good for your health.

68

Seneca:	Friendship is a sovereign antidote against all calamities.

Andre Maurois: People are what you make them. A scornful look turns into a complete fool a man of average intelligence. A contemptuous indifference turns into an enemy a woman who, well-treated, might have been an angel.

Ralph Waldo Emerson: An eye can threaten like a loaded and leveled gun, or it can insult like hissing or kicking; or, in its altered mood, by beams of kindness, it can make the heart dance for joy.

Jah: What you project is what you experience.

Norman Vincent Peale: Getting people to like you is merely the other side of liking them.

Carl Jung: Everything that irritates us about others can lead us to an understanding of ourselves.

Jerry Bundsen: You're no bigger than the things that annoy you.

Proverbs 27:19: Just as water reflects the face, so one human heart reflects another.

George Herbert: What your glass tells you will not be told by counsel.

Nikolai Gogol: It is no use to blame the looking glass if your face is awry.

George Herbert: The best mirror is an old friend.

David Miller: The development of cheerfulness in oneself attracts the good in life and the beauty in nature. Life is, after all, nothing but a mirror.

~~~*~~~

Chapter Five

The Mystic Bond

"We are all a bit deeper than we appear; the reasons for our actions are often more justified than they seem," Jah again arose from his guru–like pose and addressed the gathering. "You know, you can't positively tell why someone is doing what they're doing. Give people the benefit of the doubt. It's the old.... two sides to every story.... story. I frequently notice myself editing situations to fit what *I* think they should be. We give things meaning based mostly on our own thoughts and expectations. A lot of times what we imagine others doing is merely a figment of our projection, our own interpretations projected onto what others are doing. A spy thinks everyone is a spy, a thief sees everyone as out to rob him. A man who can't trust can't be trusted. Ironically the things we hate the most in others, are usually those reminding us most about ourselves. If you have intense feelings, especially unfavorable ones about someone, you're probably rejecting a negative attribute of yourself, refracted off of their magnifying mirror. Granted, they may be guilty, but it's far easier and less painful to be cognizant of it in them. Think on this and you'll see it to be true.

"To *pre* judge, is to *per* vert justice," proceeded Jah. "Whether the rationalization is based on color, race, habits, culture, religion, or whatever. Everyone, rich or poor, handsome, ugly, old, young, ambitious, or lazy, has something distinctly unique to offer. This contribution may be all but invisible to those residing on the earthly plane. On the highest level no *one* is better than any*one*, on the most real level we're all one.

"The code of the road, according to most hoboes and wandering

71

types I've known, has always been: 'Don't ask someone where they're coming from, only where they are headed.' We have to start at the bottom to climb to the top. To grow, we have to be a little uncomfortable at times, sometimes feel pain; hardships are vital to blooming fully as a person.

"To jump high our feet must first touch the ground."

Jah sparked our thoughts, "Imagine now that we've all passed on and are looking back upon our time here, reviewing, as part of the audience, our own life: the ultimate show that we produced, directed, and starred in. Proper perspective is added when we realize that we, amongst others, will someday be watching ourselves. The big picture comes clear, enabling us to avoid getting caught up in the petty and unimportant. Believe me, we'll soon be our own worst critics; let our actions now not make us feel ashamed or sorry on opening night.

"Ever been driving and someone cuts you off, making you mad enough to curse their ancestry?" I got the feeling Jah was talking directly to me. "Haven't *you* ever been in a hurry or cut someone off? Next time just wish them well, consider: 'That person must be in a real rush; I hope they get where they're going on time, and for their sake that life isn't always so hurried.' It'll be better for *you* not to get angry. Ultimately, the harshness by which we judge others is the degree of severity we'll use to judge ourselves. Could it be that we create the judges for ourselves by the judgments we proclaim on others. Go easy on others. If you want to use stringent justice, practice it on yourself. Help me to clean up my own garbage before I complain about the smell of my neighbor's cologne.

There's a story about Gandhi and a young mother:

> A mother comes to Gandhi saying, 'Gandhi, my little boy really loves and respects you, but he has a problem. He eats too much sugar. I know it's bad for him. Could you please tell him not to eat sugar.' Gandhi replied, 'Come back tomorrow.'
>
> The woman did so, but it was with a great effort, as she had to travel far. She approached Gandhi with her child the next day and again requested, 'Please Gandhi, tell my son now, about sugar.' Gandhi

answered, 'Don't eat sugar.' The women was upset and asked Gandhi, 'Why did you make me come back and travel again another day, why couldn't you have just told him that yesterday?' Gandhi merely said softly, 'Yesterday, I still ate sugar.'

"The ancient Indian prayer rings clear and true in its deep, foreboding voice:

'Grant that I may not criticize my neighbor until I have walked a mile in his moccasins.' "

~~~*~~~

Bernie Rhodes:
What is important is not where you come from but where you're going.

Oliver Wendell Holmes:
The great thing in this world is not so much where we are, but in what direction we are moving.

Homer Croy:
I've hit bottom and I've stood it. There is no place to go now but up.

Thomas Carlyle:
Out of the lowest depths there is a path to the loftiest height.

Publilius Syrus:
If you wish to reach the highest begin at the lowest.

Dr. Paul Pearsall:
The lower you are the higher you can become. That's called the rebound theory of emotion.

Jah:
To jump a wall, you need to take a few steps backward, crouch low, and get a running start.

Czech Saying:
Don't jump high in a low ceiling'd room.

Danish Proverb:	He who would leap high must take a long run.
John Barth:	Like an ox–cart driver in monsoon season or the skipper of a grounded ship, one must sometimes go forward by going back.
Melville D. Landon:	I wasn't born in a log cabin, but my family moved into one as soon as they could afford it.
M. F. Carey:	You can't keep a good man down.
Robert E. Regent:	We were so poor in our youth that our parents couldn't afford window shopping.
Elbert Hubbard:	If you suffer, thank God! — It is a sure sign that you are alive.
Mildred Witte Struven:	A clay pot sitting in the sun will always be a clay pot. It has to go through the white heat of the furnace to become porcelain.
Unknown:	Diamonds are coal that went through pressure.
Robert Louis Stevenson:	The saints are the sinners who keep on trying.
Marisa Berenson:	My ultimate goal is to become a saint.
A Fortune Cookie:	Do not mistake temptation for opportunity.
Oscar Wilde:	I can resist everything except temptation.
Saint Augustine:	Oh Lord, help me to be pure, but not yet.

Benjamin Franklin: He that resolves to mend hereafter, resolves not to mend now.

Phyllis McGinley: The wonderful thing about saints is that they were human. They lost their tempers, scolded God, were egotistical or testy or impatient in their turns, made mistakes and regretted them. Still they went on doggedly blundering toward heaven.

Martin E. Marty: A saint has to be a misfit. The person who embodies what his culture considers typical or normal cannot be exemplary.

Robert Neville: Living with a saint is more grueling than being one.

Sarvepalli Radhakrishnan:
The worst sinner has a future, even as the greatest saint has a past. No one is so good or so bad as he imagines.

Johann Wolfgang von Goethe:
Treat people as if they were what they ought to be, and help them to become what they are capable of being.

Hermann Hesse: He did not treat the foreign merchant differently from the servant who shaved him, and the peddlers, from whom he bought bananas and let himself be robbed of small coins.

Elie Wiesel: No one is as capable of gratitude as one who has emerged from the kingdom of night.

The Sages of Israel: The place where one sits does not give him the glory. The individual glorifies the place.

Lao–tzu:	The great Tao flows everywhere.
	  It fulfills its purpose silently and makes
	    no claim.
	It does not show greatness,
	  And is therefore truly great.

Leonardo da Vinci:	Among the great things which are to be found among us, the Being of Nothingness is the greatest.
Lao–tzu:	So, too, the wise may become great, By becoming small.
Paul Valéry:	God made everything out of nothing. But the nothingness shows through.

Rumi:	Knock, And He'll open the door.
	  Vanish, And He'll make you shine like
	    the sun.
	Fall, And He'll raise you to the heavens.
	  Become nothing, And He'll turn you into
	    everything!

Albert Einstein:	The true value of a human being is determined primarily by the measure and sense in which he has attained liberation from the self.
Morihei Ueshiba:	Nothing less than becoming one with the universe will suffice.

~~~*~~~

T. S. Eliot:	The only wisdom we can hope to acquire
	  Is the wisdom of humility; humility is
	    endless.

Unknown:	God wisely designed the human body so that we can neither pat our own backs nor kick ourselves too easily.
A. J. Liebling:	If you just try long enough and hard enough, you can always manage to boot yourself in the posterior.
Rabbi Yose:	Go down to come up and up to come down — if a man has humbled himself he will be exalted, but if he has exalted himself he will be humbled.
Proverbs 27:1:	Do not boast about tomorrow, for you do not know what a day may bring.
W. G. Benham:	Neither crow nor croak.
Benjamin Franklin:	Never praise your cider or your horse.
Jordan S. Metzger:	Braggers lose their luck.
Tommy Sledge:	Kamikaze pilots had to do all of their bragging ahead of time.
Jim Bouton:	The older they get the better they were when they were younger.
Dizzy Dean:	It ain't bragging if you can do it.
Hillel:	He who advertises his name, loses it.
Muhammad Ali:	I'm young, I'm fast, I'm pretty, and I can't possibly be beat.
Dana Carvey:	I'm thirty years old, but I read at the thirty–four year old level.

Oscar Levant:	What the world needs is more geniuses with humility. There are so few of us left.
Jerry Lewis:	People hate me because I am a multifaceted, talented, wealthy, internationally famous genius.
Bob Marley:	They gave me star treatment when I was making a lot of money. But I was just as good when I was poor.
Henry Ford:	You can't build a reputation on what you're GOING to do.
Don Mattingly:	His reputation preceded him before he got here.
Yiddish Proverb:	He who is known for an early riser may lie abed till noon.

"The Mary Tyler Moore Show"

Ted Baxter:	It's a great experience to appear before a federal grand jury. I told them I was the best newsman in the country.
Murray Slaughter:	You didn't.
Ted Baxter:	I had to. I was under oath.
Don King:	Sometimes I amaze myself. I say this humbly.
Golda Meir:	Don't be so humble, you're not that great.
Muhammad Ali:	When you're as great as I am, it's hard to be humble.
Ted Turner:	If I only had a little humility I would be perfect.

Jackie Gleason:	I have no use for humility. I am a fellow with an exceptional talent.
Stevie Wonder:	How can you even think of being conceited — with the universe as large as it is?

~~~*~~~

Confucius:	Let the superior man never fail reverently to order his own conduct, and let him be respectful to others, and observant of property — then all within the four seas will be his brothers.
Unknown:	Always obey your superiors, if you have any.
Thomas Fuller:	It is the property of fools, to always be judging.
Hillel:	Judge not thy fellow until thou art come into his Position.
Franz Kafka:	Only our concept of Time makes it possible for us to speak of the Day of Judgment by that name; In reality it is a summary court in perpetual session.
Albert Camus:	Do not wait for the last judgment. It takes place every day.
Matthew 7:1:	Judge not that ye be not judged.
G. K. Chesterton:	One sees great things from the valley, only small things from the peak.
W. S. Gilbert:	Things are seldom what they seem. Skim milk masquerades as cream.

Boy George:	What I'm really trying to do is point out that not everything is what it seems.
Jean Renoir:	Everyone has his reasons.
William James:	The art of being wise is the art of knowing what to overlook.

~~~*~~~

William Childs Westmoreland:	We met the enemy, and he was us.
Jack Parr:	Looking back, my life seems like one long obstacle race, with me as its chief obstacle.
Napoleon:	No one but myself can be blamed for my fall. I have been my own greatest enemy — the cause of my own disastrous fate.
Sally Kempton:	It is hard to fight an enemy who has outposts in your head.
Barry Beck:	We have only one person to blame, and that's each other.
Thomas à Kempis:	How seldom we weigh our neighbor in the same balance with ourselves.
George Eliot:	When Death, the great reconciler has come, it is never our tenderness we repent of, but our severity.
Louis Nizer:	When a man points a finger at someone else, he should remember that four of his fingers are pointing at himself.
Benjamin Franklin:	Clean your fingers before you point at my spots.

Matthew 7:3–5:	Why do you look at the speck of sawdust in your brother's eye and pay no attention to the plank in your own eye? How can you say to your brother, "Let me take the speck out of your eye," when all the time there is a plank in your own eye? You hypocrite, first take the plank out of your own eye, and then you will see clearly to remove the speck from your brother's eye.
Chinese Proverb:	Do not use a hatchet to remove a fly from your friend's forehead.
Salvador Dali:	Have no fear of perfection. You'll never reach it.
George Fisher:	When you aim for perfection, you discover it's a moving target.
Johnny Cash:	I guess the record shows I'm far from perfect — but I want to keep trying.
Werner Erhard:	You are perfect exactly the way you are.

~~~*~~~

Yiddish Proverb:	Let everyone sweep in front of his own door, and the whole world will be clean.
Aldous Huxley:	There's only one corner of the universe you can be certain of improving and that's your own self.
Robert Davies:	If a man wants to be of the greatest possible value to his fellow-creatures, let him begin the long, solitary task of perfecting himself.

81

Norman Douglas:	A man who reforms himself has contributed his full share toward the reformation of his neighbor.
Mark Twain:	Nothing so needs reforming as other peoples habits.
Chilean Saying:	That which is a sin in others is a virtue in ourselves.
Benjamin Franklin:	Search others for their virtues, thyself for thy vices.
William Hazlitt:	Those who are at war with others are not at peace with themselves.
Axel Munthe:	A man can stand a lot as long as he can stand himself.
Sanhedrin:	First correct yourself and then correct others.
Dr. Albert Schweitzer:	Example is not the main thing in influencing others. It is the only thing.

François de La Rochefoucauld:

If we had no faults of our own, we should take less pleasure in noticing the faults of others.

William Shakespeare:	Take each man's censure, but reserve thy judgement.
Benjamin Franklin:	Observe all men; thyself most.
Lao–tzu:	Mastering others requires force; Mastering the self requires enlightenment.

Buddha: Greater is he who conquers himself than he who conquers a thousand.

Gian Carlo Menotti: A man only becomes wise when he begins to calculate the approximate depth of his ignorance.

"The Flintstones"
Barney Rubble: It takes a smart man to know he's stupid.

Lao–tzu: Knowing ignorance is strength. Ignoring knowledge is sickness.

Daniel J. Boorstin: The greatest obstacle to discovery is not ignorance — it is the illusion of knowledge.

Tao Te Ching: The more you know the less you understand.

Harry S. Truman: The only things worth learning are the things you learn after you know it all.

Vladimir Nabokov: I am sufficiently proud of my knowing something to be modest about my not knowing everything.

Arnold H. Glasow: The fewer the facts, the stronger the opinion.

~~~*~~~

Albert Einstein: The true value of a human being is determined primarily by the measure and sense in which he has attained liberation from the self.

Tibetan Saying: Recognition is the key to liberation.

Laurence Olivier:	I'm not sure what I'm like and I'm not sure I want to know.
Confucius:	The real man has to look his heart in the eye.
Lao tzu:	He who knows others is clever, but he who knows himself is enlightened.
Muhammad:	Whoever knows himself knows God.
Socrates:	Know thyself.
Johann Wolfgang von Goethe:	Know thyself? If I knew myself, I'd run away.
Hasidic Proverb:	The man who has confidence in himself gains the confidence of others.
Camillo Di Cavour:	The man who trusts men will make fewer mistakes than he who distrusts them.
Frank Crane:	You may be deceived if you trust too much, but you will live in torment if you do not trust enough.
Henry L. Stimson:	The only way to make a man trustworthy is to trust him.
Jah:	Those who can't trust, can't be trusted.
William Shakespeare:	This above all: To thine own self be true, And it must follow, as the night the day, Thou canst not then be false to any man.
William M. Gaines:	Don't lie.
Yiddish Saying:	Truth is the safest lie.

Sam Rayburn:	Son, always tell the truth. Then you'll never have to remember what you said the last time.
David Mamet:	Always tell the truth — it's the easiest thing to remember.
Mark Twain:	When in doubt, tell the truth.
Swahili Proverb:	The lie has seven endings.
Mark Twain:	If you tell the truth you don't have to remember anything.
French Saying:	Lairs need good memories.
Abraham Lincoln:	No man has a good enough memory to be a successful lair.
Unnamed Politician:	It is indeed fitting that we gather here today to pay tribute to Abraham Lincoln, who was born in a log cabin that he built with his own hands.
Gerald Ford:	If Lincoln were alive today, he'd roll over in his grave.
Bette Midler:	I never know how much of what I say is true.
Unknown:	Be straightforward in the way you dodge issues.
Popeye:	Honesty is the best policy and spinach is the best vegetable.
Samuel Butler:	I do not mind lying, but I hate inaccuracy.

Ronald Louis Ziegler:	I never knowingly lied, but certainly history shows that many things I said were incorrect.
Earl Bush:	[You reporters] should have printed what he meant, not what he said.
Marion Barry:	There are two kinds of truth. There are real truths and there are made–up truths.
Dennis Rappaport:	I don't want to tell you any half–truths unless they're completely accurate.
Sir Boyle Roche:	Half the lies our opponents tell about us are not true.
Joseph Chamberlain:	The honorable member did not want the truth; the honorable member had asked for facts.
Frank Lloyd Wright:	The truth is more important than the facts.
The New York World:	Send all the details. Never mind the facts.
Edith Sitwell:	The public will believe anything, so long as it is not founded on truth.
"Bonanza" Mrs. Looney:	One way to confound your enemies is to tell them the truth. Did you ever notice how little attention people pay to the truth?
Hoss Cartwright:	Yeah, now that you mention it.
"My Favorite Martian" Uncle Martin:	Always tell the truth; it's the world's best lie.

"Taxi"

Alex Reiger: Louie, when you walk into that hearing room, you're going to be under oath. You know what that means?

Louie DePalma: Yeah. It means they gotta believe you. I love this country.

"Night Court"

Judge Harry Stone: I told them the truth and they fell for it.

Clive James: Nothing I have said is factual except the bits that sound like fiction.

Mark Twain: Why *shouldn't* truth be stranger than fiction? Fiction, after all, has to make sense.

Sir Arthur Conan Doyle: When you have eliminated the impossible, whatever remains, *however improbable,* must be the truth.

Groucho Marx: There is one way to find out if a man is honest — ask him. If he says yes, you know he is crooked.

H. L. Mencken: It is hard to believe that a man is telling the truth when you know that you would lie if you were in his place.

Michael Curtiz: If I told you the truth, I'd be a hypocrite.

Bosnian Saying: One who lies for you will also lie against you.

~~~*~~~

A Fortune Cookie: Love truth, but pardon error.

87

Tolstoy:	All, everything I understand, I understand only because I love.
St. Augustine:	Insomuch as love grows in you, so in you beauty grows. For love is the beauty of the soul.
Leviticus 19:18:	Thou shalt love thy neighbor as thyself.
Eric Hoffer:	It is easier to love humanity as a whole than to love one's neighbor.
"All in the Family" Archie Bunker:	I got nothin' against mankind. It's people I can't stand.
Abraham Lincoln:	You have more of a feeling of personal resentment than I have.... A man doesn't have time to spend half his life in quarrels. If any man ceases to attack me, I never remember the past against him.
Confucius:	To be wronged or robbed is nothing, unless you continue to remember it.
Edith Cavell:	I must have no hatred or bitterness toward anyone.
Eric Hoffer:	Passionate hatred can give meaning and purpose to an empty life.
Dwight D. Eisenhower:	I make it a practice to avoid hating anyone.
Eldridge Cleaver:	The price of hating other human beings is loving oneself less.
Zsa Zsa Gabor:	I have never hated a man enough to give his diamonds back.

Mark Twain: Let us not be too particular: it is better to
                       have old secondhand diamonds than none at
                       all.

Abraham Lincoln: With malice toward none; with charity for
                       all...

"Kung Fu"
Caine: As far as possible, without surrender, be on
                       good terms with all.

Schopenhauer: If possible, no animosity should be felt for
                       anyone.

Lillian Carter: I was born loving everybody.

Winnie the Pooh (A. A. Milne):
                       Everybody is alright really.

Louis Armstrong: I got a simple rule about everybody. If you
                       don't treat me right, shame on you.

Booker T. Washington: I shall never permit myself to stoop so low
                       as to hate any man.

Laurence Jones: I have no time to quarrel, no time for
                       regrets, and no man can force me to stoop
                       low enough to hate him.

J. G. C. Brainard: Hate no one; hate their vices, not them-
                       selves.

                       ~~~*~~~

Cecil: If there is any person whom you dislike,
                       that is the one of whom you should never
                       speak.

Alice Roosevelt Longworth:
If you haven't anything nice to say about anyone, come and sit by me.

Jean Paul Richter:
A man never discloses his own character so clearly as when he describes another's.

Unknown:
People with small minds talk about other people.
People with average minds talk about events.
People with great minds talk about ideas.

Marie Curie:
Be less curious about people and more curious about ideas.

Schopenhauer:
Vulgar people take huge delight in the faults and follies of great men.

Benjamin Disraeli:
Little things affect little minds.

Agatha Christie:
It is completely unimportant. That is why it is so interesting.

Dorothy Parker:
I don't care what is written about me so long as it isn't true.

Proverbs 3:30:
Do not quarrel with anyone without cause, when no harm has been done to you.

Colton:
We hate some persons because we do not know them; and we will not know them because we hate them.

Bette Davis:
You've got to know someone pretty well to hate them.

Lavater:
Thousands are hated, while none are loved, without a real cause.

Buddha:	Hatred does not cease by hatred, but only by love; this is the eternal rule.
Oscar Wilde:	Always forgive your enemies; nothing annoys them so much.
H. More:	If I wanted to punish an enemy, it should be by fastening on him the trouble of constantly hating somebody.
John Tillotson:	Malice and hatred are very fretting, and make our minds sore and uneasy.

~~~*~~~

Jawaharlal Nehru:	I want nothing to do with any order, religion or otherwise, which does not teach people that they are capable of becoming happier and more civilized, on this earth...
Groucho Marx:	I'd never join any club that would accept a person like me.
Roger Caras:	Two would actually do it — two magic words that could replace all the religions in the world — two wonderful words that embrace all the powers and all of the energy we need to survive with each other and with our planet and with all the world's living creatures — *don't hurt.*
The Dalai Lama:	... our prime purpose in this life is to *help* others. And if you can't help them at least don't hurt them.

Jah:	The Buddha's disciple Ananda once inferred to his master that half of Buddha's teachings consisted merely in the practice of lovingkindness. The Buddha replied "It was not half, but the whole of my teaching."
Benjamin Franklin:	He that falls in love with himself will have no rivals.
Robert Morley:	It is a great help for a man to be in love with himself... To fall in love with yourself is the first secret of happiness. I did so at the age of four–and–a–half. Then if you're not a good mixer you can always fall back on your own company.
Virginia Woolf:	But when the self speaks to the self, who is speaking?
Polish Saying:	Wherever you go, you can't get rid of your self.
Elizabeth Barrett Browning:	How do I love thee? Let me count the ways.
Henry Winkler:	A human being's first responsibility is to shake hands with himself.
Cornelius Tacitus:	It is human nature to hate him whom you have injured.
Hillel:	If I am not for myself, who is for me. And if I am only for myself, what am I? And if not now — when?

Rabbi Jonah:

Let no man say, "Today I am busy with my work; tomorrow I will turn to the task of perfecting myself." ... That particular day has vanished utterly... It can never again be recovered.

~~~*~~~

Fyodor Dostoevsky:

Until you have become really in actual fact a brother of everyone, brotherhood will not come to pass. Only by brotherhood will liberty be saved.

Makhpiya–luta "Red Cloud" Sioux Chief:

... I am poor and naked, but I am the chief of the nation. We do not want riches but we do want to train our children right. Riches would do us no good. We could not take them with us to the other world. We do not want riches. We want peace and love.

Martin Luther King, Jr.:

I have a dream that my four little children will one day live in a nation where they will not be judged by the color of their skin, but by the content of their character.

Zen Story:

Wealthy patrons invited Ikkyu to a banquet. Ikkyu arrived dressed in his beggar's robes. The host, not recognizing him, chased him away. Ikkyu went home, changed into his ceremonial robe of purple brocade, and returned. With great respect, he was received into the banquet room. There, he put his robe on the cushion, saying, "I expect you invited the robe, since you showed me away a little while ago," and left.

The Talmud:	Don't consider the vessel, but what is in it.
Desmond Tutu:	A person is a person because he recognizes others as persons.
"Horton The Elephant" (Dr. Seuss):	Because, after all, A person's a person no matter how small.
Elie Wiesel:	Mankind must remember that peace is not God's gift to his creatures; peace is our gift to each other.

U. S. A. Dry Pea and Lentil Council Slogan:
All We Are Saying Is Give Peas A Chance.

California Egg Commission:
Give Eggs A Break

"Wings of Desire"
Wim Wenders and Peter Handke:
My heros are no longer the warriors and kings, but the things of peace, each equally good.

Robin Jenkins:	It is not the goodness of saints that makes us feel there is hope for humanity: it is the goodness of obscure men.
Edmund Burke:	No one made a bigger mistake than he who did nothing because he could do only a little.
Adlai Stevenson, II:	The journey of a thousand leagues begins with a single step. So we must never neglect any work of peace within our reach, however small.

Margaret Mead:	Never doubt that a small group of thoughtful, committed citizens can change the world. Indeed, it's the only thing that ever has.
United Jewish Appeal:	Speak now, so that we never again pay the price of silence.
Coretta Scott King:	... to do nothing when we have the capacity to act is morally and socially wrong.
Edmund Burke:	The only thing necessary for the triumph of evil is for good men to do nothing.
Rev. Martin Niemoeller:	In Germany, the Nazis first came for the communists, and I didn't speak up because I wasn't a communist. Then they came for the Jews, and I didn't speak up because I wasn't a Jew. Then they came for the trade unionists, and I didn't speak up because I wasn't a trade unionist. Then they came for the Catholics, but I didn't speak up because I was a Protestant. Then they came for me, and by that time there was no one left to speak for me.
Elie Weisel:	Whatever happens to one people effects all people... I plead against indifference.
Martin Luther King, Jr.:	Injustice anywhere is a threat to justice everywhere.
Bertrand Russell:	It's co–existence or no existence.

Francis Bowes Sayre:	Humanity cannot go forward, civilization cannot advance, except as the philosophy of force is replaced by that of human brotherhood.
Yasutani Roshi:	The fundamental delusion of humanity is to suppose that I am here and you are out there.
Alan Paton:	There is only one way in which one can endure man's inhumanity to man and that is to try, in one's own life, to exemplify man's humanity to man.
Martin Luther King, Jr.:	I want to be the white man's brother, not his brother–in–law.
Mother Teresa:	We draw the circle of our family too small.
Empedocles:	The nature of God is a circle of which the center is everywhere and the circumference is nowhere.
Maya Angelou:	... Fundamentally we are more alike, my friends, than we are unalike.
Declaration Of Independence:	We hold these truths to be self–evident, that all men are created equal...
Tom Landry:	God doesn't make any losers.
Malachi 2:10:	Have we not all one father? Hath not one God created us?
Dr. Bronner:	... we're All–One or none!

Elie Wiesel: A fanatic is one who doesn't know that ultimately we are all in the same boat.

Will Rogers: My forefathers didn't come over on the Mayflower, but they met the boat.

Abraham Lincoln: I don't know who my grandfather was; I am much more concerned to know what his grandson will be.

John Comenius: We are all citizens of one world; we are all of one blood. To hate a man because he was born in another country, because he speaks a different language, or because he takes a different view on this subject or that, is a great folly. Desist, I implore you, for we are all equally human...

Ed McGaa: Think of your fellow men and women as holy people who were put here by the Great Spirit. Think of being related to all things!

Thomas Carlyle: The mystic bond of brotherhood makes all men one.

Norman Cousins: What was most significant about the lunar voyage was not that men set foot on the moon, but that they set eye on the earth.

Confucius: All under Heaven, one family.

~~~*~~~

Chapter Six

Flashing Into Cognition

"It was the poet Kabir," said Jah, "who once wrote:

'In the midst of the Water the fish feels thirsty.
I listen to this and I feel like laughing.'

"Kabir's fish, craving happiness, and thirsting for wisdom and enlightenment, misses the fact that both perpetually surround him. I once knew a fish more advanced than Kabir's, who left the water to explore the land," Jah related. "Returning he exclaimed, 'How wonderful to be back in the water! Here we can breathe and live happily.' Naturally, the other fish, who had never left the sea, understood none of what he meant, some even considered him crazy.

"Similarly I've heard humans say: 'Ya don't know what ya got till it's gone.' Meanwhile what they're yearning for is within. Pleasure is often erroneously confused with happiness. The best and most gratifying oasis to strive for lies within our inner selves, it has been there all along and will unceasingly endure. Any security, beyond that inside, is a momentary mirage. There can be no absolute security on this side, because there *is* no such thing in the physical, material world. Sometimes it takes a full circle around the globe to find delight in our own living room. A full circle is the path to enlightenment! To prize what we have, it helps to view it from aloft, to get the big picture from afar."

He moved his eyes up and to the left, while his head tilted slightly right, as if what he'd said reminded him of something. He spoke softly:

"There once was a man by the name of Isaac Yekel; he was a poor man but faithful, one might even have called him spiritual. Isaac lived on the poor side of Cracow, Poland, a long time ago. One night, while he lay sleeping with his family in his simple hut, he had a dream; in the dream he met a person. This person beseeched him to go to Prague, for there, he was told, was a certain bridge which led to the palace of the king. Under this bridge there lay a buried treasure of which no one knew!

Isaac considered himself a sensible man and thought it ludicrous to listen to a dream, and besides... Prague was a distant journey. The next night he had the dream again, clear as day. A third night he dreamt it a third time. Each time it was more real than real, like he was genuinely there; soon the dream haunted even his waking hours. He felt driven to pursue it, if only to see if the place really existed, and besides... he had never been to Prague.

He found the bridge all right, and indeed it led to the king's palace. Everything was just as in his dream, he was ecstatic, except for one thing, to his dismay the bridge was guarded heavily both night and day. This was no small problem, the king's soldiers were humongous... and well armed.

Isaac had brought a pick and shovel, but who would dare to dig on this, the property of the king? Treasure is nice, but you can't spend it in the dungeon. Still obsessed, he went to the bridge at all hours, awaiting his chance. He'd forgotten about his family and work, all that mattered right now was finding out if the dream was real.

After a time, the head of the guards, who turned out to be an amiable sort, asked him nicely if he were looking for something or waiting for someone. In desperation Isaac told him of the dream which had brought him. The captain laughed, 'You came all this way on account of a dream? You've worn out your shoes. I too have had dreams. If I had listened to them all, I would have had to travel long ago to a poor section of Cracow to dig under a stove for a treasure in the hut of a peasant named Isaac. How ridiculous! Do you know how common the name Isaac is in Cracow?'

Isaac knew. Growing up in Cracow a lot of his friends were also named Isaac. He also knew what to do next. Thanking the guard he hurried home. Hardly did he have his coat off when he began to dig. Sure enough the treasure had been there all along.

"Take this story to heart, and make it your own. Some things cannot be found anywhere in the world except within your own place.

"If you *seek*, the *sec*–ret, *seek*–it,... within.

"You have the knowledge, just toss away the shield that blocks understanding. It is within us to be awakened now, to be enlightened *now*, if only we believe it can be done."

~~~*~~~

Joyce Grenfell: There is no such thing as the pursuit of happiness, but there is the discovery of joy.

James Oppenheim: The foolish man seeks happiness in the distance, the wise grows it under his feet.

Lord Houghton: A man's best things are nearest him, lie close about his feet.

John Burroughs: The lure of the distant and the difficult is deceptive. The great opportunity is where you are.

Aldous Huxley: Our goal is to discover that we have always been where we ought to be.

Pindar:	Seek not, my soul, the life of the immortals; but enjoy to the full resources that are within thy reach.
Dale Carnegie:	Strange that we so seldom recognize happiness until it has passed, that we rarely recognize it when it is on our doorstep.
John Howard Tayne:	Mid pleasures and palaces though we may roam, Be it ever so humble, there's no place like home.
Robert Pirsig:	The only Zen you find on the top of the mountains is the Zen you bring up there.
Dogen:	If you cannot find the truth right where you are, where else do you expect to find it?
Zen Master Baso:	You have your own treasure house. Why do you search outside?
Richard P. Feynman:	I wonder why. I wonder why. I wonder why I wonder. I wonder why I wonder why I wonder why I wonder!
D. H. Lawrence:	Oh, for the wonder That bubbles into my soul.
Thomas Carlyle:	The man who cannot wonder is but a pair of spectacles behind which there is no eye.
Japanese Proverb:	The frog who has never seen the sea thinks the well a fine stretch of water.

"Mary Tyler Moore Show"

Mary Richards: I'm an experienced women; I've been around... Well, all right, I might not have been around, but I've been... nearby.

Irving Howe: The knowledge that makes us cherish innocence makes innocence unobtainable.

James Baldwin: Experience, which destroys innocence, also leads one back to it.

Rainer Werner Fassbinder:
    I long for a little naiveté but there's none around.

R. Buckminster Fuller: Dare to be naive.

Henri Matisse: Study, learn, but guard the original naiveté.

Winston Churchill: I am always ready to learn although I do not always like being taught.

William Least Heat Moon:
    I can't say, over the miles, that I had learned what I had wanted to know because I hadn't known what I wanted to know. But I *did* learn what I didn't know I wanted to know.

Werner Erhard: The goal of the training is "getting it," but you don't "get it" in the training. You get that you've got it in the training.

Jah: Got it.

~~~*~~~

Stanislaus I: To believe with certainty, we must begin with doubting.

Sacha Guitry: The little I know, I owe to my ignorance.

Marcel Proust: We don't receive wisdom; we must discover it for ourselves after a journey that no one can take for us or spare us.

Dag Hammarskjöld: The longest journey
  Is the journey inwards
Of him who has chosen his destiny.

Charles De Gaulle: We may as well go to the moon, but that's not very far. The greatest distance we have to cover still lies within us.

David Carradine: Happiness depends on mental health and inner peace more than any outside factors.

The Wall Street Journal Comics:
After deep meditation I've decided that there can be no inner peace without financial security.

Tom Robbins: There's a certain Buddhistic calm that comes from having money in the bank.

Miss Piggy: I think that it is worth keeping in mind that the businessmen who run banks are so worried about holding on to things that they put little chains on all their pens.

Aristotle: Happiness seems to require a modicum of external prosperity.

Michael Davis: I started out with nothing. I still have most of it.

George S. Kaufman and Moss Hart:
You Can't Take It with You.

Anna R. Brown Lindsay:
We may let go all things which we cannot carry into the eternal life.

Emanuel:
Do not give permanent reality to temporary things.

Meher Baba:
When the mind soars in pursuit of the things conceived in space, it pursues emptiness. But when the man dives deep within himself, he experiences the fullness of existence.

Epictetus:
The essence of philosophy is that a man should so live that his happiness shall depend as little as possible on external things.

Baba Ram Dass:
The game is not about becoming somebody, it's about becoming nobody.

Lao–tzu:
Freedom from desire leads to inner peace.

Nikos Kazantzakis:
I fear nothing, I hope for nothing, I am free.

Ralph Waldo Emerson:
A political victory, a rise in rents, the recovery of your sick, or the return of your absent friend, or some other quite external event, raises your spirits, and you think good days are preparing for you. Do not believe it. It can never be so. Nothing can bring you peace but yourself.

General Douglas MacArthur:
There is no security on this earth, there is only opportunity.

James Thurber:	There is no safety in numbers, or in anything else.
Germaine Greer:	Security is when everything is settled, when nothing can happen to you; security is a denial of life.
John F. Kennedy:	The one unchangeable certainty, is that nothing is unchangeable or certain.
Lao–tzu:	The sage attends to the inner and not to the outer.
Unknown:	Security is an inside job.
Luke 17:21:	The kingdom of God is within you.
P. D. Ouspensky:	People who make the same guess that you have made have certain advantages and certain disadvantages in comparison with other people who guess nothing. Their advantage is that they can be taught what other people cannot be taught, and their disadvantage is that, for them, time becomes very limited.
Sir Thomas Browne:	We carry with us the wonders we seek with out us.

~~~*~~~

Basho:	Do not seek to follow in the footsteps of the men of old; seek what they sought.
Unknown:	Happiness is where it is found, and seldom where it is sought.
Bertrand Russell:	Happiness is not best achieved by those who seek it directly.

Edith Wharton:	If only we'd stop trying to be happy we'd have a pretty good time.
Eric Hoffer:	The search for happiness is one of the chief sources of unhappiness.
Horace:	You traverse the world in search of happiness, which is within the reach of every man; a contented mind confers it all.
Richard Bach:	If your happiness depends on what some body else does... you do have a problem.
R. H. Blyth:	Any enlightenment which requires to be authenticated, certified, recognized, congratulated, is (as yet) a false, or at least incomplete one.
Henry Miller:	No man is great enough or wise enough for any of us to surrender our destiny to. The only way in which anyone can lead us is to restore to us the belief in our own guidance.
André Gide:	Believe those who are seeking the truth; doubt those who find it.
Archimedes:	Eureka! I have found it!
Kahlil Gibran:	Say not, "I have found the truth," but rather, "I have found a truth."
Robert Pirsig:	The truth knocks on the door and you say, "Go away, I'm looking for the truth," and so it goes away. Puzzling.
Winston Churchill:	Men stumble over the truth from time to time, but most pick themselves up and hurry off as if nothing happened.

Steven Wright:	I was once walking through the forest alone and a tree fell right in front of me, and I didn't hear it.
Joseph McCarthy:	That's the most unheard–of thing I ever heard of.
Will Rogers:	Everything is changing. People are taking the comedians seriously and the politicians as a joke.
Gelett Burgess:	To appreciate nonsense requires a serious interest in life.
James Nathan Miller:	There is no such thing as a worthless conversation, provided you know what to listen for.
Pascal:	All man's miseries derive from not being able to sit quietly in a room alone.
Franz Kafka:	You do not need to leave your room. Remain sitting at your table and listen.
"Kung Fu" Grasshopper: Master Po:	 How is it you hear these things? How is it you do not?
Yakov Smirnoff:	Soon after I came to America, I went to Tennessee. They are always checking your hearing there. They keep saying, "Now, you come back. You hear?"
Baba Ram Dass:	The quieter you become, the more you can hear.

Ryokan: At night, deep in the mountains, I sit in meditation. The affairs of men never reach here: Everything is quiet and empty, All the incense has been swallowed up by the endless night. My robe has become a garment of dew. Unable to sleep I walk out into the woods. — Suddenly, above the highest peak, the full moon appears.

Jonathan Edwards: ... there is something in the unruffled calm of nature that overawes our little anxieties and doubts: the sight of the deep–blue sky, and the clustering stars above, seems to impart a quiet to the mind.

Karlfried Graf Durckheim: All the masters tell us that the reality of life — which our noisy waking consciousness prevents us from hearing — speaks to us chiefly in silence.

Thomas Merton: It is in silence, and not in commotion, in solitude and not in crowds, that God best likes to reveal himself.

Wu–Tzu: Talking about Zen all the time is like looking for fish tracks in a dry riverbed.

William Wordsworth: When from our better selves we have too
        long
  Been parted by the hurrying world, and
        droop,
Sick of its business, of its pleasures tired,
  How gracious, how benign, is Solitude.

William Penn: True silence is the rest of the mind; it is to the spirit what sleep is to the body, nourishment and refreshment.

Thomas Carlyle:	Silence is the element in which great things fashion themselves together.
Wittgenstein:	Whereof one cannot speak, thereof one must be silent.
Aldous Huxley:	After silence that which becomes nearest to expressing the inexpressible is music.
Igor Stravinsky:	Music is the sole domain in which man realizes the present.
Ned Rorem:	Intelligence is silence, truth being invisible. But what a racket I make in declaring this.
Jordan S. Metzger:	The louder a person is... the less important is what he is saying.
Robert Frost:	We dance round in a ring and suppose, But the Secret sits in the middle and knows.
William Rose Benét:	And now there is merely silence, silence, silence, saying All we did not know.

~~~*~~~

Lao–tzu:	How do I know the universe is like this? By looking!
Alan Watts:	Normally, we do not so much look at things as overlook them.
George Seferis:	They were lovely, your eyes, but you didn't know where to look.

Anne Saslow: It is not the color of your eyes that makes you clever. It is what you teach your eyes to see that does.

Helen Keller: To be blind is bad, but worse is to have eyes and not to see.

Swift: There is none so blind as they that won't see.

Max Ernst: Such is the vocation of man: to deliver himself from blindness.

William Shakespeare: Love looks not with the eyes, but with the mind.

P. D. Ouspensky: A veil has suddenly fallen, and life has sparkled with a thousand lights, while the dark calumnies and lies which made love so frightening have rolled away like a cloud.

Terrence Rattigan: What a lovely world we're in, if only we'd let ourselves see it.

Old Adage: When a pickpocket meets a saint, he sees only his pockets.

Elizabeth Barrett Browning:
Earth's crammed with heaven,
    And every common bush afire with God:
But only he who sees takes off his shoes.

Ralph Waldo Emerson: To the dull mind nature is leaden. To the illumined mind the whole world burns and sparkles with light.

William Blake: A fool sees not the same tree that a wise man sees.

Joyce Kilmer:	I think that I shall never see A poem lovely as a tree.

Ogden Nash:	I think that I shall never see
	    A billboard lovely as a tree.
	Indeed, unless the billboards fall
	    I'll never see a tree at all.

Joyce Kilmer:	Poems are made by fools like me, But only God can make a tree.
William Shakespeare:	Tongues in trees, books in running brooks, sermons in stones, and God in everything.
Mary Howitt:	He is happiest who hath power, To gather the wisdom from a flower.

William Blake:	To see a World in a grain of sand,
	    And a Heaven in a wild flower:
	Hold infinity in the palm of your hand,
	    And eternity in an hour.

Gizan:	Coming and going, life and death:
	    A thousand hamlets, a million houses.
	Don't you get the point?
	    Moon in the water, blossom in the sky.

Dogen:	Enlightenment is like the moon reflected on the water. The moon does not get wet, nor is the water broken. Although its light is wide and great, the moon is reflected even in a puddle an inch wide. The whole moon and the entire sky are reflected in one dew drop on the grass.
"Kung Fu" Master Po:	Grasshopper, look beyond the game, as you look beneath the surface of the pool to see its depths.

Henry James:	Try to be one of the people on whom nothing is lost.
Chinese Saying:	When you say one thing, the clever person understands three.
Shunryu Suzuki:	When you understand one thing through and through, you understand everything.
Peter Matthiessen:	In this very breath that we take now lies the secret that all great teachers try to tell us.
Spinoza:	The more we understand individual things, the more we understand God.
William Gilbert:	Look for knowledge not in books but in things themselves.
An Indian Prayer:	Let me learn the lessons you have hidden in every leaf and rock.
Anne Saslow:	Deep in the woods, but not too deep, (because no one should ever go too deeply into anything).
Jewish Proverb:	As you are at seven, so you are at seventy.
Matsuo Basho:	Learn the rules well, and then forget them.
Zen Saying:	When an ordinary man attains knowledge, he is a sage; when a sage attains understanding, he is an ordinary man.
Shunryu Suzuki:	Zen is not some kind of excitement, but concentration on our usual everyday routine.

Dogen:	Four and fifty years
	    I've hung the sky with stars.
	Now I leap through —
	    What shattering!

Carlos Castaneda:	Things don't change. You change your way of looking, that's all.
Zen Saying:	Before a person studies Zen, mountains are mountains and waters are waters; after a first glimpse into the truth of Zen, mountains are no longer mountains and waters are not waters; after enlightenment, mountains are once again mountains and waters once again waters.
Zen Saying:	Before you study Zen, a bowl is a bowl and tea is tea. While you are studying Zen, a bowl is no longer a bowl and tea is no longer tea. After you've studied Zen, a bowl is again a bowl and tea is tea.
"Zen Mondo" Monk:	I have just entered the monastery; please give me some guidance.
Chao–chou:	Have you eaten your rice gruel?
Monk:	Yes, I've eaten.
Chao–chou:	Then go wash your bowl.
Thich Nhat Hanh:	While washing the dishes one should only be washing the dishes, which means while washing the dishes one should be completely aware of the fact that one is washing the dishes.

Reverend William Wood:
> I was trying to wash today's dishes and yesterday's dishes and dishes that weren't even dirty yet... I have ceased trying to wash tomorrow's dirty dishes today.

Rick Fields:
> When we pay attention, whatever we are doing — whether it be cooking, cleaning or making love — is transformed and becomes part of our spiritual path.

Colette:
> What a wonderful life I've had! I only wish I'd realized it sooner.

Carl Jung:
> Your vision will become clear only when you can look into your own heart...
> Who looks outside, dreams; who looks inside, awakes.

Paul Reps:
> We are most asleep when awake.

Ramakrishna:
> The fabled musk deer searches the world over for the source of the scent which comes from itself.

Jorge Luis Borges:
> Through the years, a man peoples a space with images of provinces, kingdoms, mountains, bays, ships, islands, fishes, rooms, tools, stars, horses and people. Shortly before his death he discovers that the patient labyrinth of lines traces the image of his own face.

Josh Billings:
> If you find happiness by hunting for it, you will find it as the old woman did her lost spectacles — on her own nose all the time.

Zen Saying:
> Zen is like looking for the spectacles that are sitting on your nose.

| William Barrett: | It is the familiar that usually eludes us in life. What is before our nose is what we see last. |
| Belva Plain: | All [life] is pattern... but we can't always see the pattern when we're part of it. |

~~~*~~~

Chapter Seven

90 Years

"The past has happened," Jah observed, "but with new understanding it need not have any bearing on future actions. In other words, start anew, undertake unexplored, life enriching endeavors, habits, and routines.

"I'm not *required* to repeat who I was yesterday — that was yesterday. Today I set the paradigm, looking past rutted routines, patterns, and addictions; asking myself: must they continue to confine?

"Like the tried and true story of the fleas in the jar, unmeaningful traditions cloud the daily order of business:

> A little boy with a slingshot in his back pocket whose dirty face shall remain nameless, put a bunch of fleas in a jar. He punched small holes in the top, and put it on. The fleas tried to jump out, but kept hitting their heads. Finally they stopped.
>
> Later his little sister felt sorry for the tiny critters. She crept up and quietly removed the top while her brother slumbered nearby.
>
> The boy didn't even hear her. Neither did the fleas, which was too bad for the fleas. Since they were conditioned to believe that they couldn't escape their predicament, they didn't even attempt another flight. After all, their previous breakout efforts had never proved fruitful, why bother. The fleas forgot another important principle of the earthly plane: that change in the fourth dimension, that of time, brings

change in the other three. They stayed in the jar for the rest of their brief lives.

"As the cage born canary believes the world is a cage," Jah proceeded, "legions of the world's people harbor a skewed perception of true reality; as in Jalalu'ddin Rumi's story known as, *The Disagreement as to the Description and Shape of the Elephant:*

'The elephant was in a dark house; some Hindus had brought it for exhibition.

'In order to see it, many people were going, everyone, into that darkness.

'As seeing it with the eye was impossible, (each one) was feeling it in the dark with the palm of his hand. The hand of one fell on its trunk: he said, "This creature is like water–pipe."

'The hand of another touched its ear: to him it appeared to be like a fan.

'Since another handled its leg, he said, "I found the elephant's shape to be like a pillar."

'Another laid his hand on its back: he said, "Truly, this elephant was like a throne."

'Similarly, whenever anyone heard (a description of the elephant), he understood (it only in respect of) the part that he had touched.

'On account of the (diverse) place (of the object) that they viewed their statements differed: one man entitled it "*Dal* [crooked]," another "*Alif* [straight]."

'If there had been a candle in each one's hand, the difference would have gone out of their word.

'The eye of sense–perception is only like the palm of the hand: the palm hath not power to reach whole of him (the elephant).' "

Jah continued on, "There's a great deal beyond the narrow range of perception we use to observe our universe. Had we lived in past ages, our belief in the light spectrum beyond red, orange, yellow, green, blue, indigo, and violet may have earned us the designation of heretic or witch. Today's science enables us all to rationally accept the existence of ultraviolet and infrared light. Dogs hear vibratory frequencies well above the limits of our own ears. Let these two samples serve as proof of the many things not detected with our limited senses. This holding true for our senses, our minds too are limited in what they sense. There have been those in history whose sensory perception has exceeded that of the common man. We, too, can strengthen our senses and minds to emulate them. Meanwhile, remember: there is more out there than one experiences. Remaining skeptical is wise. So–called 'experts' exploit, dilute, or just don't thoroughly understand fields which border the normal sciences; no reason for us to throw out the baby with the bath water. The world does not make sense without influence from undetected forces. Doubting the existence of things because they're beyond present perception is literally narrow–minded. Of course most folks thought Columbus was crazy when he asserted that the world was round.

"There is an escape from any cage. You have the right of choice, the power to change, mastery to be what you want, and the prerogative to be happy. An open mind allows analyzation of a present system of living. A free thinker flows with new routines. Writer John Lee went through some trying times in his life, toward the end of his problems he told of a dream:

> '... I heard voices outside the prison door. The only thing I had to do to be free was to walk to the door and gently pull it open. The first thought I had was that the door may have been unlocked for a long time.'

Jah wrapped it up, "Enduring a way of life you detest, is more degrading and deploring than deciding to deviate. Eliminating the abhorrent aspects of life and making a new beginning, although it sometimes entails postponing gratification, can pay in the long run.

"What if you had only six months to live? Considering all aspects of life, including mind, body, and spirit, resolve to list your activities into three categories: The things you **want to** do, the things you **have to** do, and the things you **neither** want to nor have to do. Do this part — then cross off all the things in the third category and never look back.

"Citing Socrates, 'An examined life is the only one worth living... Know thyself.' Studying habits, and assessing present systems of living, will put you a decade ahead in your thinking."

~~~*~~~

Jordan S. Metzger: Earth is a boot camp for the universe.

George Leonard: In the terms of game theory, we might say the universe is so constituted as to maximize the play.

David Carradine: We have come here to better ourselves. We can't do this and still remain the same as we were.

Robin Williamson: All that's been has led us hither. All that's here must lead us on.

Yogi Berra (on the phone):
     Where are you?
Joe Garagiola: Some guys say to tell you I'm at the library.
Yogi Berra: Oh, you ain't too far, just a couple of blocks. Only don't go that way, come this way.

Friedrich Wilhelm Nietzsche:
     You have your way. I have my way. As for the right way, the correct way, and the only way, it does not exist.

Henry Wadsworth Longfellow:
     Not enjoyment, and not sorrow,
       Is our destined end or way;
     But to act, that each to–morrow
       Find us farther than to–day.

The Sanskrit: Today, well–lived, makes every yesterday a dream of happiness, and every tomorrow a vision of hope.

Confucius:	Only the most absolute sincerity under heaven can effect any change.
Lao–tzu:	What is more malleable is always superior over that which is immovable. This is the principle of controlling things by going along with them, of mastery through adaption.
Shirley Hufstedler:	A man cannot be very kind unless he is also very strong.
Jerry Rubin:	Most men act so tough and strong on the outside because on the inside, we are scared, weak, and fragile.
Franco Zeffirelli:	You must be as tough as rubber and as soft as steel.
Dudley Martineau:	It takes a lot of courage to allow ourselves to be vulnerable, to be soft.
Louise Nevelson:	True strength is delicate.
Leigh Hunt:	Patience and gentleness is power.
Jean Paul Getty:	The meek shall inherit the earth, but not its mineral rights.
Bill Muir:	If the meek are going to inherit the earth, our offensive lineman are going to be land barons.
Kaicho Nakamura:	Gentleness, sometimes doesn't sound strong. But you have to have a strong personality and strong determination to *be* gentle.

The Talmud:	Be ever soft and pliable like a reed, not hard and unbending like a cedar.
Jujitsu Saying:	Bend like the willow; don't resist like the oak.
Lao–tzu:	A tree that is unbending is easily broken.
H. G. Bohn:	Better bend than break.

~~~*~~~

Muhammad Ali:	The man who views the world at fifty the same as he did at twenty has wasted thirty years of his life.
Unknown:	By the time wisdom becomes conventional wisdom, it may no longer be wisdom.
Jack Tanner:	What is counted as truth in one age is counted as myth in the next.
Judge Learned Hand:	How often the deepest convictions of one generation are the rejects of the next.
A Fortune Cookie:	The philosophy of one century is the common sense of the next.
Arthur C. Clarke:	The facts of the future can hardly be imagined ab initio by those who are unfamiliar with the fantasies of the past.
David C. McCullough:	A nation that forgets its past can function no better than an individual with amnesia.
Paul Harvey:	In times like these, it helps to recall that there have always been times like these.

| Paul Valery: | The trouble with our times is that the future is not what it used to be. |

Paul Valery: The trouble with our times is that the future is not what it used to be.

Gerald Ford: Things are more like they are now than they have ever been.

Ogden Nash: Progress might have been all right once, but it's gone on too long.

Richard Daley: We must restore to Chicago all the good things it never had.

Saul Bellow: By the time the latest ideas reach Chicago, they're worn thin and easy to see through.

Abraham Isaac Kook: The old must be made new, and the new must be sanctified.

Abraham Joshua Heschel:
Our concern is not how to worship in the catacombs, but how to remain human in the skyscrapers.

George Santayana: Those who cannot remember the past are condemned to repeat it.

Mark Twain: The past does not repeat itself, but it rhymes.

Oscar Wilde: The one duty we owe to history is to rewrite it.

Unknown: The easiest way to change history is to become a historian.

Norman Cousins: History is a vast early warning system.

John Wayne: Tomorrow is the most important thing in life. Comes into us at midnight very clean. It's perfect when it arrives and it puts itself in our hands. It hopes we've learned something from yesterday.

Robert Louis Stevenson:

As yesterday is history, and tomorrow may never come, I have resolved from this day on, I will do all the business I can honestly, have all the fun I can reasonably, do all the good I can willingly, and save my digestion by thinking pleasantly.

Patrick Henry: I know of no way of judging the future by the past.

Guy Bellamy: Hindsight is an exact science.

Richard Sasuly: No one has ever bet enough on a winning horse.

~~~*~~~

A. P. Herbert: I wish I hadn't broke that dish,
    I wish I was a movie–star,
I wish a lot of things, I wish,
    That life was like the movies are.

William O'Rourke: Regret is an odd emotion because it comes only upon reflection. Regret lacks immediacy, and so its power seldom influences events when it could do some good.

Oscar Wilde: Do not be afraid of the past. If people tell you that it is irrevocable, do not believe them.

Soyen Shaku: Do not regret the past. Look to the future.

Unknown: A little girl I once knew asked her mother why she cut off one end of the roast before putting it into the oven. The mother said, "Because that's the way my mother, your grandmother, used to do it. We'll have to ask her." Off they went to grandmother's house, only to find that grandma did it because her mother did it. The three generations then traipsed off to great–grandmother's house in order to seek the wisdom of the ages. When posed with the question, great–grandma simply chuckled, "Why, dear, the pan was too small."

Cecil Beaton: Routines have their purposes, but the merely routine is the hidden enemy of high art.

Montesquieu: Useless laws weaken the necessary laws.

George Lois: Creativity can solve almost any problem. The creative act, the defeat of habit by originality, overcomes everything.

Norman Podhoretz: Creativity represents a miraculous coming together of the uninhibited energy of the child with its apparent opposite and enemy, the sense of order imposed on the disciplined adult intelligence.

Leopold Stokowski: I don't believe in tradition. It is a form of laziness.

Oliver Wendell Holmes:
    Don't be "consistent," but be simply true.

Liewelyn Powys: Alter your manner of life ten times if you wish.

Mark Twain:	Loyalty to a petrified opinion never yet broke a chain or freed a human soul.
Elizabeth Bowen:	If you look at life one way, there is always cause for alarm.
Alain:	Nothing is more dangerous than an idea, when it's the only one we have.
Dan Quayle:	I stand by all the misstatements.
Piet Koornhoff:	And what is more, I agree with everything I have just said.
A Fortune Cookie:	Ideas are like children: there are none so wonderful as your own.
Michel Eyquem de Montaigne:	
	Nothing is so firmly believed as what we least know.
M. Scott Peck, M.D.:	Spiritual growth is a journey out of the microcosm into an ever greater macrocosm... we must continually expand our knowledge and our vision... spiritual growth demands that we actively seek the threatening and unfamiliar, and deliberately challenge what we have been taught and hold dear.
Erik H. Erikson:	All "graduations" in human development mean the abandonment of a familiar position... all growth... must come to terms with this fact.
Confucius:	When you have faults, do not fear to abandon them.

Dr. Wayne W. Dyer:	That's how you change behavior, by wandering into the unknown rather than staying with the familiar. Fear of moving into new territory... is all in your mind.
Jake Johannsen:	I'm originally from Iowa. It took a long time for me to realize we were free to go.
P. D. Ouspensky:	It would be too simple if we could do such things. There is something in us that keeps us where we find ourselves. I think this is the most awful thing of all.
"Zen Mondo" Zen Master: Seeker of liberty: The Zen Master:	Who binds you? No one binds me. Then why seek liberation?
Confucius:	To see what is right, and not to do it, is want of courage, or principle.
Everett Dirksen:	I am a man of fixed and unbending principles, the first of which is to be flexible at all times.
"Bloom County" Berke Breathed Opus:	Well. That was two and a half weeks ago. So young and foolish was I in my youth...
Unknown:	Every day is a new life to a wise man.
Baal Shem Tov:	The world is new to us every morning — this is God's gift; and every man should believe he is reborn every day.

Mark Twain:	Be careful to get out of an experience all the wisdom that is in it — not like the cat that sits down on a hot stove. She will never sit down on a hot stove lid again — and that is well; but also she will never sit down on a cold one anymore.
C. S. Lewis:	Five senses; an incurably abstract intellect; a haphazardly selective memory; a set of preconceptions and assumptions so numerous that I can never examine more than a minority of them — never become even conscious of them all. How much of total reality can such an apparatus let through?
Hermann Hesse:	There is no reality except the one contained within us. That is why so many people live such an unreal life. They take the images outside them for reality and never allow the world within to assert itself.
M. Scott Peck, M.D.:	Most of us fail to transcend the influence of our particular culture, parents, and a childhood experience... Human beings... have vastly different views of reality. Yet each one believes that his or her view is the correct one, since it is based on the microcosm of personal experience...
Rabbi Philip S. Berg:	We are looking at the world through tiny peepholes — our eyes and our ears... our bodies.
Japanese Saying:	You can't see the whole sky through a bamboo tube.

~~~*~~~

Alan Keightley: Once in awhile it really hits people that they don't have to experience the world in the way they have been told to.

Algis Juodikis: Can a blue man sing the whites?

Jules Feiffer: Artists can color the sky red because they know it's blue. Those of us who aren't artists must color things the way they really are or people might think we're stupid.

Paul Gauguin: It is the eye of ignorance that assigns a fixed and unchangeable color to every object; beware of this stumbling block.

Louis Nizer: A fine artist is one who makes familiar things new and new things familiar.

Anais Nïn: It is the function of art to renew our perception. What we are familiar with we cease to see. The writer shakes up the familiar scene, and as if by magic, we see a new meaning in it.

Pablo Picasso: I paint objects as I think them, not as I see them.

Tom Bodett: All in how ya look at it, I guess.

Laurie Anderson: You don't have to be a surrealist to think the world is strange.

Lewis Carroll: "The time has come," the Walrus said,
   "To talk of many things:
Of shoes — and ships — and sealing
     wax —
   Of cabbages — and kings —
And why the sea is boiling hot —
   And whether pigs have wings."

Chuang–tzu:	These words may seem strange, but many years from now we might meet someone who can explain them, unexpectedly, some morning or evening.
Isaac Bashevis Singer:	The supernatural is like the ocean, while the so–called natural is only a little island on it. And even this little island is a great riddle.
Robert Pirsig:	We take a handful of sand from the endless landscape of awareness around us and call that handful of sand the world.
Jane Wagner:	After all, what is reality anyway? Nothin' but a collective hunch.
Darryl Dawkins:	Nothing means nothing, but it isn't really nothing because nothing is something that it isn't.
R. D. Laing:	Any experience of reality is indescribable!
William Blake:	If the doors of perception were cleansed every thing would appear to man as it is, infinite.
Aldous Huxley:	This given reality is an infinite which passes all understanding and yet admits of being directly and in some sort totally apprehended.
Kurt Vonnegut:	Thinking doesn't seem to help very much. The human brain is too high–powered to have many practical uses in this particular universe.
Henri Bergson:	Some other faculty than the intellect is necessary for the apprehension of reality.

Joseph Campbell:	There is no way you can use the word "reality" without quotation marks around it.
Henry David Thoreau:	Shams and delusions are esteemed for soundest truths, while reality is fabulous.
Jean Giono:	Reality pushed to its extreme ends in unreality.
Jacques Barzun:	If it were possible to talk to the unborn, one could never explain to them how it feels to be alive, for life is washed in the speechless real.
Robert Linssen:	Reality is where we are from moment to moment.
Robert Pirsig:	*Any* intellectually conceived object is *always* in the past and therefore *unreal*. Reality is always the moment of vision *before* the intellectualization takes place. *There is no other reality.*
Bumper Sticker:	Question Reality.
Liza Minnelli:	Reality is something you rise above.
"Calvin and Hobbes" Bill Watterson Calvin (taking a test):	1. What important event took place on December 16, 1773?
Calvin:	I do not believe in linear time. There is no past and future: all is one, and existence in the temporal sense is illusory. This question therefore, is meaningless and impossible to answer.
Calvin:	When in doubt, deny all terms and definitions.

Steve Allen:	Nothing is quite as funny as the unintended humor of reality.
Jordan S. Metzger:	How do we know that life isn't just one big virtual reality?
"The Twilight Zone" Rod Serling:	We know that a dream can be real, but who ever thought that reality could be a dream?
Louise Nevelson:	What we call reality is an agreement that people have arrived at to make life more livable.
Jamie Wyeth:	They don't allow anything but realism there.
T. S. Eliot:	Human kind cannot bear very much reality.
Woody Allen:	Cloquet hated reality, but realized it was still the only place to get a good steak.
Jean Anouilh:	I like reality. It tastes of bread.
Shlomo Riskin:	That reality has more than one face doesn't mean that there is more than one reality.
Santayana:	One real world is enough.
Andrew Wyeth:	True reality goes beyond reality itself.
Elvis Presley:	I'm all mixed up and I can't keep up with everything that's happening.
Robert Frost:	I'm not confused, I'm just well mixed.
Harold Ross:	I don't want you to think I'm not incoherent.

132

Elliott Abrams:	I never said I had no idea about most of the things you said I said I had no idea about.
David Bowie:	I've come to the realization that I have absolutely no idea what I'm doing half the time.
Albert Einstein:	I must confess that at the very beginning when the Special Theory of Relativity began to germinate in me, I was visited by all sorts of nervous conflicts. When young I used to go away for weeks in a state of confusion, as one who at that time had yet to overcome the state of stupefaction in his first encounter with such questions.
Jah:	Any questions?
Gregory Ratoff:	Let me ask you a question, for your information.
Yogi Berra:	If you ask me anything I don't know, I'm not going to answer.

Sir Arthur Conan Doyle:

My name is Sherlock Holmes. It is my business to know what other people don't know.

"Wings of Desire"
Wim Wenders and Peter Handke:

When the child was a child it was the time of these questions:
Why am I me, and why not you?
Why am I here, and why not there?
When did time begin, and where does space end? Isn't life under the sun just a dream?

James Thurber:	It is better to know some of the questions than all of the answers.
Yogi Berra:	I wish I had an answer to that because I'm getting tired of answering that question.
Kim Anderson:	I think we're on the road to coming up with the answers that I don't think any of us in total feel we have the answers to.
Mike Wallace:	There are no indiscreet questions, there are only indiscreet answers.
William Baker:	In a general way, we try to anticipate some of your questions so that I can respond "no comment" with some degree of knowledge.
Elie Wiesel:	I came to philosophy because of the questions. I left because of the answers.
Francis Bacon:	A little philosophy inclineth man's mind to atheism; but depth in philosophy bringeth men's minds about to religion.
Jah:	Why ask why, instead ask, what now.
Yo–Yo Ma:	Always ask why you're doing anything. Be kind, especially if you have a gift. Be honest. Take risks.
Gib Lewis:	There's a lot of uncertainty that's not clear in my mind.
George Eliot:	Blessed be the man who, having nothing to say, abstains from giving wordy evidence of the fact.

Hubert Horatio Humphrey:

I've never thought my speeches were too long: I've enjoyed them.

Robert F. Wagner:

I have reiterated over again what I have said before.

Yogi Berra:

It was déjà vu all over again.

Steven Wright:

Right now I'm having amnesia and déjà vu at the same time.

Ron Fairly:

Last night I neglected to mention something that bears repeating.

J. Curtis McKay:

I'm for abolishing and doing away with redundancy.

Phil Walden:

That's the old American way — if you got a good thing, then overdo it.

Harry S. Truman:

If you can't convince them, confuse them.

Daniel Boone:

I can't say I was ever lost, but I was bewildered once for three days.

"Shoe" (Jeff MacNelly)
Shoe: He's lost in thought.
Roz: Yeah. And like most men, he won't ask for directions.

"The Wizard of Oz"
Dorothy: Toto, I don't think we're in Kansas anymore.

J. R. R. Tolkien:

Not all those that wander are lost.

Henry David Thoreau:	If a person lost would conclude that after all he is not lost, he is not beside himself, but standing in his own old shoes on the very spot where he is, and that for the time being he will live there; but the places that have known him, they are lost — how much anxiety and danger would vanish. I am not alone if I stand by myself. Who knows where in space this globe is rolling? Yet we will not give ourselves up for lost, let it go where it will.
Digby Diehl:	If you wander around in enough confusion, you will soon find enlightenment.
Jack Kerouac:	I had nothing to offer anybody except my own confusion.
Duane Michals:	You don't know what's going on.
Minnie Marx:	Where else can people who don't know anything make a living.
Marc Chagall:	Me, I do not understand Chagall.
Pearl Bailey:	I never ask myself how I do what I do. After all, how does it rain?
Johnny Depp:	I pretty much try to stay in a constant state of confusion just because of the expression it leaves on my face.
Axl Rose:	I don't know my own telephone number.
Ernest Hemingway:	If you're looking for messages, try Western Union.
Arthur Miller:	I always doubted that writers ever really understand more than anyone else.

Henry Miller:	This urge to make everything profound. What nonsense!
Sigmund Freud:	There are times when a cigar is only a cigar.
Edmund Gerald Brown, Jr.:	In this business a little vagueness goes a long way.
Johann Wolfgang von Goethe:	Do not, I beg you, look for anything behind phenomena. They are themselves their own lesson.
Sartre:	Things are entirely what they appear to be and *behind them* ... there is nothing.
J. Krishnamurti:	Freedom from the desire for an answer is essential to the understanding of a problem.
Nicholas Cage:	Thank you. That just doesn't help me at all.
Cornella Otis Skinner:	One learns in life to keep silent and draw one's own confusions.

~~~*~~~

| James Baldwin: | We take our shape, it is true, within and against that cage of reality bequeathed to us at our birth; and yet it is precisely through our dependence on this reality that we are most endlessly betrayed. |
| Mexican Saying: | Though a cage may be made of gold, it is still a cage. |

Michel Eyquem De Montaigne:
We must push against a door to find out whether it is bolted or not.

Virginia Woolf:
The eyes of others our prisons; their thoughts our cages.

Dennis Allen:
Help! I'm being held prisoner by my heredity and environment!

Osage Saying:
If you want a place in the sun, you must leave the shade of the family tree.

Jules Feiffer:
I grew up to have my father's looks, my father's speech patterns, my father's posture, my father's opinions, and my mother's contempt for my father.

Queen Elizabeth II:
I learned the way a monkey learns — by watching its parents.

Hebrew Proverb:
Do not confine your children to your own learning, for they were born in another time.

William Shakespeare:
There are more things in heaven and earth, Horatio, than are dreamt of in your philosophy.

Bruce Lee:
You're Filipino, Dan, but don't make the mistake of embracing everything that's Filipino, then you'll miss the whole universe.

M. Scott Peck, M.D.:
The path to holiness lies through questioning everything.

Ken Kesey:
Take what you can use and let the rest go by.

~~~*~~~

Cicero:	Control Thyself.
Bhagavad–Gita:	For the uncontrolled there is no wisdom. For the uncontrolled no concentration. For the unconcentrated no peace. For the unpeaceful no happiness can be.
Julie Andrews:	Some people regard discipline as a chore. For me, it is a kind of order that sets me free to fly.
Will Durant:	In my youth I stressed freedom, and in my old age I stress order. I have made the great discovery that liberty is a product of order.
Pope:	Order is Heaven's first law.
Francis Bacon:	He who will not apply new remedies must expect old evils.
Tuli Kupferberg:	When patterns are broken, new worlds can emerge.
William Somerset Maugham:	The unfortunate thing about this world is that good habits are so much easier to get out of than bad ones.
Dr. Rob Gilbert:	First we form habits, then they form us. Conquer your bad habits, or they'll eventually conquer you.
Unknown:	Never open the door to a little vice lest a great one enter with it.
Elbert H. Hubbard:	Cultivate only the habits you are willing should master you.

Zen Saying:	Be master of mind rather than mastered by mind.
Epictetus:	The man who masters himself is free.
William Shakespeare:	No one is free who is not master of himself.
Richard Feynman:	The first principle is that you must not fool yourself — and you are the easiest person to fool.
Henry David Thoreau:	It is as hard to see one's self as to look backwards without turning around.
Simone Weil:	Attachment is the great fabricator of illusions; reality can be attained only by someone who is detached.
François de La Rochefoucauld:	The opinions of our enemies, come nearer to the truth about us than do our own opinions.
Jah:	We believe what we want to believe.
John Dryden:	With how much ease believe we what we wish!
Demosthenes:	Nothing is easier than self–deceit. For what each man wishes, that he also believes to be true.
Julius Caesar:	Men willingly believe what they wish.
Marcel Pagnol:	The most difficult secret for a man to keep is the opinion he has of himself.
John Le Carre:	People are very secretive creatures — secret even from themselves.

Demosthenes:	Nothing is easier than self–deceit.
Barry Switzer:	Some people are born on third base and go through life thinking they hit a triple.
Samuel Goldwyn:	I don't want any yes–men around me. I want everybody to tell me the truth even if it costs them their jobs.
Dick Cavett:	It's a rare person who wants to hear what he doesn't want to hear.
Albert Einstein:	There is far too great a disproportion between what one is and what others think one is.
Marcus Aurelius:	The first rule is to keep an untroubled spirit. The second is to look things in the face and know them for what they are.

~~~*~~~

Baba Ram Dass:	There are no accidents whatsoever in the universe.
Ancient Proverb:	When the student is ready — the teacher will appear.
Baba Ram Dass:	The next message you need is always right where you are.
Chinese Proverb:	Teachers open the door. You enter by yourself.
Reverend R. Inaman:	A great teacher never strives to explain his vision — he simply invites you to stand beside him and see for yourself.

Kahlil Gibran:	I have learned silence from the talkative, tolerance from the intolerant, and kindness from the unkind; yet strange, I am ungrateful to those teachers.
Walt Whitman:	Have you learned lessons only of those who admired you, and were tender with you, and stood aside for you? Have you not learned great lessons from those who rejected you, and braced themselves against you, or disputed the passage with you?
George Bernard Shaw:	If you teach a man anything, he will never learn.
Louis Armstrong:	There are some people that if they don't know, you can't tell 'em.
Timothy E. Thatcher:	I can teach a man to sail, but I can never teach him why.
S. I. Hayakawa:	It is not true that we have only one life to live; if we can read, we can live as many more lives and as many kinds as we wish.
Ezra Pound:	Properly, we should read for power. Man reading should be man intensely alive. The book should be a ball of light in one's hand.
E. M. Forster:	The only books that influence us are those for which we are ready and which have gone a little farther down our particular path than we have yet gone ourselves.
Clifton Fadiman:	When you reread a classic you do not see more in the book than you did before; you see more in you than there was before.

Christopher Morely: When you sell a man a book you don't sell him just twelve ounces of paper and ink and glue — you sell him a whole new life.

New York State Lottery Slogan: Hey, you never know.

"B.C." Johnny Hart

First Ant: Harold plans his whole life strictly by the book.

Second Ant: What Book is that?

First Ant: The TV Guide.

"Leave It To Beaver"

Beaver Cleaver: You know something? If you couldn't read, you couldn't look up what was on television.

Joseph Wood Krutch: [A] book... unlike a television program, moving picture, or any other "modern means of communication"... can wait for years, yet be available at any moment when it happens to be needed.

J. W. Eagan: Never judge a book by its movie.

Abraham Lincoln: People who like this sort of thing will find this the sort of thing they like [Of a book].

Anatole France: Never lend books, for no one ever returns them: the only books I have in my library are books that other folks have lent me.

Francoise Sagan: The one thing I regret is that I will never have time to read all the books I want to read.

Henry David Thoreau:	Read the best books first or you may not have a chance to read them all.
Nora Ephron:	I always read the last page of a book first so that if I die before I finish I'll know how it turned out.
Unknown:	I read part of it all the way through.

~~~*~~~

Mort Sahl:	The more you stay the same, the more they say you've changed.
James Baldwin:	People can cry much easier than they can change.
I Ching:	When the way comes to an end, then change — having changed, you pass through.
Ronald Reagan:	I don't think my positions have changed at all.
Freddie Laker:	The man that doesn't change his mind doesn't think.
Dan Quayle:	I believe we are on an irreversible trend toward more freedom and democracy. But that could change.
Bertolt Brecht:	Because things are the way they are things will not stay the way they are.
Marlin Fitzwater:	This strategy represents our policy for all time. Until it's changed.

John Kenneth Galbraith:

> In the choice between changing one's mind and proving there's no need to do so, most people get busy on the proof.

George Bernard Shaw: The longer I live the more I see that I am never wrong about anything, and that all the pains I have so humbly taken to verify my notions have only wasted my time.

Judy Sporles: If there is an opinion, facts will be found to support it.

Dale Carnegie: ... if we bother with facts at all, we hunt like bird dogs after the facts that bolster up what we *already* think — and ignore all the others! We want only the facts that justify our acts — the facts that fit in conveniently with our wishful thinking and justify our preconceived prejudices!

William James: A great many people think they are thinking when they are merely rearranging their prejudices.

Earl Landgrebe: Don't confuse me with the facts. I've got a closed mind.

Tony Glynn: The only thing I'm doing different is I'm not doing anything different.

Ellen Glasgow: The only difference between a rut and a grave is their dimensions.

Edna St. Vincent Millay:

> It is not true that life is one damn thing after another — it's one damn thing over and over.

Benjamin Franklin:	Some people die at twenty–five and aren't buried until they are seventy–five.
Old Saying:	Some people live ninety years, and some people live one year, ninety times.
"Kung Fu" Master Po:	Time is carving you, Grasshopper. Let yourself be shaped according to your true nature.
Lesléa Newman:	You can carve out a life for yourself.
Vachel Lindsay:	Change not the mass, but change the fabric of your own soul and your own visions, and you change all.
P. D. Ouspensky:	... nothing will change by itself. I have already told you that in order to change anything you must first change yourself.
John Berger:	Nothing forces us to remain what we were.

~~~*~~~

Chapter Eight

Where You're Going

"**T**hink ahead." Jah's voice bounced in an echo off the glassy smooth lake. "So many people tell me, 'If I only knew then what I know now,' or 'If I were your age again.' " His cupped hand shielded his mouth, as he winked at me he whispered, *If they only knew.*

~~~*~~~

John Goddard: Without a plan you'll postpone living until you're dead.

John Goddard: You need a plan for everything, whether it's building a cathedral or a chicken coop.

Dr. Robert H. Schuller: Where there are no dreams, people perish.

Paula Poundstone: I used to work at The International House of Pancakes. It was a dream, and I made it happen.

Shlomo Riskin: Our own redemption must begin with a dream, no matter how distant, no matter how elusive it may seem.

Jah: You can't make your dream come true if you don't have a dream.

Marilyn VanDerbur:	The vital, successful people I have met all had one common characteristic. They all had a plan.
I Ching:	It furthers one to have someplace to go.
Denis Waitley:	... the mind is a specific biocomputer, it needs specific instructions and directions. The reason most people never reach their goals is that they don't define them, learn about them, or ever seriously consider them as believable or achievable. Winners can tell you where they are going, what they plan to do along the way, and who will be sharing the adventure with them.
Harvey Mackay:	A goal is a dream with a deadline.
Jah:	Let also your plan be for the best for all involved as well.
Mignon McLaughlin:	For the happiest life, days should be rigorously planned, nights left open to chance.
John L. Beckley:	Most people don't plan to fail; they fail to plan.
Unknown:	If you fail to plan, you're planning to fail.
William Feather:	No plan is worth a damn unless somebody makes it work.
Benjamin Boofer:	If you want to make good ingots, you got to have ingot molds.
Dan Quayle:	We are not ready for any unforeseen event that may or may not occur.

City Councilman:	I move, Mr. Chairman, that all fire extinguishers be examined ten days before every fire.
John Ciardi:	Intelligence recognizes what has happened. Genius recognizes what will happen.
Steven Wright:	I'm a peripheral visionary. I can see into the future, but *way* off to the side.
Wayne Gretzky:	Most hockey players skate to where the puck is. I skate to where the puck is going to be.
James J. Kilpatrick:	Find out where the people want to go, then hustle yourself around in front of them.
Aristotle Onassis:	The secret to business is to know something that nobody else knows.
Norman Cousins:	Wisdom consists of the anticipation of consequences.
Bernard M. Baruch:	We can't cross a bridge until we come to it; but I always like to lay down a pontoon ahead of time.
Jewish Proverb:	A wise man lowers a ladder before he jumps into a pit.
Alexander Pope:	Fools rush in where angels fear to tread.
Agnes Allen:	Almost anything is easier to get into than to get out of.
Jah:	The fish who jumps at the worm gets caught first.

Jewish Proverb:	A fool takes two steps where a wise man takes none.
German Proverb:	Better ask twice than go wrong once.
Jewish Proverb:	The wise measure ten times before cutting once; fools cut ten times before measuring once.
Joseph Joubert:	Never cut what you can untie.
Master Doshin:	The wiseman does nothing: The fool ties himself up.

<p align="center">~~~*~~~</p>

Lord Peter Thorneycroft:

> Some men go through life absolutely miserable because, despite the most enormous achievement, they just didn't do one thing.

Stanislaw J. Lec:	Think before you think!
B. C. Forbes:	Think and you won't sink.
Don Marquis:	If you make people think they're thinking, they'll love you; but if you really make them think, they'll hate you.
George Bernard Shaw:	Few people think more than two or three times a year; I have made an international reputation for myself by thinking once or twice a week.
Henry Ford:	Thinking is the hardest work there is, which is the probable reason why so few engage in it.

Thomas Edison:	There is no expedient to which a man will not resort to avoid the labor of thinking.
Dan Quayle:	What a waste it is to lose one's mind — or not to have a mind. How true that is.
B. C. Forbes:	Acting without thinking is like shooting without aiming.
Robert Browning:	The aim, if reached or not, makes great the life.
James Russell Lowell:	Not failure, but low aim, is crime.
Cicero:	When you are aspiring to the highest place, it is honorable to reach the second or even the third rank.
Antonio Porchia:	If you do not raise your eyes, you will think you are the highest point.
Sir Walter Scott:	Look for a gown of gold, and you will at least get a sleeve of it.

Inscription at Williams College:

> Climb high
> > Climb far
> Your goal the sky
> > Your aim the star.

Robert Townsend:	If you shoot for the stars and hit the moon it's okay. But you've got to shoot for something. A lot of people don't even shoot.
Oscar Wilde:	We are all in the gutter, but some of us are looking at the stars.
A Wise Man:	The mariners do not expect to reach the stars, but they use them to steer by.

George Bernard Shaw: Hell is to drift, heaven is to steer.

Welsh Saying: Those not ruled by the rudder will be ruled by the rocks.

~~~*~~~

Ralph Waldo Emerson: Every spirit makes its house, but afterwards the house confines the spirit.

Ray Kroc: If you think small, you'll stay small.

Helen Keller: One can never consent to creep when one feels an impulse to soar.

Henry David Thoreau: If you have built castles in the air, your work need not be lost; that is where they should be. Now put the foundations under them.

Yugoslavian Saying: Grain by grain, a loaf; stone by stone, a castle.

Johann von Schiller: Keep true to the dreams of thy youth.

William Hazlitt: Happy those who live in the dream of their own existence, and see all things in the light of their own minds; who walk by faith and hope; to whom the guiding star of their youth still shines from afar, and into whom the spirit of the world has not entered!

Eleanor Roosevelt: The future belongs to those who believe in the beauty of their dreams.

Alexander Bogomoletz:
One must not lose desires. They are mighty stimulants to creativeness, to love and to long life.

Thomas Merton: The biggest human temptation is... to settle for too little.

George William Miller: Don't rationalize mediocrity. There is no penalty for overachievement.

William Somerset Maugham:
Only a mediocre person is always at his best.

Daniel Hudson Burnham:
Make no little plans; they have no magic to stir men's blood, and probably themselves will not be realized.

Theodore Roosevelt: Far better it is to dare mighty things, to win glorious triumphs even though checkered by failure, than to rank with those poor spirits who neither enjoy nor suffer much because they live in the gray twilight that knows neither victory nor defeat.

~~~*~~~

Paul Tournier: Acceptance of one's life has nothing to do with resignation; it does not mean running away from the struggle. On the contrary, it means accepting it as it comes, with all the handicaps of hereditary, of suffering, of psychological complexes and injustices.

Bob Uyeda: You can always succeed at giving up.

B. C. Forbes: The only hopeless failure is the person who has ceased to strive for success.

Malcolm S. Forbes:	When you cease to dream you cease to live.
Anatole France:	To accomplish great things, we must dream as well as act.
Napoleon Hill:	Cherish your visions and your dreams as they are the children of your soul; the blueprints of your ultimate achievements.
Jordan S. Metzger:	Believe in your dreams, don't leave your dreams.
Claude Pepper:	Life is like riding a bicycle. You don't fall off unless you stop pedaling.
Hannah More:	Obstacles are those frightful things you see when you take your eyes off of the goal.
Scandinavian Proverb:	He who lets the small things bind him, leaves the great undone behind him.
H. L. Hunt:	Decide what you want, decide what you are willing to exchange for it. Establish your priorities and go to work.
Paul Tillich:	Decision is a risk rooted in the courage of being free.

John–Roger and Peter McWilliams:
> You can have anything you want, but you can't have everything you want.

Dr. Robert H. Schuller: Today's decisions are tomorrow's realities. Plan your future... you have to live with it.

Samuel Johnson:	The future is purchased by the present.
Mignon McLaughlin:	What you have become is the price you paid to get what you used to want.

Road Sign in Upstate New York:
> Choose your rut carefully; you'll be in it for the next ten miles.

George Bernard Shaw:
> Take care to get what you like or you will be forced to like what you get.

Samuel Butler:
> We grow weary of those things (and perhaps soonest) which we most desire.

Dr. Wayne W. Dyer:
> The essence of greatness is the ability to choose personal fulfillment in circumstances where others choose madness.

Elvis Costello:
> I'm not even sure what I want, but that's not the point — it's that I want it *now*.

Don Marquis:
> Ours is a world where people don't know what they want and are willing to go through hell to get it.

Eric Hoffer:
> We can never have enough of that which we really do not want.

Emma Goldman:
> I'd rather have roses on my table than diamonds on my neck.

Moshe Weber:
> Better the love of a father [God] than houses and cars.

Brigitte Bardot:
> I have been very happy, very rich, very beautiful, much adulated, very famous and very unhappy.

"Cheers"
Sam Malone:
> A lot of people may not know this, but I'm quite famous.

Krishnamurti: We all want to be famous people, and the moment we want to *be* something we are no longer free.

Gabrielle "Coco" Chanel:
How many cares one loses when one decides not to be something but to be someone.

Lily Tomlin: I always wanted to be somebody, but I should have been more specific.

~~~*~~~

Hermann Hesse: He saw them toiling, saw them suffer and grow gray about things that to him did not seem worth the price — for money, small pleasures and trivial honors.

Oliver Goldsmith: A life of pleasure is... the most unpleasing life in the world.

John D. Rockefeller, Jr.:
I can think of nothing less pleasurable than a life devoted to pleasure.

De Witt Clinton: Pleasure is a shadow, wealth is vanity, and power is pageant.

Harry Emerson Fosdick:
Happiness is not mostly pleasure; it is mostly victory.

Varnhagen: I always give much away, and so gather happiness instead of pleasure.

Charles Dickens: Minds, like bodies, will often fall into a pimpled, ill–conditioned state from mere excess of comfort.

Gloria Steinem:	The only thing I can't stand is discomfort.
Confucius:	The superior man thinks always of virtue; the common man thinks of comfort.
André Gide:	One doesn't discover new lands without consenting to lose sight of the shore for a very long time.
Charles Kingsley:	We act as though comfort and luxury were the chief requirements of life, when all that we need to make us happy is something to be enthusiastic about.
Mae West:	Too much of a good thing is wonderful.
Aesop:	We would often be sorry if our wishes were gratified.
Benjamin Disraeli:	The feeling of satiety, almost inseparable from large possessions, is a surer cause of misery than ungratified desires.
Samuel Johnson:	Our desires always increase with our possessions. The knowledge that something remains yet unenjoyed impairs our enjoyment of the good before us.
Satya Saibaba:	Man's many desires are like the small metal coins he carries about in his pocket. The more he has, the more they weigh him down.
Henry Miller:	If there is to be any peace, it will come through being, not having.

Helen Keller:	Many persons have a wrong idea of what constitutes true happiness. It is not attained through self–gratification but through fidelity to a worthy purpose.
Willa Cather:	That is happiness: to be dissolved into something complete and great.
Washington Irving:	Great minds have purposes, others have wishes.
Robert Byrne:	The purpose of life is a life of purpose.
Interviewer:	You've written hundreds of books. What would you do if you had only six months to live?
Isaac Asimov:	Type faster.
Benjamin Franklin:	If you would not be forgotten, As soon as you are dead and rotten, Either write things worthy reading, Or do things worth the writing.
William James:	The best use of life is to invest it in something which will outlast life.
Chinese Proverb:	If we don't change the way we are going — we will end up where we are headed.
Akabia Ben Mahalalel:	Know whence thou art come, and whither thou art going.
Yogi Berra:	You've got to be very careful if you don't know where you are going, because you might not get there.
Laurence J. Peter:	If you don't know where you're going, you will probably end up somewhere else.

Woodrow Wilson: All things come to him who waits —
provided he knows what he is waiting for.

~~~*~~~

Chapter Nine

Smoke Screen

"Thought sculptures destiny." Jah's eyebrows raised as he spoke, "Think a while on this. Your inner dialog is your own hypnotic suggestion, and the 'tape' plays constantly. When talking to yourself, instead of intonating: 'Why can't I do this?' It's preferable to proclaim: 'I know I can be good at this.'

"Thought precedes action. I had a judo instructor who once advised: 'You can't do anything, no matter what it is, without first thinking about it.' Think about that.

"I've seen people reflect despondently on successes they might have known, had they known more. You **can** know today what you will understand tomorrow, or at least some of it sooner. Of course there are things that only time can reveal, but I'm talking about growing, not tomorrow's racing form."

He closed his eyes, "Picturing in my mind what I want to be in ten years, I envision how I'll get there, then try to get there sooner; I visualize and act now the way I see myself in the ideal future. It's amazing, we play a role and we fulfill a self–fulfilling prophecy."

Jah enlightened us further, "The minute our minds are committed to a heading, the journey embarks to that destination. Habits, subconscious routines, and daily rituals, what we do every day, will either enslave or enhance us. Small steps lead to big accomplishments. Big accomplishments can guide to greater happiness. If I want to be a great artist, then in my mind I make myself a great artist now. With the mind–set of a great artist, half the battle is won. I'm not advocating a trek up Everest without being physically ready, or traveling by limo when not yet a millionaire mogul. Nevertheless my understanding increases as I meditate, think, concentrate, or pray on the aspiration. In order to realize the future today, we must imagine the prototypical path for us and begin living it today.

"When pondering aspirations and desires," Jah stipulated, "it's best to think multi–dimensionally, considering not just one or two, but an integrated plan of grand proportions. Everything is written down, then broken down. Notes are made to focus on achievable steps, so that these workable measures are done each day.

"Physical targets might encompass health, fitness, and beauty. Mental goals include such things as wisdom, material wealth, and knowledge. Spiritual ambitions could consist of where you want to be in terms of family, happiness, understanding of our world and its people, and God. When choosing between the spiritual and material, my credo has long been, 'Live in both worlds.'

"Neglect to think on all levels and someday you will awake to discover all your goals conquered, yet your life barren and empty. Believe it. As the Chinese are known to proclaim: *If we don't change the way we are going — we will end up where we are headed.* Plan on making a mass of money but ignore exercise or the spiritual side, and you'll end up an unhealthy millionaire.

"James Baldwin said it best, 'Be careful what you set your heart upon — for it will surely be yours.' "

~~~*~~~

Ralph Lauren: I can do any thing I want.

Edward Sorel: At what I do, I am the best there is.

Dr. Seuss: And the fools that I saw were none other
                           than you.
                           Who seem to have nothing else better to
                           do
                           Than sit here and argue who's better than
                           who!

Franklin D. Roosevelt: Never underestimate a man who
                        overestimates himself.

Jewish Proverb:	When you must you can.
Samuel Beckett:	I can't go on. You must go on. I'll go on.
Eleanor Roosevelt:	What one has to do usually can be done.
Jah:	So why not now?
Ralph Waldo Emerson:	Hitch your wagon to a star.
John Goddard:	It can be done. It should be done. It shall be done.
United States Army:	Be all that you can be.
Marva Collins:	I repeat these words to myself each day before beginning my day, "Be all that you can be..."
Barry Goldwater:	It's a great country, where anybody can grow up to be president... except me.
Yogi Berra:	He can run any time he wants. I'm giving him the red light.
Jim Patterson:	I did the traffic at a very very small–town radio station. The the whole report was one sentence: "The light is green."
Joe Frank Harris:	Anyone can be elected governor. I'm proof of that.
Pat Brown:	This is the worst disaster in California since I was elected.
Epictetus:	You are a principal work, a fragment of God himself, you have in yourself a part of Him. Why then are you ignorant of your high birth?

Helen Keller:	Never bend your head. Always hold it high. Look the world straight in the eye.
Eleanor Roosevelt:	No one can make you feel inferior without your consent.
"Pogo" Walt Kelly:	We have met the enemy and he is us.
Mark Twain:	A man cannot be comfortable without his own approval.
Hillel:	If I am not for myself, who is for me?
Henry David Thoreau:	What a man thinks of himself, that it is which determines, or rather indicates, his fate.
Bernard Baruch:	No man can humiliate me or disturb me, I won't let him.
Ene Riisna:	A friend is someone who makes me feel totally acceptable.
Stewart E. White:	Do not attempt to do a thing unless you are sure of yourself; but do not relinquish it simply because someone else is not sure of you.
Marva Collins and Civia Tamarkin:	Character is what you know you are, not what others think you are.
"Doctor Who" Doctor Who:	Good looks are no substitute for a sound character.

"The Bugs Bunny Show"

Pepe Le Pew: You know, it eez possible to be too attractive.

Lao–tzu: The truly great man dwells on what is real and not what is on the surface. On the fruit and not the flower.

Gertrude Stein: Rose is a rose is a rose is a rose.

Tommy Lasorda: The difference between the impossible and the possible lies in a person's determination.

Dag Hammarskjöld: Never measure the height of a mountain until you have reached the top. Then you will see how low it was.

Martha Grimes: We don't know who we are until we see what we can do.

John Wooden: Do not let what you cannot do interfere with what you can do.

Eleanor Roosevelt: You must do the thing you think you cannot do.

Mark Twain: Apparently there is nothing that cannot happen.

~~~*~~~

Dorothy Parker: Four be the things I'd been better without: Love, Curiosity, Freckles, and Doubt.

William Shakespeare: Our doubts are traitors, and make us lose the good we oft might win by fearing to attempt.

Kahlil Gibran:	Doubt is a pain too lonely to know that faith is his twin brother.
Old Saying:	Fear knocked at the door. Faith answered. No one was there.
Henry Ward Beecher:	Faith is nothing but spiritualized imagination.
William James:	Faith is one of the forces by which men live.
Kathryn Kuhlman:	Faith is that quality or power by which the things desired become the things possessed.
Sir Rabindranath Tagore:	

Faith is the bird that sings when the dawn is still dark.

Cervantes:	He who sings frightens away his ills.
Rubem Alves:	Hope is hearing the melody of the future. Faith is to dance to it.
Samuel Butler:	You can do very little with faith, but you can do nothing without it.
José Ortega Y. Gasset:	Our life is at all times, and before all else, the consciousness of what we can do.
Kathryn Kuhlman:	You cannot have faith without results anymore than you can have motion without movement.
Matthew 17:20:	If ye have faith as a grain of mustard seed... nothing shall be impossible unto you.

Sören Kierkegaard:	Prayer does not change God, but changes him who prays.
Mahatma Gandhi:	Without prayer I should have been a lunatic long ago.
John Stuart Mill:	One person with belief, is equal to a force of ninety–nine who have only interests.
Frank Lloyd Wright:	The thing always happens that you really believe in; and the belief in a thing makes it happen.
John Dryden:	For they conquer who believe they can.
Vergil:	They are able because they think they are able.

~~~*~~~

Maxwell Maltz:	Of all the traps and pitfalls in life, self–disesteem is the deadliest, and the hardest to overcome, for it is a pit designed and dug by our own hands, summed up in the phrase, "It's no use — I can't do it."
Mary Kay Ash:	If you think you can, you can. And if you think you can't, you're right.
John Cage:	If someone says 'can't,' that shows you what to do.
Tom Dempsey:	They never told me I couldn't.
Henry Ford:	I am looking for a lot of men who have an infinite capacity to not know what can't be done.

Harry Emerson Fosdick:
>The world is moving so fast these days that the man who says it can't be done is generally interrupted by someone doing it.

Robert Orban:
>We have enough people who can tell it like it is — now we could use a few who tell it like it can be.

Robert Heinlein:
>Always listen to experts. They'll tell you what can't be done and why. Then do it.

Arthur C. Clarke:
>When a distinguished but elderly scientist says that something is possible he is almost certainly right. When he says it is impossible, he is very probably wrong.

Konrad Lorenz:
>It is a good morning exercise for a research scientist to discard a pet hypothesis every day before breakfast. It keeps him young.

Peter Medawar:
>I cannot give any scientist of any age better advice than this: the intensity of a conviction that a hypothesis is true has no bearing over whether it is true or not.

Alfred North Whitehead:
>The "silly question" is the first intimation of some totally new development.

Charles F. Kettering:
>A man must have a certain amount of intelligent ignorance to get anywhere.

Albert Einstein:
>Imagination is more important than knowledge.

Jeno F. Paulucci:
>It pays to be ignorant, for when you are smart you already know it can't be done.

Dorothea Brande: Act as if it were impossible to fail.

Thomas Carlyle: Every noble work is at first impossible.

Fritz Perls: Learning is discovering that something is possible.

Book of the Han Dynasty:
Nothing is impossible to a willing mind.

A. H. Weiler: Nothing is impossible for the man who doesn't have to do it himself.

Lewis Carroll: Why, sometimes I've believed as many as six impossible things before breakfast.

Oscar Wilde: I can believe anything, provided it is incredible.

Bovee: The method of the enterprising is to plan with audacity, and execute with vigor; to sketch out a map of possibilities; and then to treat them as probabilities.

John Lilly: In the province of the mind, what one believes to be true either is true or becomes true within limits to be found experientially and experimentally. These limits are beliefs to be transcended.

Huang Po: Learn how to be entirely unreceptive to sensations arising from external forms, thereby purging your bodies of receptivity to externals.

Arthur C. Clarke: The only way to find the limits of the possible is by going beyond them to the impossible.

Charles F. Kettering:	The Wright Brothers flew right through the smoke screen of impossibility.
Telegram from The Wright Brothers:	Success... four flights Thursday morning/... average speed through air thirty–one miles/longest fifty–nine seconds/inform press/home Christmas.
George Winters:	If God had really intended men to fly, he'd make it easier to get to the airport.
R. Buckminster Fuller:	Dare to be naive.
Bobby Kennedy:	Some men see things as they are, and say why; I dream of things that never were, and say why not.
Ralph Waldo Emerson:	Great men are they who see that the spiritual is stronger than any material force; that thoughts rule the world.
Sister Mary Tricky:	I think I am, therefore I am, I think.
Cyril Connolly:	We must select the illusion which appeals to our temperament and embrace it with passion, if we want to be happy.
Sam Keen:	We have to move from the illusion of certainty to the certainty of illusion.
Woody Allen:	I am plagued by doubts. What if everything is an illusion and nothing exists? In that case, I definitely overpaid for my carpet.
Buddha:	When one sees that everything exists as an illusion, one can live in a higher sphere than ordinary man.

Jordan S. Metzger:	It does but it doesn't.
Will Durant:	As we acquire more knowledge, things do not become more comprehensible, but more mysterious.
Gary Zukov:	And physics and mysticism converge in striking parallels, leading back full circle.
M. Scott Peck, M.D.:	A hundred years ago paradox meant error to the scientific mind, but now it is widely recognized that at a certain level reality is paradoxical.
Lao–tzu:	The truth often sounds paradoxical.
Cyril Connolly:	Truth is a river that is always splitting up into arms that reunite. Islanded between the arms, the inhabitants argue for a lifetime as to which is the main river.
Niels Bohr:	There are trivial truths and great truths. The opposite of a trivial truth is painful false. The opposite of a great truth is also true.
Jordan S. Metzger:	It is but it isn't.
Japanese Saying:	The reverse side also has a reverse side.
Robert Leroy Ripley:	Believe It or Not.
Jimmy Durante:	Deserde conditions dat prevail.
Walter Cronkite:	And that's the way it is.
"Quantum Leap" Al (The Bartender):	Sometimes... "That's the way it is"... is the best explanation.

Steven Wright: It's a small world, but I wouldn't want to paint it.

~~~*~~~

George F. Will: The universe is not only stranger than we suppose, it is stranger than we suppose.

Marcus Aurelius: How ludicrous and outlandish is astonishment at anything that may happen in life.

Lewis Thomas: Statistically, the probability of any one of us being here is so small that you'd think the mere fact of existing would keep us all in a contented dazzlement of surprise.

Maharishi Mahesh Yogi:
Because the self is of unmanifested nature, and because man's life is always in the field of the manifested, it is not to be wondered at if some people hear about it with great surprise, and others are not able to understand it at all.

Albert Einstein: There are only two ways to live your life. One is as though nothing is a miracle. The other is as though everything is a miracle.

Pablo Picasso: Everything is miraculous. It is miraculous that one does not melt in one's bath.

Andre Gidé: A wise man is astonished by anything.

Ludwig Wittgenstein: *That* the world is, is the mystical.

Albert Einstein: The most beautiful thing we can experience is the mysterious.

Rachel Carson:	Every mystery solved brings us to the threshold of a greater one.
Albert Einstein:	The most incomprehensible thing about the world is that it is comprehensible.
Chaim Weizmann:	Einstein explained his theory to me everyday, and on my arrival I was fully convinced that he understood it.
Lord Byron:	I wish he would explain his explanation.
Albert Einstein:	It should be possible to explain the laws of physics to a barmaid.
Paul Varley:	The advantage of the incomprehensible is that it never loses its freshness.
David Stone:	One man's 'simple' is another man's 'huh'?
Freeman Teague, Jr.:	Nothing is so simple it cannot be misunderstood.
Albert Einstein:	Everything should be made as simple as possible, but not simpler.
Vauvenargues:	When a thought is too weak to be expressed simply, simply drop it.
Frederick Lewis Allen:	Everything is more complicated than it looks to most people.
Sir Arthur Conan Doyle:	Like all Holmes's reasoning the thing seemed simplicity itself when it was once explained.

Albert Szent–Gyoergyi Von Nagyraypolt:
Discovery consists in seeing what everybody has seen and thinking what nobody has thought.

W. L. Bragg:
The essence of science lies not in discovering facts but in discovering new ways of thinking about them.

Albert Einstein:
The whole of science is nothing more than a refinement of everyday thinking.

Arthur C. Clarke:
Experience has shown that the most important results of any technological breakthrough are those that are not obvious.

Albert Einstein:
Concerns for man and his fate must always form the chief interest of all technical endeavors. Never forget this in the midst of your diagrams and equations.

Stephen Hawking:
I want to understand the universe, how it came into being. Otherwise, life just seems pointless.

Woody Allen:
I'm astounded by people who want to 'know' the universe when it's hard enough to find your away around Chinatown.

Stephen Hawking:
... why it is that we and the universe exist.

Georges Poulet:
To understand is almost the opposite of existing.

Lao–tzu:
To know that you do not know is the best. To pretend to know when you do not know is disease.

Maha Sthavira Sangharakshita:

> To know what we do not know is the beginning of wisdom.

Harold Pinter:

> Apart from the known and the unknown, what else is there?

Jack Kerouac:

> I don't know. I don't care. And it doesn't make any difference.

Fred Hoyle:

> There is a coherent plan in the universe, though I don't know what it's a plan for.

~~~*~~~

Isaiah:

> In quietness and confidence will be your strength.

Midget Farrelly:

> An extra bit of confidence... can carry you through, and you can do things that are just about impossible.

Henry David Thoreau:

> Men die of fright and live of confidence.

Daniel Maher:

> Confidence is courage at ease.

Mark Twain:

> All you need in this life is ignorance and confidence, and then success is sure.

"Forrest Gump"
Forrest Gump (Winston Groom):

> Remember what I told you? Don't let anybody tell you they're better than you.

Henry David Thoreau:

> What a man thinks of himself, that it is which determines or rather indicates his fate.

Dr. Robert H. Schuller: ... the average bottom–of–the–ladder person is potentially as creative as the top executive who sits in the big office. The problem is, the person at the bottom–of–the–ladder doesn't trust his own brilliance, and doesn't therefore believe in his own ideas.

Carlos Castaneda: The average man seeks certainty in the eyes of the onlooker and calls that self–confidence.

Henry David Thoreau: If one advances confidently in the direction of his dreams, and endeavors to live the life he has imagined, he will meet with a success unexpected in common hours.

Dick Rutan: What you can do is limited only by what you can dream.

~~~*~~~

Mark Twain: Thousands of geniuses live and die undiscovered — either by themselves or by others.

"Calvin and Hobbes"
Bill Watterson
Calvin: I'm a genius, but I'm a misunderstood genius.
Hobbes: What's misunderstood about you?
Calvin: Nobody thinks I'm a genius.

Ralph Waldo Emerson: To believe your own thought,... that is genius.

Buddha: Good thoughts will produce good actions, and bad thoughts will produce bad actions.

Bruce Lee: My capabilities exceed my limitations.

William Ernest Henley:
                        I am the master of my fate;
                          I am the captain of my soul.

Bruce Lee: The mind is like a fertile garden, it will
                        grow anything you wish to plant —
                        beautiful flowers or weeds. And so it is
                        with successful, healthy thoughts or with
                        negative ones that will, like weeds, strangle
                        and crowd the others.

Roger Allan Raby: A bad attitude is the worst thing that can
                        happen to a group of people. It's infectious.

Charles Swindoll: Attitude is more important than facts.

Aldous Huxley: Facts do not cease to exist because they are
                        ignored.

State Department Spokesman:
                        Some of the facts are true, some are
                        distorted, and some are untrue.

Hermann A. Keyserling:
                        The greatest American superstition is belief
                        in facts.

Johnny Miller: Serenity is knowing that your worst shot is
                        still going to be pretty good.

Arthur Guiterman: He rarely Hits the Mark or Wins the Game,
                          Who says, "I Know I'll Miss!" while
                            taking Aim.

Sparky Anderson: Our pitching could be better than I think it
                        will be.

Hank Aaron:	Came up here to hit.
Bill Lee:	I'm mad at Hank Aaron for deciding to play one more season. I threw him his last home run and I thought I would be remembered forever. Now I'll have to throw him another.
Dr. Robert H. Schuller:	Commitment to excellence taps an incredible source of energy.
Pablo Picasso:	When I was a child my mother said to me, "If you become a soldier you'll be a general. If you become a monk you'll end up as the Pope." Instead I became a painter and wound up as Picasso.
Martin Luther King, Jr.:	If a man is called to be a streetsweeper, he should sweep streets even as Michelangelo painted, or Beethoven composed music, or Shakespeare wrote poetry. He should sweep streets so well that all the host of heaven and earth will pause to say, here lived a great streetsweeper who did his job well.
J. C. Penney:	Intelligence is the effort to do the best you can at your particular job; the quality that gives dignity to that job, whether it happens to be scrubbing a floor, or running a corporation.
Peter Ustinov:	If you want to do a thing badly, you have to work as hard at it as though you wanted to do it well.

W. Somerset Maugham:

> It's a funny thing about life; if you refuse to accept anything but the best, you very often get it.

Robert Schumann:

> If we were all determined to play the first violin we should never have a full ensemble. Therefore respect every musician in his proper place.

Henry David Thoreau: The squeaking of the pump sounds as necessary as the music of the spheres.

William Carlos Williams:

> so much depends
>   upon
> a red wheel
>   barrow
> glazed with rain
>   water
> beside the white
>   chickens

~~~*~~~

Norman Vincent Peale: Your enthusiasm will be infectious, stimulating and attractive to others. They will love you for it. They will go for you and with you.

Henry Chester: Enthusiasm is the greatest asset in the world. It beats money and power and influence.

Ralph Waldo Emerson: Enthusiasm is one of the most powerful engines of success. Nothing great was ever achieved without enthusiasm.

Walter Chrysler: The real secret of success is enthusiasm.

179

Charles Schwab:	A man can succeed at almost anything for which he has unlimited enthusiasm.
Ralph Waldo Emerson:	Nothing great was ever achieved without enthusiasm.
Sir Edward Appleton:	I rate enthusiasm even above professional skill.
Benjamin Disraeli:	Every production of genius, must be the production of enthusiasm.
Ingmar Bergman:	Each film is my last.
Korean Saying:	One's utmost moves the heavens.
George Sheehan:	If you want to win anything — a race, your self, your life — you have to go a little berserk.
Yogi Berra:	You give a hundred percent in the first half of the game, and if it isn't enough, in the second half you give what's left.
Danny Ozark:	Half this game is ninety percent mental.
Yogi Berra:	Baseball is 90 percent mental. The other half is physical.
Samuel Goldwyn:	You are partly one hundred percent right.
A Congressman:	These are not my figures I'm quoting. They're from someone who knows what he's talking about.
Sir Boyle Roche:	Every pint bottle should contain a quart.
Salvador Dali:	The difference between a madman and me is that I am not mad.

Vince Lombardi:	If you aren't fired with enthusiasm, you will be fired with enthusiasm.
Malcolm S. Forbes:	People who never get carried away should be.
Edwin Land:	Anything worth doing is worth doing to excess.
Norman Vincent Peale:	There is a real magic in enthusiasm. It spells the difference between mediocrity and accomplishment... It gives warmth and good feeling to all your personal relationships.
Ronnie Shakes:	I was going to buy a copy of <u>The Power of Positive Thinking</u>, and then I thought: What the hell good would that do?

~~~*~~~

George Winslow Plummer:

Life reflects your real underlying thought–form... consider what would happen if a drop of white paint were mixed with a whole tube of black paint. What would you have, black paint, of course. Now suppose a man has a head full of black thoughts. And suppose that by chance he let one little white thought into it. Obviously, his head would still be full of black thoughts.

Mark Twain:

Life does not consist mainly — or even largely — of facts and happenings. It consists mainly of the storm of thoughts that is forever blowing through one's head.

James Allen:	As you think, you travel; and as you love, you attract. You are today where your thoughts have brought you; you will be tomorrow where your thoughts take you. You cannot escape the result of your thoughts, but you can endure and learn, and accept and be glad. You will realize the vision (not the idle wish), of your heart, be it base or beautiful, or a mixture of both, for you will always gravitate towards that which you, secretly, most love. Into your hands will be placed the exact results of your thoughts; you will receive that which you earn; no more, no less. Whatever your present environment may be, you will fall, remain or rise with your thoughts, your vision, your ideal. You will become as small as your controlling desire; as great as your dominant aspiration.
Dhammapada:	All that we are is the result of what we have thought.
Ralph Waldo Emerson:	A man is what he thinks about all day long.
Claude Monet:	Nobody can count themselves an artist unless they can carry a picture in their head before they paint it.
Marcus Aurelius:	Our life is what our thoughts make it.
Unknown:	Thought sculptures destiny.
The Upanishads:	The Transmigration of life takes place in one's mind. Let one therefore keep the mind pure, and what a man thinks, he becomes.
Proverbs:	As you think so shall you be.

James Allen: A man is literally what he thinks.

Norman Vincent Peale: You are not what you think you are; but what you *think*, you are.

Herman Kahn: Think the unthinkable.

Iara Gassen: Be careful of your thoughts; they may become words at any moment.

Flip Wilson: What you see is what you get.

Norman Vincent Peale:

You can think your way to failure and unhappiness, but you can also think your way to success and happiness. The world in which you live is not primarily determined by outward conditions and circumstances, but by thoughts that habitually occupy your mind.

Bruce Lee: Do not allow negative thoughts to enter your mind, for they are the weeds that strangle confidence.

Dr. Wayne W. Dyer: The ancestor to every single action in your life is a thought.

Ayn Rand: To achieve, you need thought... You have to know what you are doing and that's real power.

Ralph Waldo Trine: Ideas have occult power. To hold yourself in this attitude of mind is to set into operation subtle, silent, and irresistible forces that sooner or later will actualize in material form what is today merely an idea.

William James:
The greatest discovery of my generation is that human beings can alter their lives by altering their attitudes of mind.

George Bernard Shaw: Imagination is the beginning of creation. You imagine what you desire, you will what you imagine, and at last you create what you will.

~~~*~~~

Theodore Roosevelt, Jr.:
All the resources we need are in the mind.

The Buddha:
Everything is based on mind, is led by mind, is fashioned by mind. If you speak and act with a polluted mind, suffering will follow you, as the wheels of the ox cart follow the footsteps of the ox. Everything is based on mind, is led by mind, is fashioned by mind. If you speak and act with a pure mind, happiness will follow you, as a shadow clings to a form.

Theodore Cuyler:
Joy is not gained by *asking* for it, but only by *acting* for it.

Dale Carnegie:
Act as if you were already happy and that will tend to make you happy.

William James:
... and by regulating the action, which is under the more direct control of the will, we can indirectly regulate the feeling, which is not.

Dale Carnegie:	Put a big, broad, honest–to–God smile on your face; throw back your shoulders; take a good, deep breath; and sing a snatch of song... If you can't sing, whistle. If you can't whistle, hum. You will quickly discover that it is physically impossible to remain blue or depressed while you are acting out the symptoms of being radiantly happy.
William James:	The more rational statement is that we feel sorry because we cry, angry because we strike, afraid because we tremble, and not that we cry, strike, or tremble because we are sorry, angry, or fearful, as the case may be.
William James:	Thus, the sovereign voluntary path to cheerfulness, if your cheerfulness be lost, is to sit up cheerfully and to act and speak as if cheerfulness were already there.
James Allen:	A man will find that as he alters his thoughts towards things and other people, things and other people will alter towards him... Let a man radically alter his thoughts, and he will be astonished at the rapid transformation it will effect in the material conditions of his life...
Émile Coué:	Day by day in every way I am getting better and better.
Benjamin N. Cardozo:	We are what we believe we are.
Guatama Buddha:	Mind is everything, we become what we think.
William Shakespeare:	Assume a virtue, if you have it not.

Vallie G. Golden:	I made this important discovery: if I do my work *as if* I really enjoy it, then I do enjoy it to some extent.
William James:	If you want a quality, act as if you already had it. Try the "as if " technique.
Benjamin Franklin:	What you would seem to be, be really.
Kurt Vonnegut:	We are what we pretend to be, so we must be careful about what we pretend to be.
Cary Grant:	I pretended to be somebody I wanted to be until finally I became that person. Or he became me.
Maurice Valency:	We are all pretending... The important thing is to maintain a straight face.
Maxwell Maltz:	Our self–image strongly held essentially determines what we become.
Lily Tomlin:	Sometimes I feel like a figment of my own imagination.
William Shakespeare:	All the world's a stage, And all the men and women merely players.
Siobhan McKenna:	You can do what you like in Shakespeare because people don't understand half of it anyway.
Josephine Hull:	Playing Shakespeare is so tiring. You never get a chance to sit down unless you're a king.
Orson Welles:	Now we sit through Shakespeare in order to recognize the quotations.

John Carradine:	Read all the Shakespeare you can; if you can play Shakespeare, you can play anything.
Harrison Ford:	I don't use any method. I'm from the let's pretend school of acting.
Jah:	Ingrid Bergman told her director, Alfred Hitchcock, that she could just not play a certain scene 'naturally.' "Then fake it," Hitchcock advised.
George Burns:	The most important thing in acting is honesty. If you can fake that, you've got it made.
Sanford Meisner:	When you go into the professional world, at a stock theater somewhere, backstage you will meet an older actor — someone who has been around awhile. He will tell you tales and anecdotes about life in the theater. He will speak to you about your performance and the performances of others, and he will generalize to you, based on his experience and his intuitions, about the laws of the stage. Ignore this man.
W. C. Fields:	You'll never make it as a juggler, m'boy. Your eyes are too sad. But don't listen to me, kid. My entire success is based on one rule: never take advice from anybody!
Palladas:	Our Life's a stage, a playground; learn to play And take nought seriously, or bear its troubles.

Spencer Tracy:	Know your lines and don't bump into the furniture.
John Wayne:	Talk low, talk slow, and don't say too much.
David Lean:	Don't act, think.

~~~*~~~

Albert Einstein:	Imagination is more important than knowledge.
Paul J. Meyer:	Whatever you vividly imagine, ardently desire, sincerely believe and enthusiastically act upon... must inevitably come to pass.
Sheilah Graham:	You can have anything you want if you want it... enough. You must want it with an inner exuberance that erupts through the skin and joins the energy that created the world.
Matthew 21:22:	All things whatsoever you shall ask in prayer, believing, you shall receive.
Ram Tirth:	Prayers are answered in the way they're asked.
James Allen:	The divinity that shapes our ends is in ourselves. It is our very self... All that a man achieves is the direct result of his own thoughts...
Thomas Carlyle:	Silence is the element in which great things fashion themselves together.
William Penn:	True silence is the rest of the mind; it is to the spirit what sleep is to the body, nourishment and refreshment.

George Winslow Plummer:

> A properly worked out thought–form, if persisted in, will *always* work... Meditate first... Then contemplate calmly and expectantly its working out... Whatever your purpose, let it also serve the purpose of the power that has brought you to the point where you are permitted to use thought–forms.

Sue Schmidt:

> I repeated the same thing over and over again: I'm going to make it. I'm going to get there. I'm going to the North Pole.

Abraham Lincoln:

> Always bear in mind that your own resolution to success is more important than any other one thing.

Gertrude Stein:

> You have to know what you want to get.

Thomas Edison:

> The capacity of the human brain is tremendous, but people put it to no use. They live sedentary mental lives.

English Proverb:

> An idle brain is the devil's workshop.

William James:

> Men habitually use only a small part of the powers which they possess and which they might use under appropriate circumstances.

Ananda Mitra:

> It is a commonly accepted fact that we human beings are utilizing only a fraction of our mental potential... We are like a small family of squatters who have taken over a vast palace but prefer to live in a corner of the basement.

| Smiley Blanton: | The truth is that all of us attain the greatest success and happiness possible in this life whenever we use our native capacities to their greatest extent. |
| George Ohsawa: | People are always looking for miraculous power, overlooking the fact that they already have it. |

~~~*~~~

Chapter Ten

The Shadow

Jah spoke up, "Giving up the idealism of the heart because of outside pressure or other people's perceptions of reality, is not cool. The majority of these people, having failed, have terminated attempts to attain their ideal dreams, and will be quick to call you idealistic. We often act the way we do because we figure we're supposed to do it. A signal of falling into this cage is discovering yourself saying the words, 'should' or 'supposed to' in a sentence. Who says I should? Who says they're right? I say: always obey your superiors... if you have any. Whenever I espy myself using the word 'should,' a buzzer goes off in my brain and I think again, questioning: Why 'should' I?"

Jah pushed on adding, "It's too easy to settle, sometimes we all get sad and despondent. Our targets seem remote and we grasp at instant gratification to make us happier temporarily. We settle and live the rest of life in the secure snare of superfluous, miserable mediocrity. I hear you when you lose faith, plateaus in progress can be long and mundane, but you could be verging on a major breakthrough. I don't care if you're ninety–two, you only become old when you let all your hopes fade to dreams.

"Here's a conversation I once had with a buddy of mine:

'I'm always working,' he started.
'Why are you working?' I asked.
'To buy things,' he said.
'Why?' I beseeched.
'It makes me feel happy and free,' was his answer.
'Why aren't you happy and free?' I questioned.

It took him a moment to answer, 'Because I am always working.'

"Which reminds me of a story from down in the islands:

An island man used to enjoy fishing each day in the pristine, light turquoise waters of his native shore. One day a tourist happened by and inquired as to his pursuit.

'What're you doing,' asked the tourist.

The fisherman looked up, his eyes wondering who could ask something so obvious, 'I'm trying to get a fish to feed my family some dinner.'

'That's what I figured, but I never could understand you island people, why give up after just one fish, if you catch two you could eat one and sell the other. Soon you'd have enough to buy a pole.'

'Why would I need a pole?' inquired the fisherman.

'Well,' lectured the vacationer, 'with a pole you can cast the line into deeper water, there's a *slew* of fish out there. In the same amount of time you'd be able to catch more fish. By selling the ones you don't need, soon you'd be able to afford a boat.'

'What do I need with a boat?'

'With a boat you could go to the cove, beyond the reef you'd get even more fish, there'd be enough money to buy a net.'

'Yes,' said the fisherman, getting the idea now. 'With a net I could bring my two daughters, together we could round up many fish.'

'Right!' exclaimed the excited, fast–talking tourist. 'After a time you'd get another boat and hire more people to fish. Then, of course, a third boat and so on. Soon you could get an ocean going vessel, take on more people, and before you know it you'd have an entire fleet. There's virtually no competition here, the field is wide open. Eventually you could have a major fishing operation with corporate offices, secretaries, accountants, mechanics, the works. You could sit back and run the place, why it would practically run itself! You wouldn't have to work much at all.'

'What would I do then,' demanded the native fisherman.

'You could do anything you want my friend, you'd be a rich man. Don't you know that with money comes freedom!? You could forget your troubles, head for pristine waters and relax — just go fishing. You could languish in the sun all day long. You'd be a man of leisure.'

The fisherman gave a small shrug and quipped dryly, 'That's what I do now,' and modestly went back to his work."

~~~*~~~

Jewish Proverb: Some of the most well–trodden roads lead nowhere.

Mae West: I always like to try the one I've never tried before.

Walter Pater: What we have to do is to be forever curiously testing new opinions and courting new impressions.

Dizzy Gillespie: It took me all my life to learn the biggest music lesson of them all — what not to play.

Louis Armstrong: Never play a thing the same way twice.

Robert Schumann: In order to compose, all you need to do is remember a tune that nobody else has thought of.

Frank Capra: Don't follow trends, start trends.

Edgard Varese:	An artist is never ahead of its time but most people are far behind theirs.
Ned Rorem:	Art means to dare — and to have been right.
Douglas MacArthur:	It's the orders you disobey that make you famous.
Earl Warren:	Everything I did in my life that was worthwhile I caught hell for.
Jordan S. Metzger:	You don't always have to park between the lines.

<center>~~~*~~~</center>

Frank Capra:	A hunch is creativity trying to tell you something.
Mark Twain:	A man with a new idea is a crank until the idea succeeds.
Samuel Goldwyn:	I had a great idea this morning, but I didn't like it.
Irving Thalberg:	Never take any one man's opinion as final. Never take your own opinion as final.
"Beaches" Bette Midler:	Well, enough about me. Let's talk about you. What do you think about me?
John Cage:	... [do] not be dependent on anyone's opinion,... never, never look to another person for that sort of support.
Samuel Goldwyn:	When I want your opinion, I'll give it to you.

Henry Miller:	When one is trying to do something beyond his known powers it is useless to seek the approval of friends. Friends are at their best in moments of defeat.
John Cage:	I think he felt my reaction to it was not sufficiently enthusiastic.
Jean Sibelius:	Pay no attention to what the critics say: no statue has ever been put up to a critic.
Abraham Lincoln:	If I were to try to read, much less to answer, all the attacks made on me, this shop might as well be closed for any other business. I do the very best I know how — the very best I can; and I mean to keep on doing so until the end. If the end brings me out all right, then what is said against me won't matter. If the end brings me out wrong, then ten angels swearing I was right would make no difference.
Kenneth Tynan:	A critic is a man who knows the way but can't drive the car.
Igor Stravinsky:	The only true comment on a piece of music is another piece of music.
Arturo Toscanini:	If you want to please the critics, don't play too loud, too soft, too fast, too slow.
Laurence Olivier:	Don't be afraid to be outrageous; the critics will shoot you down anyway.

Jah:	A politician once went to see Calvin Coolidge to complain that another politician had insulted him, telling him that he could "Go to hell." Mr. Coolidge replied stoically, "I have looked up the law, Senator, and you don't have to go."
Eleanor Roosevelt:	Do what you feel in your heart to be right — for you'll be criticized anyway. You'll be "damned if you do, and damned if you don't."
Woody Allen:	In the afternoons, Gertrude Stein and I used to go antique hunting in the local shops, and I remember once asking her if she thought I should become a writer. In the typically cryptic way we were all enchanted with, she said, "No." I took that to mean yes and sailed for Italy the next day.
Tibetan Saying:	The wise understand by themselves; fools follow the reports of others.
Kermit The Frog:	It's okay to take advice, but be careful what you believe. Keep your little, globed eyes open.
Guatama Buddha:	Believe nothing no matter where you read it, or who said it — even if I have said it — unless it agrees with your own reason and your own common sense.
Ella Wheeler Wilcox:	You have heard me quote from Plato A thousand times no doubt; Well, I have discovered that he did not know What he was talking about.

Ralph Waldo Emerson:	Stay at home in your mind. Don't recite other people's opinions.
J. Krishnamurti:	Discard all theologies and belief... The whole principle that someone else knows and you do not know, that the one who knows is going to teach you.
Jawaharlal Nehru:	I want nothing to do with any order, religious or otherwise, which does not teach people that they are capable of becoming happier and more civilized.
George Burns:	I was always taught to respect my elders and I've now reached the age when I don't have anybody to respect.
Dennis Wolfberg:	There's one advantage to being one hundred and two. There's no peer pressure.
Timothy Leary:	Think for yourself and question authority.
Ralph Waldo Emerson:	Every burned book enlightens the world.
Walt Whitman:	Resist much, obey little.
John Leo:	Reality is just something that a good journalist hangs his opinions on, so ignore the external world as much as possible and report your own views.
John Osborne:	Never believe in mirrors or newspapers.
Iris Murdoch:	A bad review is even less important than whether it is raining in Patagonia.
Chinese Proverb:	One dog barks at something, and a hundred bark at the sound.

Graffiti:	One thousand lemmings can't be wrong.
Albert Einstein:	Great spirits have always encountered violent opposition from mediocre minds.
One of Albert Einstein's teachers:	It doesn't matter what he does, he will never amount to anything.
Albert Einstein:	To punish me for my contempt for authority, Fate made me an authority myself.
William Cowper:	To follow foolish precedents, and wink With both our eyes, is easier than to think.
Walter Lippmann:	Where all think alike, no one thinks very much.
Meister Eckhart:	Only the hand that erases can write the true thing.
Daniel S. Greenberg:	Don't ask the barber whether you need a haircut.
Huang Po:	Observe things as they are and don't pay attention to other people.
Tom Wicker:	To know things as they are is better than to believe things as they seem.
Bodhidharma:	People of this world are deluded. They're always longing for something, always, in a word, seeking. But the wise wake up. They choose reason over custom.

e. e. cummings: To be nobody–but–yourself — in a world
                      which is doing its best, night and day, to
                      make you everybody else — means to fight
                      the hardest battle which any human being
                      can fight; and never stop fighting.

Ralph Waldo Emerson: It is easy in the world to follow the world's
                      opinions; it is easy in solitude to follow our
                      own; but the great man is he who in the
                      midst of the crowd keeps with perfect
                      sweetness the independence of solitude.

Takuan: If you follow the present–day world, you
                      will turn your back on the Way; if you
                      would not turn your back on the Way, do
                      not follow the world.

George Bernard Shaw: My dear sir, I quite agree with you. But
                      who are we among so many?

Jah: In a society where everyone is wrong, it
                      doesn't mean that any*one* has the right to be
                      wrong.

Mark Twain: Whenever you find that you are on the side
                      of the majority, it is time to reform (or
                      pause and reflect).

M. Scott Peck, M.D.: Spiritual growth demands that we actively
                      seek the threatening and unfamiliar, and
                      deliberately challenge what we have been
                      taught and hold dear. The path to holiness
                      lies through questioning everything.

                      ~~~*~~~

Keith W. Hall: The word 'necessary' seldom is.

Lenny Bruce:	The "what should be" never did exist, but people keep trying to live up to it. There is no "what should be" there is only what is.
A Bumper Sticker:	Why be normal.
Unknown:	Eagles fly alone.
Unknown:	Better to be alone than in bad company.
Seumas MacManus:	If you will walk with lame men you'll soon limp yourself.
Malay Saying:	Where there's a carcass, there will be vultures.
Laotian Saying:	Live with vultures, become a vulture; live with crows, become a crow.
Japanese Saying:	It is better to be the head of a chicken than the rear end of an ox.
Maximillian Sikinger:	It is better to be a hungry coyote than to be a satisfied dog.
Benjamin Franklin:	He that lieth down with dogs, shall rise up with fleas.
E. Wilson:	If you ain't the lead dog, the scenery never changes.
The Book Of Koheleth 9:4:	For a living dog is better than a dead lion.
Pirkay Avot:	Better a tail to the lions than a head to foxes.
Elizabeth Kenny:	It's better to be a lion for a day than a sheep all your life.

Jean Giraudoux:	Only the mediocre are always at their best.
Noel Coward:	I'll go through life either first class or third, but never in second.

~~~*~~~

Herbert Bayard Swope:	I cannot give you the formula for success, but I can give you the formula for failure — which is: Try to please everybody.
Donald Rumsfeld:	If you try to please everybody, somebody is not going to like it.
Arnold Lobel:	Satisfaction will come to those who please themselves.
Christopher Morley:	There is only one success... to be able to spend your life in your own way, and not to give others absurd maddening claims upon it.
Sheldon Solomon:	We know that people with low self–esteem tend to be very conforming. They are apt to alter their behavior to suit others and to look to other people for cues about how to behave in social situations.
Adlai Stevenson II:	A free society is one where it is safe to be unpopular.
James A. Daar:	Regardless of what you say or do, some of the people will hate you all of the time.
Robert F. Kennedy:	One fifth of the people are against everything all the time.

Mark Twain:	Keep away from people who try to belittle your ambitions. Small people always do that, but the really great make you feel that you, too, can become great.
Manuel Benitez Perez:	Bravery is believing in yourself, and that thing nobody can teach you.
Manuel Benitez Perez:	Where is the university for courage?... The university for courage is to do what you believe in!
Laurence Olivier:	Have a very good reason for everything you do.
C. S. Lewis:	I am doing work which is worth doing. It would still be worth doing if nobody paid for it. But as I have no private means, and need to be fed and housed and clothed, I must be paid while I do it.
Francesco Scavullo:	If you want to do it, do it!
William S. Burroughs:	What you want to do is eventually what you will do anyway. Sooner or later.
Martin Luther:	To go against one's consciences is neither safe nor right. Here I stand. I cannot do otherwise.
Ralph Waldo Trine:	There are many who are living far below their possibilities because they are continually handing over their individualities to others. Do you want to be a power in the world? Then be yourself. Be true to the highest within your soul, and then allow yourself to be governed by no customs or conventionalities or arbitrary man–made rules that are not founded on principle.

Samuel Johnson:	Almost every man wastes part of his life in attempts to display qualities which he does not possess.
Arthur Schopenhauer:	We forfeit three–fourths of ourselves to be like other people.
Woody Allen:	My one regret in life is that I'm not someone else.
Richard Nixon:	Don't try to take on a new personality; it doesn't work.
Janis Joplin:	Don't compromise yourself. You are all you've got.
Duke Ellington:	The wise musicians are those who play what they can master.
Miles Davis:	Sometimes you have to play a long time to be able to play like yourself.
Mikhail Baryshnikov:	I do not try to dance better than anyone else. I only try to dance better than myself.
Peter Sellers:	If you ask me to play myself, I will not know what to do. I do not know who or what I am.
Ralph Waldo Emerson:	There comes a time in every man's education when he realizes that envy is ignorance, and imitation suicide.
Yogi Berra:	That's his style of hitting. If you can't imitate him, don't copy him.
Dale Berra:	The similarities between me and my father are different.

Chinese Proverb:	You can put two men to sleep in the same bed, but you can't make them dream the same dream.
Tallulah Bankhead:	Nobody can be exactly like me. Sometimes even I have trouble doing it.
Martha Graham:	You are unique, and if that is not filled then something has been lost.
Martin Mull:	Why be influenced by a person when you already are one?
Edith Sitwell:	Why not be oneself? That is the whole secret of a successful appearance. If one is a greyhound, why try to look like a Pekingese?
Frank J. Giblin:	Be yourself. Who else is better qualified?
Marcus Aurelius:	How much trouble he avoids who does not look to see what his neighbor says or does or thinks.
Henry David Thoreau:	If a man does not keep pace with his companions, perhaps it is because he hears a different drummer. Let him step to the music which he hears, however measured or far away.
Albert Einstein:	Small is the number of them that see with their own eyes and feel with their own hearts.
Ralph Waldo Emerson:	Whoso would be a man must be a nonconformist... Nothing is at last sacred but the integrity of your own mind.

Amy Vanderbilt:	One face to the world, another at home, makes for misery.
William Wordsworth:	The world is too much with us; late and soon,
	Getting and spending, we lay waste our powers:
	Little we see in nature that is ours.
	We have given our hearts away.

~~~*~~~

Tseng:	Looking straight into the heart and acting thence is the root; the wealth is a by–product.
Edna Kerr:	The greatest tragedy I know of, is that so many young people never discover what they really want to do. I think no one else is so much to be pitied as the person who gets nothing at all out of his work but his pay.
Old Saying:	Most people spend the first half of their lives giving up their health for money, and the second half of their lives they give their money to regain their health.
Chuck Close:	Don't trade a life for a BMW.
Aesop:	Beware lest you lose the substance by grasping at the shadow.
Bob Dylan:	What's money? A man is a success if he gets up in the morning and goes to bed at night and in between does what he wants to do.

| George Ohsawa: | One who lives with the "spirit of miracles" is one who... does not spend his life for earning money, but only for what he really wants to do... He is most happy when he finds the order of the universe in his daily life and in small unnoticeable things. |

"Welcome Back, Kotter"

| Gabe Kotter: | The way I figure it, leaving a job you really love for one that pays more money isn't necessarily a promotion. |

| Christopher Morley: | There is only one success — to be able to spend your life in your own way. |

| Sir James M. Barrie: | Nothing is really work unless you would rather be doing something else. |

"Peanuts" Charles Schultz

| Charlie Brown: (On the school bus) | Wake up, Sally... We're at school... |

| Sally: | Keep going, driver... Once more around the park! |

| Richard Bach: | The more I want to get something done, the less I call it work. |

| Thomas A. Edison: | I never did a day's work in my life. It was all fun. |

| Noel Cowrad: | Work is much more fun than fun. |

| Maxsim Gorky: | When work is a pleasure, life is a joy! When work is a duty, life is slavery. |

| Thomas Carlyle: | Blessed is he who has found his work. |

| Samuel Johnson: | When making your choice in life, do not neglect to live. |

Katherine Hepburn: Life is to be lived. If you have to support yourself, you had bloody well better find some way that is going to be interesting.

Alexander Graham Bell: Know what work you want to do and go after it. The young man who gets ahead must decide for himself what he wishes to do. From his own tastes, his own enthusiasm, he must get the motive and the inspiration which are to start him on his way to a successful life.

Mark Twain: The secret of success is making your vocation your vacation.

Robert Frost: My goal in life is to unite my avocation with my vocation...

Harry Emerson Fosdick: Every boy is a gambler when he chooses a vocation. He must stake his life on it.

Garry Trudeau: I've been trying for some time now to develop a life–style that doesn't require my presence.

David M. Goodrich: If you enjoy what you are doing, you may work long hours, but it won't seem like work at all. It will seem like play.

William Shakespeare: If all the year were playing holidays, to sport would be as tedious as work.

Claude Adrien Helvétius: What makes men happy is liking what they have to do. This is a principle on which society is not founded.

François de La Rochefoucauld:
>People rarely succeed at anything unless they have fun doing it.

Ernst F. Schumacher:
>They're spending their time rearranging the deck chairs on the Titanic.

William James:
>The greatest use of life is to spend it for something that will outlast it.

John Ruskin:
>When love and skill work together, expect a masterpiece.

Robert Louis Stevenson:
>If a man loves the labor of his trade, apart from any questions of success or fame, the gods have called him.

Margaret Young:
>Often people attempt to live their lives backwards; they try to have more things, or more money in order to do more of what they want, so they will be happier. The way it actually works is the reverse. You must first be who you really are, then do what you need to do, in order to have what you want.

"Alf"
Alf:
>Like my old skleenball coach used to say, "Find out what you don't do well, then don't do it."

Frantz Fanon:
>If the building of a bridge does not enrich the awareness of those who work on it, then that bridge ought not to be built.

John Ruskin:
>The highest reward for man's toil is not what he gets for it, but what he becomes by it.

Robert Graves: There's no money in poetry, but then there's no poetry in money either.

Man Ray: The streets are full of admirable craftsman, but so few practical dreamers.

Abraham Maslow: A musician must make music, an artist must paint, a poet must write, if he is to be ultimately at peace with himself.

George Winslow Plummer:

Follow the rules given and picturize yourself doing the exact work you desire to do, regardless of money. Always think of yourself as opulent. Many a financially poor man is so rich in courage and stamina that he is bound to rise out of his poverty. Many a rich man is so poor in spirit that his money is the only thing that gets him by, and he frequently loses that. But the opulent man, the one who, rich or poor, is conscious of his fullness of the good things of life, health, spirit, resilience, the ability to feel himself one with all God's creation, a brother and friend to all and able to feel the beauty of a sunset, the rhythm of a symphony, the language of trees and flowers and animals, will sooner or later enjoy, physical and spiritually, all the things this world can shower upon him, simply because he is a part of all good things and by the Law of Attraction they will come to him. He can have "infinite riches in a single room."

Herb Caen: ... remember, I have a short attention span.

Anne Saslow: He does go on a bit, doesn't he?

Michael Philips:	Money will come to you when you are doing the right thing.
Henry Miller:	I have no money, no resources, no hopes. I am the happiest man alive.
Charles H. Spurgeon:	It is not how much we have, but how much we enjoy, that makes happiness.
Henry David Thoreau:	Love your life, as it is. You may perhaps have some pleasant, thrilling, glorious hours, even in a poorhouse. The setting sun is reflected as brightly from the windows of the almshouse as from the rich man's abode.
Benjamin Franklin:	Wealth is not his who has it, but his who enjoys it.
Cleveland Amory:	The New England conscience doesn't keep you from doing what you shouldn't — it just keeps you from enjoying it.
Saadi:	Roam abroad in the world, and take thy fill of its enjoyments before the day shall come when thou must quit it for good.
The Talmud (Kidushin):	A person in the world–to–come will have to account for those [permitted pleasures] that his eyes had seen, but which he failed to partake of.

~~~*~~~

Dr. Bernie Siegel:	Each person has to figure out how they want to contribute to life.

Ralph Waldo Emerson: If a man can write a better book, preach a better sermon, or make a better mousetrap than his neighbor, though he builds his house in the woods the world will make a beaten path to his door.

"Field of Dreams"
W. P. Kinsella: If you build it they will come.

Sandra Carey: Never mistake knowledge for wisdom. One helps you make a living; the other helps you make a life.

Jah: There is the legendary story of the traveler. He discovered a mine of gold and precious stones in the desert. Elated he began the journey home, burdened with the treasures and tortured by thirst, he experienced a mirage, envisioning an oasis on the horizon. After exhausting his last energies to reach it, he expired finding to his great anguish that it was merely more gold.

Bion: He has not a acquired a fortune; the fortune has acquired him.

Arthur Miller: You specialize in something until one day you find it is specializing in you.

Anne Morrow Lindbergh: The most exhausting thing in the world is being insincere.

Ashley Montagu: Human beings are the only creatures who are able to behave irrationally in the name of reason.

Margaret Fuller:	Men, for the sake of getting a living, forget to live.
Robert Cochrane:	Don't be a salary slave! Do it now!
Erich Fromm:	The danger of the past was that men became slaves. The danger of the future is that men may become robots.
Simone Weil:	Man alone can enslave man.
Irving Berlin:	What the hell do you want to work for somebody else for? Work for yourself!
Leon Sokolsky:	Those who have never made a mistake work for those who have dared to.
John Atkinson:	If you don't run your own life, somebody else will.
Tallulah Bankhead:	If I had to live my life again, I'd make the same mistakes, only sooner.
A Fortune Cookie:	Do not let ambitions overshadow your accomplishments.
German Proverb:	Who begins too much accomplishes little.
Swahili Proverb:	To the person who seizes two things, one always slips from his grasp!
Bernard Baruch:	Always do one thing less than you think you can do.
Morris Mandel:	Always put off until tomorrow what you shouldn't do at all.

Denis Waitley: Instead of tackling the most important priorities that would make us successful and effective in life, we prefer the path of least resistance, and do things simply that will relive our tension, such as shuffling papers and majoring in minors.

~~~*~~~

Solomon Ibn Gabirol: When told of a man who had acquired great wealth, a sage replied, "Has he also acquired the days in which to spend it?"

Antoine de Saint–Exupéry: Although human life is priceless, we always act as if something had an even greater price than life. ... But what is that something?

Lao–tzu: He who knows he has enough is rich. One must know when to stop.

Marshall McLuhan: The winner is one who knows when to drop out in order to get in touch.

Harry Golden: What I admire about Shakespeare is that he was a guy who said when he made enough he was going to quit, and when he made enough, he did quit.

George Winslow Plummer:

Many times in the passing years have I heard people say: "Wait till I have made enough money and then I want to devote my entire time to humanitarian work." And I have watched and waited, and I have never seen *one* of them acquire what he considered enough to enable him to relax and devote himself to the really useful side of life. Yet many of them have made what the world calls 'wealth.'

Seneca:

Not he who has little, But he who wishes more, is poor.

Henry David Thoreau:

That man is the richest whose pleasures are the cheapest.

Pirkay Avot:

Who is rich? He who rejoices in his portion.

Alexander Solzhenitsyn:

Own only what you can always carry with you; know languages, know countries, know people. Let your memory be your travel bag.

"Kung Fu"
Master Po:

Know when to let go of those things which do not serve you, but force *you* to serve them.

J. Paul Getty:

I find all this money a considerable burden.

William K. Vanderbilt:

Inherited wealth is a real handicap to happiness.

Nathan Meyer Rothschild:

Poor unhappy me! A victim to nervousness and fancied terrors! And all because of my money.

Joe Dominguez and Vicki Robin:

... It is becoming increasingly clear that, beyond a certain minimum of comfort, money is not buying us the happiness we seek.

Seneca:

When we have provided against cold, hunger, and thirst, all the rest is but vanity and excess.

"Forrest Gump"
Forrest Gump (Winston Groom):

Now Mama said there's only so much money a man really needs, and the rest is just for showing off.

Glenda Jackson:

I used to believe that anything was better than nothing. Now I know that sometimes nothing is better.

Christina Onassis:

Sometimes when you have everything, you can't really tell what matters.

John Peers:

A man with one watch knows what time it is. A man with two watches is never sure.

The Huai Nan Tzu:

The King of Ts'u, when he went to hunt the hare, provided himself with two jade ornaments on his girdle, in case one should break in the chase; but the very fact of two being in juxtaposition, one knocking against the other, made it all the more easy for them both to be broken.

E. W. Helms:	Happy the man with one coat; he always knows what to wear.
Henry David Thoreau:	I say, beware of all enterprises that require new clothes, and not rather a new wearer.
Henry David Thoreau:	The cost of a thing is the amount of what I call life, which is required to be exchanged for it immediately or in the long run.
The Chofetz Chaim:	People say, "Time is money," but I say, "Money is time," for every luxury costs so many precious hours of your life.
Socrates:	Often when looking at a mass of things for sale, he would say to himself, "How many things I have no need of."
Elizabeth Larsen:	The only way to really get more free time is to stop buying all of these things that sell our fantasies back to us. Whether it's a picnic basket or clothes available in colors like java, lagoon, and yam, it all takes money.
Fred Stoller:	Why pay a dollar for a bookmark? Why not just use the dollar as a bookmark?
Benjamin Franklin:	In short, I conceived that a great part of the miseries of mankind are brought upon them by the false estimates they have made of the value of things.
Maimonides:	Man's obsession to add to his wealth and honor is the chief source of his misery.

~~~*~~~

Juliet Schor: Our problem is that what we want changes with income. As we get used to luxury, it becomes a necessity.

The Gulistan of Moslih Eddin Saadi:

If of thy mortal goods thou art bereft,
And from thy slender store two loaves
alone to thee are left,
Sell one, and with the dole
Buy hyacinths to feed thy soul.

Ralph Waldo Emerson: The sky is the daily bread of the eyes.

Unknown: Simplicity is the ultimate sophistication.

John Fowles: Stained glass, engraved glass, frosted glass; give me plain glass.

Konrad Adenauer: As soon as you are complicated, you are ineffectual.

Henry David Thoreau: Our life is frittered away by detail... Simplicity, simplicity, simplicity!

Thomas À Kempis: Constantly choose rather to want less, than to have more.

William Ellery Channing:

To live content with small means; to seek elegance rather than luxury, and refinement rather than fashion; to be worthy, not respectable, and wealthy, not rich; to study hard, think quietly, talk gently, act frankly; to listen to stars and birds, to babes and sages, with open heart; to bear all cheerfully, do all bravely, await occasions, hurry never. In a word, to let the spiritual, unbidden and unconscious, grow up through the common. This is to be my symphony.

Dale Carnegie:	Let's not get so busy or live so fast that we can't listen to the music of the meadow or the symphony that glorifies the forest. Some things in the world are far more important than wealth; one of them is the ability to enjoy simple things.
Nikos Kazantzakis:	How simple and frugal a thing is happiness: a glass of wine, a roast chestnut, a wretched little brazier, the sound of the sea... All that is required to feel that here and now is happiness is a simple, frugal heart.
Jordan S. Metzger:	Think high. Live Simple. Not the opposite.
Horace:	He will always be a slave who does not know how to live upon a little.
Marcus Aurelius:	Remember this, that very little is needed to make a happy life.
Unknown:	The best things in life money cannot buy.
Chinese Saying:	You can't buy an inch of time with an inch of gold.
French Saying:	All the treasures of the earth can't bring back one lost moment.
Juliet Schor:	The medieval peasant had much more free time than the professional today.

~~~*~~~

Bill Vaughan:	Money won't buy happiness, but it will pay the salaries of a large research staff to study the problem.

Herman Mankiewicz and Orson Welles:
> It's no trick to make a lot of money, if all you want to do is make a lot of money.

"Ziggy" Tom Wilson:
> Money really isn't everything! ... if it was, what would we <u>buy</u> with it?

Josh Billings:
> Money will buy a pretty good dog, but it won't buy the wag of his tail.

Malcolm Forbes:
> Money isn't everything as long as you have enough.

"Forrest Gump"
Forrest Gump (Winston Groom):
> I didn't have to think about money no more... which was good, I guess. One less thing.

Nepalese Saying:
> Wealth is both an enemy and a friend.

H. Roy Kaplan:
> I've talked to hundreds of lottery winners and I have found very few who had any idea what to do with the money, or who got great happiness from it.

Elsie Stapleton:
> I have often seen it happen that an increase in income accomplished nothing but an increase in spending — and an increase in headaches.

Kin Hubbard:
> It's pretty hard to tell what does bring happiness. Poverty an' wealth have both failed.

Dave Barry:
> It is better to be rich and healthy than poor and sick.

Jean Kerr:	You don't seem to realize that a poor person who is unhappy is in a better position than a rich person who is unhappy. Because the poor person has hope. He thinks money would help.
Rabelais:	Half the world does not know how the other half lives.
Sophie Tucker:	I've been rich and I've been poor; rich is better.
Joe E. Lewis:	It doesn't matter if you're rich or poor, as long as you've got money.
Sister Mary Tricky:	Rich people are just poor people with money.
Gabrielle "Coco" Chanel:	There are people who have money and people who are rich.
Pablo Picasso:	I'd like to live like a poor man with lots of money.
Walter Hagen:	I never wanted to be a millionaire. I just wanted to live like one.

"The Beverly Hillbillies"

Mrs. Fenwick:	Your banker tells me you're worth forty million dollars. Why do you drive around in that truck and dress as you do and eat grits and hog jowls?
Jed Clampett:	Well, the way I look at it, Widow, if ya got it, spend it!
Alfred Hitchcock:	Actually, I have no regard for money. Aside from its purchasing power, it's completely useless as far as I'm concerned.

Woody Allen: Money is better than poverty, if only for financial reasons.

Jules Renard: I finally know what distinguishes man from the other beasts: financial worries.

Danish Saying: It's no disgrace to be poor, but it can be inconvenient.

Jackie Mason: I have enough money to last me the rest of my life — unless I buy something.

Henny Youngman: I've got all the money I'll ever need — if I die by four o'clock.

Artemus Ward: Let us all be happy and live within our means, even if we have to borrow the money to do it with.

Gus Kahn and Raymond B. Egan:
There's nothing surer,
  The rich get rich and the poor get poorer,
In the meantime,
  In between time,
Ain't we got fun.

Deuteronomy 8:3: One does not live on bread alone, but by every thing that comes out of the mouth of the Lord does one live.

Aesop: Beware lest you lose the substance by grasping at the shadow.

Henry David Thoreau: Many men go fishing all of their lives without knowing that it is not fish they are after.

Quentin Crisp:	It's no good running a pig farm badly for thirty years while saying, "Really I was meant to be a ballet dancer." By that time pigs will be your style.
Golda Meir:	I may not have been a great prime minister, but I would have been a great farmer.
Laurence Olivier:	I think I would have liked to have been a farmer.
African Bushman:	Why should we take up farming when there are so many mongongo nuts in the world?
Grant Wood:	All the really good ideas I ever had came to me while I was milking a cow.
Herman Mankiewicz:	I don't know how it is that you start working at something that you don't like, and before you know it you're an old man.
George Burns:	I'd rather be a failure at something I enjoy than be a success at something I hate.
Dr. Albert Schweitzer:	I am just a simple doctor. All I wanted to do... was to found a small hospital.
Martin Scorsese:	I just wanted to be an ordinary parish priest.
Duchess of Windsor:	I would like to be the head of an advertising agency.
Martina Navratilova:	My wish is to have enough money so that I never have to play another set of tennis if I don't want to.
Katherine Hepburn:	Life is to be lived. If you have to support yourself, you had bloody well better find some way that is going to be interesting.

Shirley Conran:	Life is too short to stuff a mushroom.
Graffiti:	The prospect of tomorrow's joy will never console me for today's boredom.
Friedrich Nietzsche:	Is not life a hundred times too short for us to bore ourselves?

~~~*~~~

Chapter Eleven

It Might Have Been!

"It is essential to do what is feared in life, or fear is in charge of life," Jah observed. "A wise fortune cookie once stated with a Chinese accent: Better to face unknown, than to always be in uncertainty.

"Reacting to appease feelings of fear is tempting, but we must resist abdicating control to the norms and negative attitudes of those around us if we want to control our own world. Of course, it's befitting to be considerate, and important to follow the golden rule, but it's literally ludicrous to think that all of the people can be pleased all of the time. You've got to be free to do what you want to do, not what the masses prescribe; there are too many of them and only one of you.

"The crowd is easy to follow, but those who follow the crowd will never be followed by them. I mostly flow opposite the undercurrent of the crowd; they're usually wrong," Jah admitted. "When a hundred million people believe in a foolish idea, it doesn't lend it any wisdom! Ever notice that the people in charge generally aren't sure what's happening themselves; often ulterior interests are at the forefront. Why mimic them? Nietzsche said, 'Most won't wander from the herd because it is warm and they are lazy.'

"To rise above the rut of everyday life, we need to recognize the traps that we set for ourselves so we can escape and avoid them. Move with the herd and you'll get no further then they. You'll be average."

Jah was ready for another story:

"Someone once asked "Dear Abby" for an

opinion; contemplating whether or not to go back to college to become a doctor; they were torn by indecision.

'If I go back to college and get my degree, then go to medical school, do my internship, and finally get into the practice of medicine — it will take me seven years. But Abby, in seven years, I will be forty–three years old! What do you think?'

Abby's reply? 'And how old will you be in seven years if you don't go back to college?'

"The sun will set there everyday," Jah's forefinger and thumb touched his chin, his eyes looking thoughtfully toward the west, "if ever you must choose between doing something and doing nothing remember that, and realize:

"The next seven years will go by anyway.

"If you must choose between two alternatives remember the credo:

"When in doubt, do both. More often than not the choices are not mutually exclusive.

"Nadine Stair put it most eloquently in her deathbed vignette, *If I Had My Life to Live Over*:

'I'd dare to make more mistakes next time. I'd relax. I would limber up. I would be sillier than I have been on this trip. I would take fewer things seriously. I would take more chances. I would take more trips. I would climb more mountains and swim more rivers. I would eat more ice cream and less beans. I would perhaps have more actual troubles, but I'd have fewer imaginary ones.

'You see, I'm one of those people who live sensibly and sanely, hour after hour, day after day. Oh, I've had my moments, and if I had it to do over again, I'd have more of them. In fact, I'd try to have nothing else. Just moments, one after another, instead of living so many years ahead of each day. I've been one of those persons who never goes anywhere without a thermometer, a hot water bottle, a raincoat, and a parachute. If I had to do it again, I would travel lighter than I have.

'If I had my life to live over, I would start bare-foot earlier in the spring and stay that way later in the fall. I would go to more dances. I would ride more merry–go–rounds. I would pick more daisies.'

"What will you say about yourself at the end of the next seven years. When your life is in its twilight, will you say... 'I've done a lot and tried my best,' or, 'I wish I had at least given it a shot?'

"Most settle. Be strong, go for your dreams!"

~~~*~~~

William Shakespeare:

> Cowards die many times before their deaths;
>> The valiant never taste of death but once.

"Night Court"
Judge Harry Stone:

> A coward dies a hundred deaths, a brave man only once... But then, once is enough, isn't it?

Ella Fitzgerald:

> One saying of Count Basie's that I'll always remember pertains to when my husband and I broke up. Basie said, "It's just like a toothache. It hurts now, but if you take that tooth out, you'll miss it but you'll feel better."

Julius Caesar:

> It is better to suffer the worst at once, than to live in perpetual fear of it.

Norman Mailer:

> As many people die from an excess of timidity as from bravery.

Henry Miller:

> Life moves on, whether we act as cowards or heroes.

Cus D'Amato:	The hero and the coward both feel the same thing, but the hero uses his fear, projects it onto his opponent, while the coward runs. It's the same thing, fear, but it's what you do with it that matters.
Ronald Reagan:	Heros may not be braver than anyone else. They're just braver five minutes longer.
Anne Saslow:	I believe that the bravest of men do not always have the sense of one lone doe in the meadow.
Elmer Davis:	This will remain the land of the free only so long as it is the home of the brave.
Pericles:	The secret of happiness is liberty and the secret of liberty is courage.
Andrew Jackson:	One man with courage makes a majority.
Ruth Gordon:	Courage is very important. Like a muscle, it is strengthened by use.
C. S. Lewis:	Courage is not simply one of the virtues, but the form of every virtue at the testing point.
Clare Boothe Luce:	Courage is the ladder on which all the other virtues mount.
Woody Allen:	In terms of human attributes, what really counts is courage.
Erica Jong:	Everyone has talent. What is rare is the courage to follow the talent to the dark place where it leads.

Phillip Adams:
It seems to me that people have vast potential. Most people can do extraordinary things if they have the confidence or take the risks. Yet most people don't. They sit in front of the telly and treat life as if it goes on forever.

Ty Murray:
Riding bulls isn't like settin' in a recliner watching T.V., it gives you a wild rush.

Spanish Proverb:
It is not the same to talk of bulls as to be in the bullring.

John Keats:
In Endymion, I leaped head long into the sea, and thereby have become better acquainted with the soundings, the quick-sands, and the rocks, than if I had stayed upon the green shore, and piped a silly pipe, and took tea and comfortable advice.

Erica Jong:
Advice is what we ask for when we already know the answer but wish we didn't.

Alexander Solzhenitsyn:
We do not err because truth is difficult to see. It is visible at a glance. We err because this is more comfortable.

French Saying:
Good advice is often annoying — bad advice never is.

Edna St. Vincent Millay:
Please give me some good advice in your next letter. I promise not to follow it.

Ethiopian Saying:
Give advice; if people don't listen, let adversity teach them.

P. G. Wodehouse:	I always advise people never to give advice.
Jack Herbert:	We all admire the wisdom of people who come to us for advice.
George Burns:	Too bad all the people who know how to run the country are busy driving taxi cabs and cutting hair.
E. W. Howe:	A good scare is worth more to a man than good advice.
Anselm Feuerbach:	If someone gives you so–called good advice, do the opposite; you can be sure it will be the right thing nine out of ten times.
G. K. Chesterton:	I owe my success to having listened respectfully to the very best advice, and then going away and doing the exact opposite.
Tom Magliozzi:	I've never gotten any good advice. I've had to figure everything out for myself.
Oscar Wilde:	The only thing to do with good advice is to pass it on. It is never of any use to oneself.
Edward Gorey:	Pay no attention to whatever advice you receive.
George Carlin:	Most people don't pay any attention to me.
Lao–tzu:	To lead the people, walk behind them.

Josh Billings:	When a man comes to me for advice, I find out the kind of advice he wants, and I give it to him.
Harry S. Truman:	I have found the best way to give advice to your children is to find out what they want and then advise them to do it.
Frank Tyger:	The art of giving advice is to make the recipient believe he thought of it himself.
Kin Hubbard:	The worst waste of breath, next to playing a saxophone, is advising a son.
Italian Saying:	The dying cannot leave their wisdom or experience to their heirs.
O. A. Battista:	The best inheritance a parent can give to his children is a few minutes of his time each day.
Ruth E. Renkel:	Sometimes the poorest man leaves his children the richest inheritance.
Ludwig van Beethoven:	Recommend to your children virtue; that alone can make them happy, not gold.
Thomas Paine:	... virtue is not hereditary.
Anne Frank:	Parents can only give good advice or put them on the right paths, but the final forming of a person's character lies in their own hands.
Hodding Carter III:	There are only two things we can give our children. One is roots; the other is wings.
Francesco Scavullo:	If you want to do it, do it!

Walt Whitman:	This is what you shall do: Love the earth and sun and the animals, despise riches, give alms to every one that asks, stand up for the stupid and crazy, devote your income and labor to others, hate tyrants, argue not concerning God, have patience and indulgence toward the people, take off your hat to nothing known or unknown or to any man or number of men, go freely with powerful uneducated persons and with the young and with the mothers of families, read these leaves in the open air every season of every year of your life, re–examine all you have been told at school or church or in any book, dismiss whatever insults your own soul, and your very flesh shall be a great poem and have the richest fluency not only in its words but in the silent lines of its lips and face and between the lashes of your eyes and in every motion and joint of your body...
Horace:	Whatever your advice, make if brief.
Sophie Tucker:	Keep breathing.
Ben Crenshaw:	Never do anything stupid.
Miss Piggy:	Never purchase beauty products in hardware stores.
Erma Bombeck:	Never lend your car to anyone to whom you have given birth.
Unknown:	Never say never.
Keith A. Pitman:	All generalizations are untrue.

Lady Mary Wortley Montagu:
General notions are generally wrong.

Jack Jackson:
No rule is ever so good, or so well written, or covers so many contingencies that it can't be replaced by another, much better, more appropriate rule (with the exception of this rule).

Alexander Haig:
You'd better caveat that statement.

Charles Bukowski:
Never get out of bed before noon.

Unknown:
Never eat crackers in bed.

Miss Piggy:
Never eat more than you can lift.

Benjamin Franklin:
Hold your counsel before dinner; the full belly hates thinking as well as acting.

Abraham Lincoln:
Do not worry; eat three square meals a day; say your prayers; be courteous to your creditors; keep your digestion good; exercise; go slow, and easy. Maybe there are other things that your special case requires to make you happy, but, my friend, these I reckon will give you a good lift.

Cary Grant:
My formula for living is quite simple. I get up in the morning and go to bed at night. In between times, I occupy myself as best I can.

Norman Vincent Peale:
I try to eat sensibly, exercise regularly, and avoid bad habits of all kinds.

Sophie Tucker:
Keep breathing.

Garrison Keillor:	That is the secret of a good life ladies and gentlemen,... a short work week.
Robert Frost:	In three words I can sum up everything I've learned about life. It goes on.
Joseph Campbell:	People say that what we're all seeking is a meaning for life... I think that what we're really seeking is an experience of being alive... so that we can actually feel the rapture of being alive.
Woody Allen:	The meaning of life is that nobody knows the meaning of life.
Charles A. Lindbergh:	Life is like a landscape. You live in the midst of it, but can describe it only from the vantage point of distance.
Judith Martin:	Life is full of situations that cry out not to be commented upon.
William S. Burroughs:	Life is a cut–up.
Charlie Chaplin:	In the end, everything is a gag.

Maharishi Mahesh Yogi:

The purpose of life is the expansion of happiness.

Phyllis McGinley:	Pressed for rules and verities,
	    All I recollect are these:
	 Feed a cold and starve a fever.
	    Argue with no true believer.
	 Think too–long is never–act.
	    Scratch a myth and find a fact.

J. Paul Getty:	Rise early. Work late. Strike oil.

Raymond Carver:	Eat cereal for breakfast and write good prose.
Malay Saying:	Don't use an ax to embroider.
George Carlin:	Well, some people need practical advice you know.
Samuel Johnson:	Advice is seldom welcome. Those who need it most, like it least.
Benjamin Franklin:	Wise men don't need advice. Fools don't take it.
Latin Saying:	A word to the wise, may be sufficient.

~~~*~~~

Martin Luther King, Jr.:	
	So I'm happy tonight. I'm not worried about anything. I'm not fearing any man.
A Fortune Cookie:	Think like a philosopher; act like a king.
"History of the World — Part I" Mel Brooks:	It's good to be 'da' king.
Woodrow Wilson:	I would rather lose in a cause that will someday win, than win in a cause that will someday lose!
Gandhi:	The enemy is fear. We think it is hate; but it is fear.
Ida Tarbell:	I know no companion so terrible as fear.
Henry David Thoreau:	Nothing is so much to be feared as fear.

Michel Eyquem De Montaigne:
>The thing I fear most is fear.

Franklin Delano Roosevelt:
>The only thing we have to fear is, fear itself.

Francis Bacon: Nothing is terrible except fear itself.

Duke of Wellington: The only thing I am afraid of is fear.

Underdog: There's no need to fear — Underdog is here.

Edward Moore Kennedy:
>I am glad to be an underdog.

John F. Kennedy: Let us never negotiate out of fear, but let us never fear to negotiate.

Rabbi Nachman Of Breslav:
>All the world in its entirety is a very narrow bridge, and the essential thing is not to be afraid.

Marie Curie: Nothing in life is to be feared. It is only to be understood.

Franz Kafka: The true way goes over a rope which is not stretched at any great height, but just above the ground.

George Leybourne: He flies through the air with the greatest of ease,
>   This daring young man on the flying trapeze;
>His figure is handsome, all girls he can please,
>   And my love he purloined her away!

John Goddard: To dare is to do, to fear is to fail.

Michel Eyquem De Montaigne:
He who fears he will suffer, already suffers because of his fear.

Aristotle: Fear is pain arising from the anticipation of evil.

Reporter: Were you apprehensive in the twelfth inning,

Yogi Berra: No, but I was scared.

"M*A*S*H"
Hawkeye Pierce: I'd feel a lot braver if I wasn't so scared.

"Tennessee Tuxedo"
Chumley: But Tennessee, would you be scared to be an astronaut.

Tennessee Tuxedo: No, Chumley, and neither will you.

Eddie Rickenbacker: Courage is doing what you're afraid to do. There can be no courage unless you're scared.

Elmer Davis: The first and great commandment is, "Don't let them scare you."

Lao–tzu: He who knows how to live can walk abroad without fear of rhinoceros or tiger.

Louis Pasteur: Ain't nothing in the woods going to hurt you unless... it smells that you are afraid.

Margaret Mitchell: There ain't nothing from the outside can lick any of us.

Bedouin Saying:	Truth may walk through the world unarmed.
Ernest Hemingway:	Cowardliness, as distinguished from panic, is almost always simply a lack of ability to suspend the functioning of the imagination.
James Thurber:	All men should strive to learn before they die what they are running from, and to, and why.
Ralph Waldo Emerson:	Do not be too timid and squeamish about your actions. All life is an experiment.
Gertrude Stein:	Considering how dangerous everything is, nothing is really frightening.

Samuel Ichiye Hayakawa:
> If you have ceased to be ready to face the frightening, then you become old. We weren't put on earth to behave like barnacles.

John F. Kennedy:	If we are strong, our strength will speak for itself. If we are weak, worries will be no help.

"The Bob Newhart Show"
Elliott Carlin:	I think I'm overcoming my agoraphobia.
Bob Hartley:	I didn't know you had a fear of open places.
Elliott Carlin:	I thought it was a fear of agricultural products. Anyway, wheat doesn't scare me anymore.

Bertrand Russell:	Fear is the main source of superstition, and one of the main sources of cruelty. To conquer fear is the beginning of wisdom.

Andrew W. Mathis:	It's bad luck to be superstitious.
Edmund Burke:	Superstition is the religion of feeble minds.
Unknown:	Superstition is the religion of fools.
Jah:	Breaking a mirror is only bad luck to the extent that you have to buy a new mirror.
Steven Wright:	I broke a mirror in my house. I'm supposed to get seven years bad luck, but my lawyer thinks he can get me five.
Lucretius:	For as children tremble and fear everything in the blind darkness, so we in the light sometimes fear what is no more to be feared than the things children in the dark hold in terror and imagine will come true.
William Shakespeare:	Present fears are less than horrible imaginings.
Sophocles:	To him who is in fear, everything rustles.
Dr. Robert H. Schuller:	Nothing devastates or holds people back more than the fear of failure. What would you attempt to do if you knew you could not fail?
Jim Seibel:	I'm not indecisive. Am I indecisive?
Bob Nickman:	I have mixed feelings about ambivalence.
Arlo Guthrie:	That's what it all comes down to; whether or not, when the time comes, you decide to jump in the pot.

David Lloyd George:	Don't be afraid to take a big step if one is indicated. You can't cross a chasm in two small jumps.
Eleanor Roosevelt:	The purpose of life is, after all, to live it, to taste experience to the utmost, to reach out eagerly and without fear for newer and richer experience.
Unknown:	Life is not a goblet to be drained but a measure to be filled.
Elizabeth Cochrane:	Life can be a great adventure and I'm going to make it one.
Helen Keller:	Life is either a daring adventure or nothing. Security does not exist in nature, nor do the children of men as a whole experience it. Avoiding danger is no safer in the long run than exposure.
Hugh Walpole:	Don't play for safety — it's the most dangerous thing in the world.
Elizabeth Bowen:	What I regret, on behalf of myself of long ago, is not the overweeningness, but the playing it safe.
Thea Musgrave:	In art you have to follow your hunch. You can't play it safe.
Jean-Jacques Rousseau:	Every man has the right to risk his own life in order to save it.
John F. Kennedy:	There are risks and costs to a program of action, but they are far less than the long–range risks and costs of comfortable inaction.

Shirley Williams:	There are great hazards in anything one does, but there are greater hazards in doing nothing.
Moliere:	It is not only what we do, but also what we do not do, for which we are accountable.
Stell Lefkowitz:	The only things I regret are those things I didn't do.
Harvey Mackay:	Sometimes it's risky not to take a risk.
Dr. Paul Pearsall:	I regretted that I didn't take more risks.
I. King Jordan:	Take risks; don't be afraid of failing. It's how we learn.
Maxwell Maltz:	Often the difference between a successful man and a failure is not one's better abilities or ideas, but the courage that one has to bet on his ideas, to take a calculated risk — and to act.
George Patton:	Take calculated risks, that is quite different from being rash.
Phillip Adams:	Unless you're willing to do that, to have a go, to fail miserably, and have another go, success won't happen.
Will Rogers:	Why not go out on a limb? That's where the fruit is.
Robert Frost:	It was a risk I had to take — and took.
Alexander Woolcott:	Nothing risqué, nothing gained.
Erica Jong:	And the trouble is, if you don't risk anything, you risk even more.

Sydney J. Harris:	Regret for the things we did can be tempered by time; it is regret for the things we did not do that is inconsolable.

~~~*~~~

Bertolt Brecht:	Do not fear death so much, but rather the inadequate life.
"Kung Fu" Master Po: Caine:	What is it I have told you, Grasshopper? That life is a corridor and death merely a door.
"Night Court" Bull:	Death is just nature's way of telling you, "Hey, you're not alive anymore."
Robin Williams:	Death is nature's way of saying, "Your table is ready."
Jackie Gleason's Epitaph:	And away we go!
Dolly Parton:	When I sit back in my rocker, I want to have done it all.
Cab Calloway:	I did it all. And do you know what that's called. It's called living.
Deuteronomy 30:15:	See I have set before you this day life.
Alexander Eliot:	Life is a fatal adventure. It can only have one end. So why not make it as far-ranging and free as possible?
Oscar Wilde:	One can survive everything nowadays, except death.

242

1943 Farmer's Almanac:

'Feared of dying? Were you 'feared of being born?

Woody Allen:

It's not that I'm afraid to die, I just don't want to be there when it happens.

Benjamin Franklin:

Fear not death; for the sooner we die, the longer we shall be immortal.

Susan Ertz:

Millions long for immortality who do not know what to do with themselves on a rainy Sunday afternoon.

Woody Allen:

I don't want to achieve immortality through my work. I want to achieve immortality through not dying.

David Garrick:

It is what we must all come to if we only live long enough.

Albert Einstein:

The fear of death is the most unjustified of all fears, for there's no risk of accident for someone who's dead.

Kurt Vonnegut:

When you're dead you're dead.

Bumper Sticker:

Extinct is forever.

William Faulkner:

Living is a process of getting ready to be dead for a long time.

Scottish Proverb:

Be happy while you're living, for you're a long time dead.

Ptahhotep:

Be cheerful while you are alive.

"Friends"
Chandler: I'm not dead, and yet I have no life.

Benjamin Franklin: A long life may not be good enough, but a good life is long enough.

Jean Jacques Rousseau: The man who has lived longest is not the man who has counted most years, but he who has enjoyed life most.

Dr. Paul Pearsall: It is a quality of life, your love span not your life span, that matters most.

Alfred Lord Tennyson: 'Tis better to have loved and lost
                              Than never to have loved at all.

William Makepeace Thackeray:
                              To love and win is the best thing; to love and lose the next best.

"The Princess Bride"
Wesley: Death cannot stop true love; all it can do is delay it for awhile.

Thornton Wilder: The highest tribute to the dead is not grief but gratitude.

Jimi Hendrix: It's funny the way most people love the dead. Once you are dead, you are made for life.

Arthur Ford and Ruth Montgomery:

> No person has the right to take the life within himself, any more than that of another person, since all are a part of the Godhead... [Thus,] they are what we refer to as suffering souls. They live hourly with the shame of self–destruction and rage within themselves for having failed to settle the problem while in the flesh, where it is much more easily faced (than here) [in heaven].

Unknown:

> Don't mourn for me now; don't mourn for
> me never —
> I'm going to do nothing forever and ever.

Dr. Paul Pearsall:

> If I bring any warning to your audience today, that's what you will think: did I forgive enough, did I hug enough, did I care enough, did I love enough. There is a difference between the date of dying and releasing life.

Henry John Temple:

> Die, my dear Doctor, that's the last thing I shall do!

George Simenon:

> I adore life but I don't fear death. I just prefer to die as late as possible.

"Blake's 7"
Vila Restal:

> I plan to live forever, or die trying.

George Bernard Shaw:

> Do not try to live forever. You will not succeed.

Kensal Green:

> Here Einstein lies;
>   At least, they laid his bier
> Just hereabouts —
>   Or relatively near.

Dinah Maria Mulock Craik:
> And when I lie in the green kirkyard,
> With the mould upon my breast,
> Say not that she did well or ill,
> Only, "She did her best."

Fred DeCordova (Epitaph):
> I'll be seeing you shortly.

Virgil:
> Death twitches my ear. "Live," he says, "I am coming."

Omar Khayyám:
> Ah, make the most of what we yet may spend,
> Before we too into the Dust descend;
> Dust into Dust, and under Dust, to lie,
> Sans Wine, sans Song, sans Singer, and — sans End!

Dorothy Parker (Epitaph):
> Excuse my dust.

James Cameron:
> While other people's deaths are deeply sad, one's own is sure to be a bit of a joke.

Mark Twain:
> Why is it that we rejoice at a birth and grieve at a funeral? It is because we are not the person involved.

Lawrence Durrell:
> Death is a metaphor; nobody dies to himself.

Flora Johnson:
> There is nothing like death. Everything that approaches it is a metaphor.

~~~*~~~

Socrates:
> Death may be the greatest of human blessings.

246

Francis Bacon:	It is as natural to die as to be born.
George Merriman:	Death is, to us here, the most terrible word we know. But when we have tasted its reality, it will mean to us birth, deliverance, a new creation of ourselves.
Chuang–tzu:	Li Chi was a daughter of the border chieftain Ai Feng. When Duke Hsien claimed her as his wife, she cried until her sleeves were soaked with tears. But after she had come to know the duke and had shared his palace, she laughed at her former fears and sadness. How do we know that the spirits of the dead do not do the same?
Elisabeth Kübler–Ross:	Death is simply a shedding of the physical body, like the butterfly coming out of a cocoon... It's like putting away your winter coat when spring comes.
Helen Steiner Rice:	The end of the road is but a bend in the road.
Matsuo Basho:	Every bend in the road brings me new ideas; every dawn gives me fresh feelings.
Leonardo da Vinci:	As a well–spent day brings happy sleep, so life well used brings happy death.
Fran Lebowitz:	Sleep is death without the responsibility.
Muhammad:	People sleep, and when they die they wake.

~~~*~~~

Santayana:	There is no cure for birth and death, save to enjoy the interval.

Brooke Shields:	If you're killed, you've lost a very important part of your life.
Yogi Berra:	I could've probably said that.
Isidor Feinstein Stone:	
	If you live long enough, you get accused of things you never did and praised for virtues you never had.
Yogi Berra:	I really didn't say everything I said.
British Parliamentary Speaker:	
	Mr. Speaker, if I had said that I would not have been allowed to.
Woody Allen:	I keep wondering if there is an afterlife, and if there is, will they be able to break a twenty?
Carl Jung:	We can never finally know. I simply believe that some part of the human Self or Soul is not subject to the laws of space and time.
Joseph Heller:	I've come to look upon death the same way I look upon root–canal work. Everyone else seems to get through it all right, so it couldn't be too difficult for me.

Jordan S. Metzger and Stell Lefkowitz:

> Be Forewarned And
>   Not Forlorn'd For:
> There is no Man upon this Earth,
>   Who has achieved Immortal Birth.
>
> We All must Die, this much is True.
>   We All must Die, I'm tellin' You.
> So when you lay me Down to Sleep,
>   And pray, "Dear Lord My Soul To Keep."
>
> Don't mourn me in that Old Gravestone,
>   I've left, my Dear, the better to Roam,
> I'm gone... to find a sweeter Home.
>
> We All must Die, Life's Brief and Curt,
>   So Live Life Grand, Be Alert,
> 'Cause the Words of the Wise are, "Doesn't
> Hurt."

~~~*~~~

Vladimir Nabokov: Life is a great surprise, I do not see why death should not be an even greater one.

Gracie Allen: When I was born I was so surprised I didn't talk for a year and a half.

Henry Miller: Death itself doesn't frighten me because I don't believe it's the end.

Woody Allen: I don't believe in an afterlife, although I am bringing a change of underwear.

Samuel Beckett: Do you believe in the life to come? Mine was always that.

Interviewer: Do you believe in the hereafter?
Henry David Thoreau: One world at a time.

Rowena L. Brown Edelbrock:

When I quit this mortal shore
  And mosey 'round this earth no more
Don't weep, don't sigh, don't grieve, don't sob;
  I may have struck a better job.
Don't go and buy a large bouquet
  For which you'll find it hard to pay.
Don't stand around me looking blue;
  I may be better off than you!

Unknown:

Do not stand at my grave and weep,
  I am not there, I do not sleep.
I am a thousand winds that blow;
  I am the diamond glints on snow.
I am the sunlight on ripened grain;
  I am the gentle autumn's rain.
When you awaken in the morning's hush,
  I am the swift uplifting rush
Of quiet birds in circled flight.
  I am the soft star that shines at night.
Do not stand at my grave and cry.
  I am not there; I did not die.

P. D. Ouspensky:

Nothing dies. Everything exists forever. It is we who go away from it, lose sight of it. Yesterday exists... This has not died and it cannot die. I can always go back to it. But there is a mystery about it; this mystery we call death. Yet in truth death is simply our failure to understand something. I feel this now. Why can it not always be felt?

Shunryu Suzuki:

We die, and we do not die.

Old Adage:

What the caterpillar thinks is death, to the master is a butterfly.

"Kung Fu"

Master Po:

The caterpillar is secure in the womb of the cocoon. And yet — to achieve its destiny — it must cast off its earthbound burden... to realize the ethereal beauty of the butterfly.

Norman O. Brown:

To be born is to die.

Russian Saying:

The one who is born yells; the one who dies is silent.

Winston Churchill:

I am ready to meet my Maker. Whether my Maker is prepared for the ordeal of meeting me is another matter.

A Railroad Station Sign:

Beware! To touch these wires is instant death. Anyone found doing so will be prosecuted.

Yogi Berra:

He must have made that before he died.

Humberto Cardinal Medeiros:

We just lost a Pope, which is very sad, and now we lost to the Yankees, which is also very sad.

Phil Rizzuto:

Well, that kind of puts a damper on even a Yankee win.

~~~*~~~

Grace Hansen:

Don't be afraid your life will end; be afraid that it will never begin.

Dr. Jon Kabat–Zinn:

The real problem is not that we're afraid of death, but that in some way we really shy away from life.

251

Saul Alinsky:	Once you accept your own death all of a sudden you're free to live. You no longer care about your reputation. You no longer care except so far as your life can be used tactically — to promote a cause you believe in.
Virgil Thomson:	Try a thing you haven't done three times. Once, to get over the fear of doing it. Twice, to learn how to do it. And a third time to figure out whether you like it or not.
Ralph Waldo Emerson:	Do the thing you fear and the death of fear is certain.
Dr. Albert Schweitzer:	The tragedy of life is what dies inside a man while he lives.
James Smith:	There ain't no sense in dying before your time is come.
Richard Bach:	Here is the test to find whether your mission on earth is finished: If you're alive, it isn't.
Thich Nhat Hanh:	By overcoming revulsion and fear, life will be seen as infinitely precious, every second of it worth living.
Taisendeshimaru:	Human beings are afraid of dying. They are always running after something: money, honor, pleasure. But if you had to die now, what would you want?
Sri Ramakrishna:	The world is impermanent. One should constantly remember death.

Epictetus:	What do you wish to be doing when it [death] overtakes you? ... If you have anything better to be doing when you are so overtaken, get to work on that.
Joanne Seltzer:	I wish I found less time for shaving legs and underarms, more for visiting planetariums.
Joseph Campbell:	Follow your bliss.
Ralph Waldo Emerson:	Counsel that I once heard given to a young person, "Always do what you are afraid to do."

John Greenleaf Whittier:

God pity them both! and pity us all,
  Who vainly the dreams of youth recall.
For of all sad words of tongue or pen,
  The saddest are these: "It might have been!"

~~~*~~~

Chapter Twelve

A Thin Stream

What's the use of worrying?
 It never was worthwhile,
So, pack up your troubles in your old kit–bag,
 And smile, smile, smile.

George Asaf

"Many of us are listening to the weather report too closely," Jah swiftly added. "Those busy looking for rain will find no time left for love; there is such a thing as a self–fulfilling prophecy."

~~~*~~~

The Book Of Koheleth 11:4:

Whoever observes the wind will not sow; and whoever regards the clouds will not reap.

John Kieran:

Bad weather always looks much worse through a window.

L. A. Express Weather Report:

There is some possibility of showers tonight, according to Colonel H. B. Hersey, government meteorologist, although it is probable there will be no rain.

255

William Dean Howells: Do you think it [the rain] will stop?

Mark Twain: It always has.

Announcement at a Church:
There will be a procession next Sunday afternoon in the grounds of the Monastery; but if it rains in the afternoon, the procession will take place in the morning.

Charles Dudley Warner:
Everybody talks about the weather, but nobody does anything about it.

Richard Eaton: Life is subject to change without notice.

Proverb: To worry about tomorrow is to be unhappy today.

Matthew 6:34: Take therefore no thought for the morrow: for the morrow shall take thought for the things of itself.

Dale Carnegie: By all means take thought for the morrow, yes, careful thought and planning and preparation. But have no anxiety.

Rod Steiger: It's true that tomorrow may be better — or worse. But today may not be so bad. You must appreciate the miracle that you're alive right now and forget about how, or if, you're going to live tomorrow.

Igor Stravinsky: I am in the present. I cannot know what tomorrow will bring forth. I can know only what the truth is for me today. That is what I am called upon to serve, and I serve it in all lucidity.

Robert J. Burdette: It isn't the experience of today that drives men mad. It is the remorse for something that happened yesterday, and the dread of what tomorrow many disclose.

Robert Louis Stevenson:
Anyone can carry his burden, however hard, until nightfall. Anyone can do his work, however hard, for one day. Anyone can live sweetly, patiently, lovingly, purely, till the sun goes down. And this is all that life really means.

Matthew 6:34: So do not worry about tomorrow, for tomorrow will bring worries of its own. Today's trouble is enough for today.

Robert J. Burdette: There are two days in the week about which and upon which I never worry... One... Yesterday... And the other day I do not worry about is Tomorrow.

Rex Harrison: Tomorrow is just a fiction of today.

General Colin Powell: It ain't as bad as you think; it will look better in the morning.

Swedish Saying: The afternoon knows what the morning never suspected.

John Steinbeck: It is a common experience that a problem difficult at night is resolved in the morning after the committee of sleep has worked on it.

Dale Carnegie:	If you can't sleep, then get up and do something instead of lying there and worrying. It's the worry that gets you, not the loss of sleep.
Jack Dempsey:	I would say to myself: "What a fool you are to be worrying about something that hasn't happened and may never happen. Life is short."
Latin Proverb:	Never take the antidote before the poison.
Henry Kissinger:	The history of things that didn't happen has never been written.
Yogi Berra:	It's never happened in a World Series competition, and it still hasn't.
Mark Twain:	I am an old man and have known a great many problems, but most of them never happened.
George Abbot:	Perhaps statistics would show that most calamities never happen.
Thomas Jefferson:	How much pain have cost us the evils which have never happened.
Lee Weiner:	We are all refugees of a future that never happened.
Michel Eyquem de Montaigne:	My life has been full of terrible misfortunes, most of which never happened.
Yogi Berra:	How can you say this and that when this and that hasn't happened yet?

Virgil Thomson:	I don't go around regretting things that don't happen.
James A. Garfield:	I have had troubles in my life but the worst of them never came.
James Russell Lowell:	... the misfortunes hardest to bear are those which never come.
Unknown:	Some of your griefs you have cured, And the worst you have survived; But, think of the pain you have endured From the evils that never arrived.
Solomon Ibn Gabirol:	It is a serious disease to worry over what has not occurred.
Honoré De Balzac:	After all, our worst misfortunes never happen, and most miseries lie in anticipation.
Elbert Hubbard:	If pleasures are greatest in anticipation, just remember that this is also true of trouble.

Kathryne Holcombe Farmer:

I now realize that in the past, I was being driven half mad not by today's problems but by the bitterness and anxiety over something that had happened yesterday or that I feared might happen tomorrow.

Mrs. Herbert H. Salinger:

"By the law of averages, it won't happen." That phrase has destroyed ninety per cent of my worries; and it has made the past twenty years of my life beautiful and peaceful beyond my highest expectations.

Sir William Osler: Waste of energy, mental distress, nervous worries dog the steps of a man who is anxious about the future.

Tyron Edwards: Anxiety is the rust of life, destroying its brightness and weakening its power. A childlike and abiding trust in Providence is its best preventative and remedy.

Italian Proverb: Everyone thinks his own cross is heaviest.

John W. Roper: Sympathy is never wasted except when you give it to yourself.

Jewish Proverb: I felt sorry for myself because I had no shoes — until I met a man who had no feet.

John Milton: It is not miserable to be blind, it is only miserable not to be able to endure blindness.

Epictetus: There is only one way to happiness, and that is to cease worrying about things which are beyond the power of our will.

Friedrich Christoph Oetinger:
> Give me the serenity
>   To accept the things I cannot change
> Give me the courage
>   To change the things I can;
> And the wisdom to distinguish
>   The one from the other.

Dane Gibson: If something is worrying you, decide whether you can do anything about it. If you can, then do it. If it's out of your control, then let it go. Don't waste your time and energy worrying about things you can't do anything about.

William James:	Be willing to have it so. Acceptance of what has happened is the first step to over- coming the consequences of any misfor- tune.
François de La Rochefoucauld:	Accustom yourself to the thought that the worst will befall you and that you will lose all you have.
Willis H. Carrier:	I analyzed the situation fearlessly and hon- estly and figured out what was the worst that could possibly happen as a result of this failure... After figuring out what was the worst that could possibly happen, I rec- onciled myself to accepting it, if neces- sary... From that time on, I calmly devoted my time and energy to trying to improve upon the worst which I had already accept- ed mentally.
Nat Hentoff:	There are two kinds of worries — those you can do something about and those you can't. Don't spend any time on the latter.
Mother Goose:	For every ailment under the sun, There is a remedy, or there is none; If there be one, try to find it; If there be none, never mind it.
Elsie MacCormick:	When we stop fighting the inevitable, we release energy which enables us to create a richer life.
Lin Yutang:	True peace of mind comes from accepting the worst. Psychologically, I think, it means a release of energy.

Willis H. Carrier:	After facing the worst, I immediately relaxed and felt a sense of peace that I hadn't experienced in days. From that time on, I was able to *think!*
William James:	The turbulent billows of the fretful surface leave the deep parts of the ocean undisturbed; and to him who has a hold on vaster and more permanent realities, the hourly vicissitudes of his personal destiny seem relatively insignificant things. The really religious person is accordingly unshakable and full of equanimity and calmly ready for any duty that the day may bring forth.
Dale Carnegie:	When I look at the stars and realize that the light from some of these suns takes a million years to reach my eyes, I realize how tiny and insignificant this earth is, and how microscopic and evanescent are my own little troubles. I will pass on soon; but the sea stretching for a thousand miles in all directions and the stars and spiral nebulae swarming through illimitable space above, they will continue for thousands of millions of years. I marvel that any man looking up at the stars can have an exaggerated opinion of his own importance.
Earl Wilson:	Nonchalance is the ability to remain down to earth when everything else is up in the air.
Robert Frost:	Education is the ability to listen to almost anything without losing your temper or your self–confidence.

~~~*~~~

Virginia Kelley:	I have this knack of putting bad things in the back of my head. Forget about them.
"Maverick" Pappy Maverick:	Never cry over spilt milk. It could've been whiskey.
Unknown:	It's no use crying over split milk: It only makes it salty for the cat.
W. S. Gilbert:	However, it's no use crying over spilt milk.
King George:	Teach me neither to cry for the moon nor over spilt milk.
Anne Frank:	What is done cannot be undone, but one can prevent it happening again.
Omar Khayyám:	The Moving Finger writes; and, having writ, Moves on: nor all your Piety nor Wit Shall lure it back to cancel half a Line, Nor all your Tears wash out a Word of it.
Ogden Nash:	I myself am more and more inclined to agree with Omar and Satchel Paige as I grow older: Don't try to rewrite what the moving finger has writ, and don't ever look over your shoulder.
Dr. Wayne W. Dyer:	This morning is just as over as the Peloponnesian war.
Jim Bishop:	It is difficult to live in the present, ridiculous to live in the future, and impossible to live in the past. Nothing is as far away as one minute ago.

Dale Carnegie:	We may do something to *modify the effects* of what happened 180 seconds ago; but we can't possibly change the event that occurred then.
Admiral Ernest J. King:	If a ship has been sunk, I can't bring it up.
Italian Proverb:	Since the house is on fire, let us warm ourselves.
Nancy Lopez:	I remember being upset once and telling my dad I wasn't following through right, and he replied, "Nancy, it doesn't make any difference to a ball what you do after you hit it."
Chinese Proverb:	Life unfolds on a great sheet called Time, And once finished it is gone forever.
Admiral Harold R. Stark:	Dollars cannot buy yesterday.
Francis Quarles:	One today is worth two tomorrows.

~~~*~~~

K. T. Keller:	I never worry about the future...There are so many forces that will affect the future! Nobody can tell what prompts those forces — or understand them. So why worry about them?
Ashleigh Brilliant:	The longer I live the less future I worry about.
Chinese Proverb:	Do not anxiously hope for that which is not yet come; do not vainly regret what is already past.

Sir William Osler: Live neither in the past nor in the future, but let each day's work absorb all your interest, energy and enthusiasm. The best preparation for tomorrow is to do today's work superbly well.

Henry Wadsworth Longfellow:
Look not mournfully into the past — it comes not back again; wisely improve the present — it is thine; go forth to meet the shadowy future without fear, and with a manly heart.

Carl Sandburg: I tell you the past is a bucket of ashes.

Vanessa Williams: The past just came up and kicked me.

Marshall McLuhan: The past went that–a–way.

Pearl Buck: One faces the future with one's past.

I. King Jordan: Live in the present. Don't use the past as an excuse for how to think or act.

David Russell: The present is a point just passed.

Loren Eiseley: The door to the past is a strange door. It swings open and things pass through it, but they pass in one direction only. No man can return across that threshold, though he can look down still and see the green light waver in the water weeds.

Sir William Osler: Touch a button and hear, at every level of your life, the iron doors shutting out the Past.

Dale Carnegie:	Today is the only time we can possibly live. Let's not turn it into a physical and mental hell by aimless worry about the future. Let's also stop fretting over the blunders we made yesterday.
Fredrick William Robertson:	We lose time by remorse.
Ole Helgerson:	Worry a little bit everyday and in a lifetime you will lose a couple of years. If something is wrong, fix it if you can. But train yourself not to worry. Worry never fixes anything.
William Shakespeare:	Wise men never sit and wail their loss, but cheerily seek how to redress their harms.
Francis Bacon:	That which is past is irrevocable, and wise men have enough to do with things present and to come.
Dr. Wayne W. Dyer:	It makes no sense to worry about the things that you have no control over.
Ralph W. Sockman:	Let us not bankrupt our todays by paying interest on the regrets of yesterday and by borrowing in advance the troubles of tomorrow.
Katherine Mansfield:	Make it a rule of life never to regret and never to look back. Regret is an appalling waste of energy; you can't build on it; it's only good for wallowing in.
Arthur Brisbane:	Regret for time wasted can become a power for good in the time that remains, if we only stop the waste, and the idle, useless regretting.

André Maurois:	Here we are on this earth, with only a few more decades to live, and we lose many irreplaceable hours brooding over grievances that, in a year's time, will be forgotten by us and by everybody. No, let us devote our life to worth–while actions and feelings, to great thoughts, real affections and enduring undertakings.
Pericles:	Come gentlemen, we sit too long on trifles.
Dr. Robert S. Eliot:	Rule Number 1 is, don't sweat the small stuff. Rule Number 2 is, it's all small stuff. And if you can't fight and you can't flee, flow.

"The Honeymooners"
Ed Norton:
	When the tides of life turn against you,
	   And the current upsets your boat,
	Don't waste those tears on what might have
	     been;
	   Just lay on your back and float.

Edmund Burke:	Never despair, but if you do, work on in despair.
Menander:	He who labors diligently need never despair; for all things are accomplished by diligence and labor.
Winston Churchill:	I'm too busy. I have no time for worry.
Thomas A. Edison:	As a cure for worrying, work is better than whiskey.
Jewish Proverb:	Worms eat you when you're dead; worries eat you when you're alive.

Louis T. Montant, Jr.:	Worry caused me to lose ten years of my life.
Duke Baird:	You ought to sit down and face the facts. If you devote half as much time and energy to solving your problems as you do to worrying about them, you wouldn't have any worries. Worrying is just a vicious habit you have learned.
William James:	...overtension and jerkiness and breathlessness and intensity and agony of expression... are *bad habits*, nothing more or less.
Dale Carnegie:	Tension is a habit. Relaxing is a habit. And bad habits can be broken, good habits formed.
Charles F. Kettering:	A problem well stated is a problem half solved.
Jim Birdsall:	As I look back at it now, I can see that my problem was one of confusion, a disinclination to find the causes of my worry and face them realistically.
Percy H. Whiting:	I have died more times from more different diseases than any other man, living, dead, or half dead.
Robert Frost:	The reason why worry kills more people than work is that more people worry than work.
Unknown:	Worry doesn't pay the rent.
Alfred E. Neuman:	What, me worry?

Rabbi Israel Salanter: Every kind of worrying is forbidden —
except worrying about worrying.

Jewish Proverb: Only one kind of worry is proper: to worry
because you worry so much.

Frank McKinney: It's wonderful what a run there is on worry
when you consider that it never helped any-
thing.

Swedish Proverb: Worry often gives a small thing a big
shadow.

Unknown: Worry is like a rocking chair — it keeps
you busy but it doesn't get you anywhere.

Arthur Somers Roche: Worry is a thin stream of fear trickling
through the mind. If encouraged, it cuts a
channel into which all other thoughts are
drained.

The Talmud: Worry saps a man's strength.

~~~*~~~

Chapter Thirteen

A Strange Door

Everyone was intently quiet. Was I hallucinating? I pinched myself again to see, but at the same time, Jah, acting as our conductor, sprung up once more, "All things are happening here only at this moment in time; this single chord in time's eternal symphony," began his oration. "Everything is perpetually new, beginning now, ending now. In my experience so far on this planet, I have only been able to live in the present. When I'm happy and centered in this moment, not lusting after the future somewhere or delving into the past, I'm harmonious with nature and myself.

"I'm talking about right now! Sitting exactly where you are *now* loving the luxury of reading. Remembering things you knew, pondering fresh concepts. Looking out the window meditating on a passage, loving living, loving breathing, and loving thinking.

"It's not about being happy after finals. I'm not talking about when you get out of jail, or after your tax refund check comes in the mail. I'm not talking about after the big bowling tournament on Saturday, or after the book gets published, or subsequent to the new house being built, or even after this bee gets out of my ear. There's no way to be happy later this evening or to make myself content yesterday afternoon. I can only... possibly... control now. So I'm doing, simply, that.

"Being centered in the present means doing the utmost to prize whatever we're accomplishing at this precise moment! This can be applied to taking out the garbage as well as to playing hooky on sunny fall days. Perhaps it's later than you presume. Transcending time and focusing on this chord of life's symphony, and how to make

271

it as full and robust as possible, makes each building block of the whole become part of a more perfect lifetime.

"I'm not suggesting never to plan ahead. As a tremendous advocate of planning, meditation, study, and practice, I realize that these things are infinitely more influential if we concentrate on *them* to the fullest of our abilities, without dwelling on things we'd rather be doing. Savoring the task, playing with life's intricacies, rather than riding the train with eyes fixed upon the destination highlighted on the map. The scenery is outside the window! Success is rooted in <u>suc-cession</u>. The fun and reward is not necessarily in arriving, but rather in the excursion."

"When I was six," I interrupted, "I was brushing my teeth. My mother told me, 'If you're going to do it, you might as well do it right.' "

Jah in his vast patience and calm forgave instantly my poor manners. "Every great mother knows this. Superb athletes too, can relate. They know there's no sense squandering precious workout time by practicing lackadaisically or erroneously. Time is extraordinarily valuable. When Olympians practice they picture themselves at the Olympics as Olympic champions. Striving in this way, putting in maximum energy with real focus, makes one truly outstanding. There is solely this instant to live. Strive to do your best in the present situation then sit back and revel in that interval of your existence.

"Man has not learned to relish the moment," Jah observed, "no matter how negative or mediocre it may seem as it passes. Erich Fromm said, 'Man is the only animal that can be bored.' Other animals cannot fathom any other time to live than in the present. Time is not real, so concentrate not, on it.

"During the next big storm, what if you decided to get completely wet, smiling like a madman through the rain instead of hastening with a frown to far away shelter? Smelling the taste and passion of feeling wet, radiating a genuine smile through your eyes and heart, I bet you won't get sick.

"Some people call the art of living each moment fully, being 'centered,' as in centered in the moment. Staying centered allows for concentration on the simple present. Being centered makes life smoother, since we can't act on our memories past; and we definitely can't live in illusions of the future. Being aware, thinking ahead — but living now. The worries of the future vanish along with the regrets and habits of the past.

"A fanatic, maybe humorous example, of the concept is the optimist falling from the Empire State Building. When a lady stuck her head out of the fifty–first floor and asked: 'Are you okay?' The ever–hopeful one, whizzing downward, shouted back: 'So far so good!'

"Why fear death when now we live?" Jah entreated. "An ancient Zen parable tells:

> A man was traveling when he encountered a fierce and hungry tiger. Chased by the beast, he ran, literally for his life, until he came to the edge of a cliff. There he saw a hanging wild vine, swung himself down over the edge, and began climbing down it hand over hand toward supposed safety. Suddenly he looked down and saw a second, equally famished, ferocious tiger waiting for him at the bottom of the cliff. Only the tenuous vine suspended him between the two. At that moment he saw two mice, one white, one black, slowly starting to gnaw away at the very vine from which he was clinging.
>
> Just then something caught the man's eye — a luscious, ruby–red strawberry growing just within his reach. Clinging to the vine with one arm he plucked the sweet berry with the other; and swallowing it, he uttered passionately, 'How delicious this is!'

"An enduring Hasidic anecdote relates that when Rabbi Moshe died, Rabbi Mendel of Kotzk questioned one of Moshe's disciples: 'What was most important to your mentor?' The student paused, considered, then replied: 'Whatever he happened to be doing at the moment.' "

~~~*~~~

Harry Chapin:	It's got to be the going, not the getting there that's good.
George Eliot:	Nothing is so good as it seems beforehand.

"Star Trek"

Spock:
After a time, you may find that having is not so pleasing a thing, after all, as wanting. It is not logical, but it is often true.

Jerry Rubin:
Why must we have something to look forward to? Why can't we just look at now?

Robert Townsend:
Getting there isn't half the fun — it's all the fun.

Robert Louis Stevenson:
I travel for travel's sake. The great affair is to move.

A Fortune Cookie:
It is sometimes better to travel hopefully than to arrive.

Alex Noble:
Success is not a place at which one arrives, but rather... the spirit with which one undertakes and continues the journey.

Ben Sweetland:
Success is a journey, not a destination.

Roy M. Goodman:
Remember that happiness is a way of travel, not a destination.

Burton Hillis:
Happiness is not a destination. It is a method of life.

Jordan S. Metzger:
The idea of being lost is a function of the desire to be elsewhere.

Jules Renard:
I am never bored anywhere: being bored is an insult to oneself.

Antoine De Saint–Exupéry:
He who would travel happily must travel light.

Jah:	Are you traveling light?
Neil Bartlett:	It is better to travel well–dressed than to arrive on time.
Drew "Bundini" Brown:	
	You don't look in the mirror to see life; you gotta look out of the window.
Harold M. Gibson:	Looking out the window is the most important thing if you want to know what's going on.
Yogi Berra:	You can observe a lot just by watching.
Charles Kuralt:	Thanks to the Interstate Highway System, it is now possible to travel across the country from coast to coast without seeing anything.
Todd Rundgren:	So many people go through life without a direction. They just go from stop to stop. It's like they're on a bus and the only time they get off is to p... .
Martin Mull:	Always pee before a long car trip.
Steven Wright:	One time the police stopped me for speeding and they said, "Don't you know the speed limit is 55 miles an hour?" I said, "Yeah, I know, but I wasn't going to be out that long."
Spanky McFarland:	I was stopped once for going 53 in a 35 mph zone, but I told them I had dyslexia.

Princess Anne: Perhaps the thing I might do best is to be a long–distance lorry driver.

Princess Margrethe of Denmark:
I have always had a dread of becoming a passenger in life.

"Rain Man"
Rain Man: I'm a very good driver.

French Saying: Wisemen are happy with trifles, but nothing pleases fools.

John Gunther: All happiness depends on a leisurely breakfast.

Josh Billings: Never work before breakfast; if you have to work before breakfast, get your breakfast first.

The Talmud: Sixty runners ran but did not overtake the man who breakfasted early.

George Burns: When I get up in the morning the first thing I do is get a newspaper, and I read the obituary column. If my name isn't in it I have breakfast.

Steven Wright: I went to a restaurant. It said, "Breakfast Anytime" so I ordered French toast during the Renaissance period.

~~~*~~~

Robert Browning: How good is man's life, the mere living! How fit to employ all the heart and the soul and the senses forever in joy!

William Durant: Every normal function of life holds some delight.

Admiral Richard E. Byrd:

I realized I failed to see that the simple, homely, unpretentious things of life are the most important.

George Winslow Plummer:

... he finds them equally in the song of a lark or the glad cry of a child, in a lump of soft clay or a dancing sunbeam, in the caress of a loved one or the smile of a friend.

Henry Ward Beecher: The art of being happy lies in the power of extracting happiness from common things.

Zen Saying: Unformed people delight in the gaudy and in novelty. Cooked people delight in the ordinary.

Master Rinzai: When hungry, I eat, when tired, I sleep. Fools laugh at me. The wise understand.

Al Neuharth: Eat only when you're hungry. Drink only when you're thirsty. Sleep only when you're tired.

Alice Roosevelt Longworth:

Fill what's empty. Empty what's full. And scratch where it itches.

Taisen Deshimaru: Every gesture is important. How we eat, how we put on our clothes, how we wash ourselves, how we go to the toilet, how we put our things away, how we act with other people, family, wife, work — how we are: totally, in every single gesture.

The Book Of Koheleth 9:10: All that your hand can possibly do, do with all your might.

Marcus Aurelius: Do every act of your life as if it were your last.

Charles Dickens: He did each single thing as if he did nothing else.

Tom Bodett: It's the smaller things that seem to stay with ya.

Swami Sivananda: Put your heart, mind, intellect and soul even to your smallest acts. This is the secret of success.

Pop Warner: You play the way you practice.

Wanda Landowska: I never practice; I always play.

E. B. White: I arise in the morning torn between a desire to improve (or save) the world and a desire to enjoy (or savor) the world. This makes it hard to plan the day.

Hubert Horatio Humphrey: Life was not meant to be endured but enjoyed.

John Ruskin:	You were made for enjoyment, and the world was filled with things which you will enjoy.
The Talmud (Kidushin):	
	A man will have to give account on the Judgment Day for every good [permitted] thing that he might have enjoyed and did not.
Walter Hagen:	You only get one trip through life, so don't forget to stop and smell the flowers.
Hollis Stacy:	Have a blast while you last.
Nikita Khrushchev:	Life is short. Live it up.
Seneca:	We are always complaining that our days are few, and acting as though there would be no end to them.
Susan Etrz:	Millions long for immortality who do not know what to do with themselves on a rainy Sunday afternoon.
F. Scott Fitzgerald:	"What'll we do with ourselves this afternoon?" cried Daisy, "and the day after that, and the next thirty years?"
Anatole France:	The average man, who does not know what to do with his life, wants another one which will last forever.
Arthur Guiterman:	"Man's Life is all–too–brief!" Man writes in sorrow; Yet man will sigh, "I wish it were Tomorrow!"

Charles Caleb Colton:	Many who find the day too long, think life too short.
Alain:	What is a thousand years? Time is short for one who thinks, endless for one who yearns.
Irving L. Metzger:	Life is uncertain, eat dessert first.
Sydney Smith:	Serenely full, the epicure would say, Fate cannot harm me, I have dined today.
John Dryden:	Happy the man, and happy he alone, He who can call today his own; He who, secure within, can say, Tomorrow, do thy worst, for I have lived today.
Horace:	He will through life be master of himself and a happy man who from day to day can have said, "I have lived: tomorrow the Father may fill the sky with black clouds or with cloudless sunshine."
Robert Pirsig:	When you're no longer thinking ahead, each footstep isn't just a means to an end but a unique event in itself.
Federico Fellini:	There is no end. There is no beginning. There is only the infinite passion of life.
Henry Miller:	Every moment is a golden one for him who has the vision to recognize it as such.

Robert Grudin:	Individuals we consider happy commonly seem complete in the present and we see them constantly in their wholeness: attentive, cheerful, open rather than closed to events, integral in the moment rather than distended across time by regret or anxiety.

Omar Khayyám:

Tomorrow's fate, though thou be wise,
 Thou canst not tell nor yet surmise;
Pass, therefore, not today in vain,
 For it will never come again.

Unknown: The best preparation for tomorrow is to live fully today.

Elbert Hubbard: The best way to prepare for life is to begin to live.

~~~*~~~

Johann Wolfgang von Goethe:
Nothing is worth more than this day.

Unknown: One today is worth a thousand tomorrows.

Spanish Proverb: Tomorrow is often the busiest day of the week.

Martial: Tomorrow's life is too late. Live today.

Livy: Better late than never.

Malcolm Forbes: I don't think this life is for hibernating and getting ready for the next one... you are given it for a purpose and this is to live it. Live while you are alive!

Ralph Waldo Emerson:	We are always getting ready to live, but never living.
Pascal:	So we never live, but we hope to live — and as we are always preparing to be happy, it is inevitable we should never be so.
Unknown:	It is far better to live a little as you go along, instead of working yourself to death getting ready to live.
Laurence Sterne:	Men tire themselves in pursuit of rest.
Jonathan Swift:	May you live all the days of your life.
Albert Einstein:	Life is always becoming, never being.
June Callwood:	*Never delay* — unhappiness is nurtured by the habit of putting off living until some fictional future day.
Dale Carnegie:	One of the most tragic things I know about human nature is that all of us tend to put off living. We are all dreaming of some magical rose garden over the horizon — instead of enjoying the roses that are blooming outside our windows today.
Jose Ortega Y. Gasset:	We cannot put off living until we are ready. The most salient characteristic of life is its coerciveness: it is always urgent, "here and now" without any possible postponement. Life is fired at us point–blank.

"Calvin and Hobbes"
Bill Watterson

Calvin:

That's the problem with life. It rolls along with speed you can't control. You can't go faster or slower. Fun experiences always go roaring by... while bad experiences never pass quickly enough. I wish we could choose how fast and slow events go. For example, I'd like to speed up childhood and get to driving age.

French Saying:

The first half of life is spent in longing for the second — the second half in regretting the first.

Stephen Leacock:

How strange it is, our little procession of life! The child says, "When I am a big boy." But what is that? The big boy says, "When I grow up." And then, grown up, he says, "When I get married." But to be married, what is that after all? The thought changes to "When I'm able to retire." And then, when retirement comes, he looks back over the landscape traversed; a cold wind seems to sweep over it; somehow he has missed it all, and it is gone. Life, we learn too late, is in the living, in the tissue of every day and hour.

Hasidic Proverb:

"And if not now, when?" asked Hillel. When will the "now" be? The now that is now, this moment, never existed before — from the time the world was created; and this moment will never exist again. Formerly there was another "now" and later there will be another "now", and every "now" has its own special important function.

Dale Carnegie:	You and I are standing this very second at the meeting place of two eternities: the vast past that has endured forever, and the future that is plunging on to the last syllable of recorded time. We can't possibly live in either of those eternities — no, not even for one split second.
Tennessee Williams:	Life is all memory except for the one present moment that goes by so quick you can hardly catch it going.
Corita Kent:	Life is the succession of moments, To live each one is to succeed.
Artur Rubinstein:	Of course there is no formula for success, except perhaps, an unconditional acceptance of life and what it brings.

~~~*~~~

Mme. du Deffand:	Shallow men speak of the past, wise men of the present, fools of the future.
Dr. Eric Berne:	Losers spend their lives thinking about what they're going to do. They rarely enjoy doing what they're doing.
Glenda Jackson:	I'm waiting for the day when I wake up and life is a breeze. I used to think that happened when you grew old. But it doesn't. That's just a fantasy.

Phillip Moffitt: Always the rationalization is the same —
"Once this situation is remedied, then I will
be happy." But it never works in reality:
The goal is achieved, but the person who
reaches it is not the same person who
dreamed it. The goal was static, but the
person's identity was dynamic.

Nacha Guevara: In life the things you want always arrive
after you've stopped waiting.

J. Krishnamurti: Future freedom has no reality; it is only an
idea. Reality is what is.

Jerry Brown: Life just is. You have to flow with it. Give
yourself to the moment. Let it happen.

Chuang–tzu: Flow with whatever may happen and let
your mind be free: Stay centered by
accepting whatever you are doing. This is
the ultimate.

Barbara Grizzuti Harrison:
To live exhilaratingly in and for the
moment is deadly serious work, fun of the
most exhausting sort.

Oprah Winfrey: ... doing the best at this moment puts you in
the best place for the next moment.

Corita Kent: Love the moment and the energy of that
moment will spread beyond all boundaries.

Confucius: Some have managed to do this; they have
hit the true center, and then? Very few have
been able to stay there. The process is not
understood. The men of talent shoot past it,
and the others do not get it.

"Calvin and Hobbes"
Bill Watterson

Calvin: I suppose the secret to happiness is learning to appreciate the moment. I, for example, take great pleasure in being right here, right now, doing what we're doing.

Hobbes: Of course, you're supposed to be at school.

Calvin: I couldn't appreciate those moments.

Master Han: You must learn to live in the present, not in the future or the past. Zen teaches that life must be seized at the moment. By living in the present you are in full contact with yourself and your environment, your energy is not dissipated and is always available. In the present there are no regrets as there are in the past. By thinking of the future, you dilute the present. The time to live is now.

As long as what you are doing at the moment is *exactly* what you are doing at the moment and nothing else, you are one with yourself and with what you are doing — and that is Zen; while doing something you are doing it at the fullest.

André Gide: In order to be utterly happy the only thing necessary is to refrain from comparing this moment with other moments in the past, which I often did not fully enjoy because I was comparing them with other moments of the future.

W. Somerset Maugham:

The passing moment is all that we can be sure of; it is only common sense to extract its utmost value from it; the future will one day be the present and will seem as unimportant as the present does now.

Samuel Johnson:	No mind is much employed upon the present; recollection and anticipation fill up almost all our moments.
Johann Wolfgang von Goethe:	The present moment is a powerful Goddess.
Gilda Radner:	Taking the moment and making the best of it, without knowing what's going to happen next — delicious ambiguity.

"Calvin and Hobbes"
Bill Watterson

Calvin:	"Live for the moment" is **my** motto. You never know how long you've got! You could step into the road tomorrow and — **Wham** — you get hit by a cement truck! Then you'd be sorry you put off your pleasures! That's why *I* say "Live for the moment." What's *your* motto?
Hobbes:	"Look down the road."
Mick Jagger:	Society is all wrong. All those vibrations of fear. You have to change not only the setup but the whole concept. You have to learn how to live the moment and enjoy it.

~~~*~~~

"Kung Fu"

Master Po:	The heart of the wise man is tranquil and still.
Jim Lau:	Relaxation and concentration go hand in hand.

Jochen Rindt:
You completely ignore everything and just concentrate. You forget about the whole world and just... are part of the car and the track... It's a very special feeling. You're completely out of this world. There is nothing like it.

Tom Horwitz and Susan Kimmelman:
There is a common experience in Tai Chi of seemingly falling through a hole in time. Awareness of the passage of time completely stops, and only when you catch yourself, after five or ten minutes, or five or ten seconds, is there the realization that for that period of time the world *stopped.*

Arnold Palmer:
You're involved in the action and vaguely aware of it,... not a dreamlike state but the somehow insulated state that a great musician achieves in a great performance... It is not merely mechanical, it is not only spiritual; it is something of both, on a different plane and a more remote one.

Tony Jacklin:
When I'm in this state everything is pure, vividly clear. I'm in a cocoon of concentration. And if I can put myself into that cocoon, I'm invincible... I'm living fully in the present. I'm absolutely engaged, *involved* in what I'm doing... It comes and it goes, and the pure fact that you are out on the first tee of a tournament and say, "I must concentrate today," is no good. It won't work.

Mickey Wright:
When I play my best golf, I feel as if I'm in a fog... standing back watching the earth in orbit with a golf club in your hands.

Catfish Hunter:	I wasn't worried about a perfect game going into the ninth. It was like a dream. I was going on like I was in a daze. I never thought about it the whole time. If I thought about it I wouldn't have thrown a perfect game — I know I wouldn't.
Robert Linssen:	In judo, he who thinks is immediately thrown. Victory is assured to the combatant who is both physically and mentally nonresistant.
Gertrude Stein:	Everybody gets so much information all day long that they lose their common sense.
Kurt Vonnegut:	Life happens too fast for you to ever think about it. If you could just persuade people of this, but they insist on amassing information.
Isabelle Adjani:	Life is worth being lived but not worth being discussed all the time.
Gloria Steinem:	The examined life is not worth living.
Plato:	The life which is unexamined is not worth living.
Nicolas Chamfort:	The contemplative life is often miserable. One must act more, think less, and not watch oneself live.
Santayana:	Man is not made to understand life, but to live it.
Yogi Berra:	Who can think and hit at the same time?

Georges Clenenceau:	It is as if a tennis player before returning a ball stopped to think about his views of the physical and mental advantages of tennis. You must act as you breathe.
Taisen Deshimaru:	The body moves naturally, automatically, unconsciously, without any personal intervention or awareness. But if we begin to use our faculty of reasoning, our actions become slow and hesitant. Questions arise, the mind tires and the conscious flickers and waivers like a candle flame in a breeze.
Bruce Lee:	A good martial artist puts his mind on one thing at a time.
John Brodie:	A player's effectiveness is directly related to his ability to be right there, doing that thing, in that moment. All the preparation he may have put into the game — all the game plans, analysis of movies, etc. — is no good if he can't put it into action when game time comes. He can't be worrying about the past or the future or the crowd or some other extraneous event. He must be able to respond in the here and now.

~~~*~~~

H. L. Mencken:	We are here and it is now. Further than that all human knowledge is moonshine.
Baba Ram Dass:	Be Here Now.
Abraham Maslow:	... all there, totally immersed, fascinated and absorbed in the present, in the current situation, in the here–now, with the matter–in–hand.

290

Taisen Deshimaru: If you are not happy here and now, you never will be.

Hillel: And if not now — when?

William Lyon Phelps: I live every day now as if it were the first day I had ever seen and the last I were going to see.

Horace: Carpe diem [Seize the day].

Dante: Think that this day will never dawn again.

Erma Bombeck: Seize the moment. Remember all those women on the Titanic who waved off the dessert cart.

William Butler Yeats: We must laugh and we must sing,
We are blest by everything.

Henry Miller: The aim of life is to live, and to live means to be aware, joyously, drunkenly, serenely, divinely aware.

James Thurber: Let us not look back in anger or forward in fear, but around in awareness.

Aldous Huxley: To be enlightened is to be aware, always, of total reality in its immanent otherness — to be aware of it and yet to remain in a condition to survive as an animal, to think and feel as a human being, to resort whenever expedient to systematic reasoning.

"Wings of Desire"
Wim Wenders and Peter Handke:
Most of the time I'm too aware to be sad.

Kalidasa:	For yesterday is but a dream And tomorrow is only a vision, But today well lived makes every yesterday a dream of happiness And every tomorrow a vision of hope. Look well, therefore, to this day! Such is the salutation to the dawn.
Thomas Carlyle:	Lo, here hath been dawning another blue day; Think, wilt thou let it slip useless away? Out of eternity this new day is born, Into eternity at night will return. Behold it aforetime no eye ever did; So soon it forever from all eyes is hid. Here hath been dawning another blue day; Think, wilt thou let it slip useless away?
William Wordsworth:	... Nothing can bring back the hour Of splendor in the grass, of glory in the flower.
Robert Herrick:	Gather ye rosebuds while ye may, Old Time is still a–flying, And this same flower that smiles today Tomorrow will be dying.
Michael Landon:	Somebody should tell us, right at the start of our lives, that we are dying. Then we might live life to the limit, every minute of every day. Do it! I say. Whatever you want to do, do it now! There are only so many tomorrows.
Psalm 118:24:	This is the day that the Lord has made; let us rejoice and be glad in it.

Henry David Thoreau: Live each season as it passes; breathe the
air, drink the drink, taste the fruit, and
resign yourself to the influences of each.

Henry Wadsworth Longfellow:
If spring came but once in a century instead
of once a year, or burst forth with the sound
of an earthquake and not in silence, what
wonder and expectation there would be in
all hearts, to behold the miraculous change.

Walt Whitman: Why, who makes much of a miracle?
As to me I know of nothing else but
miracles,
Whether I walk the streets of Manhattan,
Or dart my sight over the roofs of houses
toward the sky,
Or wade with naked feet along the beach
just in the edge of the water,
Or stand under trees in the woods,
Or talk by day with anyone I love, or sleep
in the bed at night with anyone I
love,
Or sit at table at dinner with the rest,
Or look at strangers opposite me
riding in the car,
Or watch honey–bees busy around the
hive of a summer forenoon,
Or animals feeding in the fields,
Or birds, or the wonderfulness of insects
in the air,
Or the wonderfulness of the sundown, or of
stars shining so quiet and bright,
Or the exquisite delicate thin curve of the
new moon in spring;
These with the rest, one and all, are to me
miracles,
The whole referring, yet each distinct and
in its place.

To me every hour of the light and dark is a
    miracle,
  Every cubic inch of space is a miracle,
    Every square yard of the surface of
    the earth is spread with the same,
  Every foot of the interior swarms with the
    same.

To me the sea is a continual miracle,
  The fishes that swim — the rocks — the
  motion of the waves — the ships
    with men in them,
What stranger miracles are there?

~~~*~~~

Arabic Saying:	Everyday of your life is a page of your history.
Bruce Lee:	The past is an illusion. You must learn to live within the present and accept yourself for what you are *now*.
Graffiti:	Time is an illusion perpetrated by the manufacturers of space.
P. D. Ouspensky:	There is no essential difference between the past and the future. We only call them by different words: *was* and *will be*. In reality, all this both "was" and "will be."
Alan Watts:	I have realized that the past and the future are real illusions, that they exist only in the present, which is what there is and all that there is.
Unknown:	By losing present time we lose all time.
Gahan Wilson:	Nothing happens next. This is it.

Alan Watts: This — the immediate, everyday, and present experience — is IT, the entire and ultimate point for the existence of a universe.

Jah: It's great to experience the experience.

Oliver Goldsmith: To enjoy the present without regret for the past, or solicitation for the future, appears to be the only general precept respecting the pursuit of happiness that can be applied with propriety to every condition of life.

Unknown: Good cheer is something more then faith in the future; it is gratitude for the past and joy in the present.

Michel Eyquem De Montaigne:
Rejoice in the things that are present, all else is beyond you.

Marcus Aurelius: Remember that a man's life lies all within this present, as 'twere but a hair's breadth of time; as for the rest, the past is gone, the future yet unseen. Short, therefore is man's life, and narrow is the corner of the earth wherein he dwells.

C. S. Lewis: The future is something which everyone reaches at the rate of sixty minutes an hour, whatever he does, whoever he be.

Unknown: We never find the future. It's always a dream. Someday, when we are old, we may realize that all these years we've been living the future every day of our lives.

Kenneth Patchen:	Now is then's only tomorrow.
Vladimir Horowitz:	My future is in my past and my past is my present. I must now make the present my future.
Denny Crum:	Most of our future lies ahead.

Henry Wadsworth Longfellow:

> Our to–days and yesterdays
>   Are the blocks on which we build...
> Build to–day, then, strong and sure,
>   With a firm and ample base;
> And ascending and secure
>   Shall to–morrow find its place.

Dean Acheson:	The best thing about the future is it only comes one day at a time.
Ida Scott Taylor:	One day at a time, — this is enough. Do not look back over the past, for it is gone; and do not be troubled about the future, for it is yet to come. Live in the present, and make it so beautiful that it will be worth remembering.
Daniel J. Boorstin:	The contemporary time is always the best time to live. It is a mistake to say the best age is one without problems.
Bill Clinton:	Though we march to the music of our time, our mission is timeless.
Saint Augustine:	What then is time? If no one asks me, I know what it is. If I wish to explain it to him who asks, I do not know.
Tom Seaver:	Yogi, what time is it?
Yogi Berra:	You mean now?

Hugh Prather:	There will never be a time when it will not be now.
Dr. Albert Schweitzer:	Truth has no special time of its own. Its hour is now — always.
Taisen Deshimaru:	Time is not a line, but a series of now–points.
Alfred Kahn:	All life is a concatenation of ephemeralities.
Sören Kierkegaard:	Life can only be understood backward, but it must be lived forward.
Ralph Waldo Emerson:	The years teach us much the days never knew.
Kurt Vonnegut:	All moments, past, present, and future, always have existed, always will exist. ... It is just an illusion we have here on Earth that one moment follows another one, like beads on a string, and that once a moment is gone, it is gone forever.
Graffiti:	Time is nature's way of preventing everything from happening at once.
Fran Lebowitz:	If God had meant for everything to happen at once, he would not have invented desk calendars.
Franz Kafka:	Only our concept of Time makes it possible for us to speak of the Day of Judgment by that name; In reality it is a summary court in perpetual session.

Eudora Welty:	The events in our lives happen in a sequence in time, but in their significance to ourselves they find their own order... the continuous thread of revelation.
Bertrand Russell:	To realize the unimportance of time is the gate of wisdom.
R. Buckminster Fuller:	Time is not the fourth dimension, and should not be so identified. Time is only a relative observation.
Henri Frederic Amiel:	Time and space are fragments of the infinite for the use of finite creatures.
Hippocrates:	Healing is a matter of time, but it is sometimes also a matter of opportunity.

"The Andy Griffith Show"

Floyd the Barber:	"Tempus edax rerum." Time heals everything. You know who said that? My Latin teacher in barber college.
Terence:	Time heals all wounds.
Jordan S. Metzger:	If time heals all wounds, and time is not real, but relative, then it is possible to heal all wounds at any time, including now.
M. F. Tupper:	Now is the constant syllable ticking from the clock of time.
Arthur Miller:	The word "now" is a bomb through the window, and it ticks.
Chinese Proverb:	Always take an emergency leisurely.

Ralph Waldo Emerson: Keep cool; it will all be over one hundred years hence.

Edwin Markham: At the heart of a cyclone tearing the sky is a place of central calm.

~~~*~~~

Chapter Fourteen

Say Little

"Who will open the next topic?" Jah asked in an easy tone.

The forest was silent. You could smell the humid, cool fragrance of pine on a summer night. Still holding the glowing sapphire, I could tell it was Andrew Jackson who stood up from amongst the great men, and with the polite manner and graciousness of a classic gentleman orator stated, "Take time to deliberate; but when the time for action arrives, stop thinking and go in."

"Thank you Mr. President, well said; we contemplate and then we act." Jah's deep voice took over. "Pros practice their golf swing in slow motion prior to hitting the course, imagining in their mind's eye what will come out during the game. Masters of the martial arts practice the same moves over a lifetime, so that if they must defend themselves, conscious thought is not present, merely action. It's possible to be too hasty and try too hard, so most of us, likewise, need to plan, theorize, and contemplate. When first learning to drive a car we think carefully about shifting, clutching... braking with just the right amount of pressure. We do this while trying to steer enough to stay out of the bushes. At the same time we try not to go through any red lights. Soon, as a result of practice, we're driving. It becomes relatively simple: we listen to the radio, gesture to passengers, and chew gum at the same time. If a child loses his ball in the road and dives in after it, we, as seasoned drivers, don't ponder... oh, gee, I think now I'll take my foot off of the accelerator, and then put it back on the brake, that way I won't hit that kid... **We Just Do It.** At some point in time there arrives a moment when we just have to jump in and take action."

Then Jah looked right at me, "For you that time is now."

~~~*~~~

Jah: To win we must begin.

N.Y. State Lottery Slogan:
                              You can't win if you ain't in.

Fran Lebowitz: I figure you have the same chance of
                              winning the lottery whether you play or not.

Eugene F. Ware: All glory comes from daring to begin.

A Fortune Cookie: If you want to get somewhere you must let
                              yourself go.

Jackie Collins: If you want to be a writer — stop talking
                              about it and sit down and write!

Henry Moore: It is a mistake for a sculptor or a painter to
                              speak or write very often about his job; it
                              releases tension needed for his work.

Arthur Godfrey: Even if you're on the right track — you'll
                              get run over if you just sit there.

Unknown: Many people have the right aim in life, they
                              just never pull the trigger.

Reggie Leach: Success is not the result of spontaneous
                              combustion. You must set yourself on fire.

Deshimaru: You must concentrate upon and consecrate
                              yourself wholly to each day, as though a fire
                              were raging in your hair.

Socrates: Let him that would move the world, first
                              move himself.

Arabian Proverb: All mankind is divided into three classes: Those that are immovable, those that are movable, and those that move.

Unknown: The follies a man regrets most are the ones he didn't commit when he could.

Gene Autry: I finally came to the conclusion that I had nothing to lose and everything to gain.

Izaak Walton: No man can lose what he never had.

Alcaeus: Nothing will come of nothing.

Samuel Johnson: Nothing will ever be attempted if all possible objections must be overcome.

Henry Wadsworth Longfellow:
> Each morning sees some task begun,
>   Each evening sees it close;
> Something attempted, something done,
>   Has earned a night's repose.

English Proverb: One of these days is none of these days.

A Fortune Cookie: Go after what you want; there's no time like the present.

Charles Buxton: You will never "find" time for anything. If you want time you must make it.

Samuel Johnson: He who waits to do a great deal of good at once, will never do anything.

Helen Keller: I long to accomplish a great and noble task, but it is my chief duty to accomplish small tasks as if they were great and noble.

Mother Teresa:	We can do no great things — only small things with great love.
George MacDonald:	Life is made up of little things. It is but once in an age that occasion is offered for doing a great deed. True greatness consists in being great in little things.
Baba Ram Dass:	If I'm saving the whale, why am I eating tuna fish?
Rebecca West:	There are jungles of people, and jungles of facts — which make it harder to recognize the great things when they do happen.

~~~*~~~

Henry James:	Until you try, you don't know what you can't do.
"Star Wars" Yoda:	Try not. Do or do not. There is no try.
T. S. Elliot:	For us there is only the trying. The rest is not our business.
Richter:	Only actions give to life its strength, as only moderation gives it its charm.
Greek Proverb:	Act quickly, think slowly.
Henri Bergson:	Think like a man of action and act like a man of thought.
Michael Cacoyannis:	You think too much, Boss.
Thomas Henry Huxley:	The great end of life is not knowledge but action.

Lao–tzu:	The Way of the sage is to act but not to compete.
Bhagavad Gita:	Action should culminate in wisdom.
Abbie Hoffman:	Action is the only reality...
John Webster:	The chiefest action for a man of spirit is never to be out of action; the soul was never put into the body to stand still.
Gilbert Keith Chesterton:	I do not believe in a fate that falls on men however they act; but I do believe in a fate that falls on them unless they act.
Unknown:	You've got to take the bull by the teeth.
W. C. Fields:	There comes a time in the affairs of men when you must take the bull by the tail and face the situation.
Conrad Hilton:	Success seems to be connected with action.
Samurai Maxim:	To know and to act are one and the same.
Ken Boswell:	I'm in a rut. I can't break myself of the habit of swinging up at the ball.
Yogi Berra:	Then swing down.
Woodie Held:	Don't forget to swing hard, in case you hit the ball.
Yogi Berra:	Swing at the strikes.
Wee Willie Keeler:	Keep your eye clear and hit 'em where they ain't.

Steve Balboni:	Hitting your first grand slam is a thrill. I'll always remember this.
Commentator:	But you hit one back in '83.
Steve Balboni:	You're right. I guess I forgot about that one.
Joe Garagiola:	Nolan Ryan is pitching much better now that he has his curve ball straightened out.
Yogi Berra:	Slump, I ain't in no slump. I just ain't hitting.
Italian Proverb:	To him who is determined it remains only to act.
Theodore Roosevelt:	There is nothing brilliant or outstanding about my record except perhaps this one thing, when I make up my mind to do a thing I act.
Henry Kissinger:	I do not believe in doing something just for the sake of action.
Benjamin Disraeli:	Action may not always bring happiness; but there is no happiness without action.
Freya Stark:	There can be no happiness if the things we believe in are different from the things we do.
Ursula K. Le Guin:	It is good to have an end to journey toward; but it is the journey that matters, in the end.
Krishnamurti:	Meditation is not a means to an end. It is both the means and the end.
Paul Goodman:	Enjoyment is a goal, it is a feeling that accompanies important ongoing activity.

~~~*~~~

Jerry Brown:	Inaction may be the highest form of action.
Claude Debussy:	Music is the space between the notes.
Artur Schnabel:	The notes I handle no better than many pianists. But the pauses between the notes — ah, that is where the art resides!
Max Eastman:	I don't know why we are in such a hurry to get up when we fall down. You might think we would lie there and rest awhile.
Henri Langlois:	Most people advance through life walking backward. Those artists who face forward are likely to be put in jail — or the madhouse.
Sören Kierkegaard:	Life can only be understood backward, but it must be lived forward.
Lowell Palmer Weicker:	Those who insist on walking backward into the future, with their faces turned resolutely to the past, run a very high risk of falling on their butts.
Casey Stengel:	If you walk backward you'll find out that you can go forward and people won't know if you're coming or going.
Wayne Hoy:	If you go slow enough, long enough, you'll be in the lead again.
Mahatma Gandhi:	There's more to life than increasing its speed.
Elia Kazan:	Don't just act; stand there.

Irving. L. Metzger: You can't catch the ball until it's hit to you.

Lefty Gomez: If you don't throw it, they can't hit it.

The Tao Te Ching: By letting go, it all gets done;
The world is won by those who let it go!

Harry Emerson Fosdick:
He who cannot rest, cannot work; he who cannot let go, cannot hold on; he who cannot find footing, cannot go forward.

"The Big Valley"
Nick Barkley: Sometimes the best way to hold onto something is to let it go.

Jesse Lair: If you want something very, very badly, let it go free. If it comes back to you, it's yours forever. If it doesn't, it was never yours to begin with.

John Berry: The bird of paradise alights only upon the hand that does not grasp.

William Saroyan: The greatest happiness you can have is knowing that you do not necessarily require happiness.

Bruce Lee: The less effort, the faster and more powerful you will be.

Takano Shigeyoshi: It goes without saying that as soon as one cherishes the thought of winning the contest or displaying one's skill in technique, swordsmanship is doomed.

Lao Tzu:	A good soldier is not violent. A good fighter is not angry. A good winner is not vengeful. A good employer is humble. This is known as the virtue of not striving.
W. Timothy Gallwey:	Concentration is not staring hard at something, it is not *trying* to concentrate.
Unknown:	A young boy traveled across Japan to the school of a famous marital artist. When he arrived at the dojo he was given an audience by the sensei. "What do you wish from me?" the master probed. "I wish to be your student and become the finest karateka in the land," the boy replied. "How long must I study?" "Ten years at least," the master answered. "Ten years is a long time," said the lad. "What if I studied twice as hard as all your other students?" "Twenty years," replied the master. "Twenty years! What if I practice day and night with all my effort?" "Thirty years," was the master's reply. "How is it that each time I say I will work harder, you tell me that it will take longer?" the boy asked. "The answer is clear. When one eye is fixed upon your destination, there is only one eye left with which to find the Way."

Mrs. Elizabeth Cleghorn Gaskell:

What's the use of watching? A watched pot never boils.

"The Addams Family"
Morticia Addams: A watched cauldron never bubbles.

Unknown:	The secret of patience... to do something else in the meantime.
A Fortune Cookie:	Patience is the key to joy.
Sam Rayburn:	The three most important words in the English language are "wait a minute."

Henry Wadsworth Longfellow:

> Let us, then, be up and doing,
> With a heart for any fate;
> Still achieving, still pursuing,
> Learn to labor and to wait.

Dr. Robert H. Schuller:

Probably nothing is more difficult than to keep waiting and working... maintaining patience and poise through dark times.

Unknown:	Haste is not always speed. We must learn to work and wait. This is like God, who perfects his work through beautiful gradations.
Augustus Caesar:	More haste, less speed.
Benjamin Franklin:	Make haste slowly.
David Carradine:	Don't be in a hurry. Haste will get you there slower, not faster.
John Wooden:	Be quick, but never hurry.
Lily Tomlin:	For fast–acting relief, try slowing down.
Jah:	You don't usually get places expeditiously by driving fastest; but by traveling at the right speed you can time the traffic lights so that they can be approached with ample momentum.

Jordan S. Metzger:	In achieving one's ambitions, it is crucial, but difficult, to properly blend patience with drive.
D. H. Lawrence:	One's action ought to come out of an achieved stillness; not to be a mere rushing on.
Paul Klee:	Nothing can be rushed. Things must grow, they must grow upward...
C. A. Stoddard:	Rapidity does not always mean progress, and hurry is akin to waste.
John Heywood:	Haste maketh waste.
Benjamin Franklin:	Take time for all things. Great haste makes great waste.
Mae West:	I've said it before and I'll say it again — I like a man that takes his time.
Gypsy Rose Lee:	Anything worth doing well is worth doing slowly.
Lord Chesterfield:	Whoever is in a hurry shows that the thing he is about is too big for him.
Mae West:	He who hesitates is last.
The Koran:	Haste is from the devil.
Thomas Shadwell:	The haste of a fool is the slowest thing in the world.
Davarian Proverb:	What is the use of running when we are on the wrong road?

"Garfield"
Jim Davis

Garfield: My Uncle Bob was quite the sage, "Slow down, take it easy." He used to say... Then he got hit by a bus.

Steven Wright: Curiosity killed the cat, but for a while I was a suspect.

"The Andy Griffith Show"

Floyd Lawson: The bus bringeth and the bus taketh away. You know, that's a lot like life.

Mel Brooks: Don't run for a bus — there'll always be another.

Satchel Paige: Avoid running at all times.

Virginia Woolf: I have lost friends, some by death... Others by sheer inability to cross the street.

Piet Hein: Here lies, extinguished in his prime,
A victim of modernity;
But yesterday he hadn't time —
And now he has eternity.

Dr. Albert Schmidt: If there is one thing I've learned in my eighty–five years, it's not to hurry.

Irvin S. Cobb: I'd rather be late for supper in this world tonight than be in some other world on time for breakfast in the morning.

Woody Allen: Death is nature's way of telling you to slow down.

Horatio Nelson: I owe all my success in life to having always been a quarter of an hour beforehand.

Swahili Proverb: Haste, haste, has no blessing.

Alexander Solzhenitsyn:
                           Hastiness and superficiality are the psychic
                           disease of the twentieth century.

Old Shaker Verse: Leave the flurry
                               To the masses;
                           Take your time
                               And shine your glasses.

Kwai–koo–tsu: Patience, the essential quality of a man.

B. C. Forbes: Patience is not only a virtue, but it pays.

Ignace Gan Paderewski:
                           I have no more patience than anyone else.
                           It's just that I use mine.

                                    ~~~*~~~

Stephen Bayne: I am rather like a mosquito in a nudist
                           camp; I know what I ought to do, but I
                           don't know where to begin.

"Alice in Wonderland"
Lewis Carroll
The King: Begin at the beginning and go on till you
                           come to the end; then stop.

Dr. Joyce Brothers: Trust your hunches. They're usually based
                           on facts filed away just below the conscious
                           level.

Herbert Hoover: Wisdom ofttimes consists of knowing what
                           to do next.

| Thomas Carlyle: | Our grand business in life is not to see what lies dimly at a distance, but to do what lies clearly at hand. |

| Chinese Proverb: | To succeed consult three old people. |

| Gunther Cohn: | My father didn't leave me much money, but he gave me a wonderful bit of advice that has paid off many times. He said, "Whenever you are challenged, do just three things. Which three? The three most important things you can think of." |

| Scott Nearing: | Do the thing you believe in. Do it with all your might. |

Johann Friedrich von Schiller:
What the inner voice says will not disappoint the hoping soul.

| Blaise Pascal: | The heart has reasons which the reason cannot understand. |

| Jordan S. Metzger: | The heart usually knows things that the head finds out later. |

| Benjamin Spock: | You know more than you think you do. |

| Michael Burke: | Good instincts usually tell you what to do long before your head has figured it out. |

| Tammy Grimes: | Trust your instincts. If you have no instincts, trust your impulses. |

Charles Maurice De Talleyrand:
Mistrust first impulses, they are always good.

Ralph Waldo Emerson:

Self–trust is the first secret of success.

Johann Wolfgang von Goethe:

As soon as you trust yourself, you will
know how to live.

Martin Luther King, Jr.:

The time is always right to do what is right.

Mark Twain:

Always do right. This will gratify some
people and astonish the rest.

Stell Lefkowitz:

You "havta" do the things you "havta" do.

Ralph Waldo Emerson:

This time, like all times, is a very good one,
if we but know what to do with it.

Rabbi Shammai:

Say little and do much.

Rabbi Natan:

The righteous say little and do much, but
the wicked say much and do not do even a
little.

Jean Jacques Rousseau:

People who know little are usually great
talkers, while men who know much say
little.

Yogi Berra:

It was hard to have a conversation with anyone, there were so many people talking.

A lady sitting next to Calvin Coolidge at dinner:

I have made a bet, Mr. Coolidge, that I
could get more than two words out of you.

Calvin Coolidge:

You lose.

E. J. Liebling:	The people who have something to say don't talk; the others insist on talking.
Robert Frost:	Half the world is composed of people who have something to say and can't, and the other half who have nothing to say and keep on saying it.
"Double Trouble" Aileen Foster:	It's like my mama always says, "Those who can, do. Those who can't, talk about it so much you want to stuff a sofa cushion up their mouths."
Bobby Seale:	Those who know don't talk; and those who talk don't know.
Chinese Saying:	The one who understands does not speak; the one who speaks does not understand.
Victor Hugo:	Strong and bitter words indicate a weak cause.
Jordan S. Metzger:	Those who know the least speak the loudest.
Louis Nizer:	Some people will believe anything if you whisper it to them.
Donovan:	The softer you sing, the louder you're heard.
Zen Saying:	Say one word with your mouth shut!
Duke Ellington:	You've got to find some way of saying it without saying it.

Marcel Marceau:	In silence and movement you can show the reflection of people. To communicate through silence is a link between the thoughts of man.
Victor Borge:	In my youth I wanted to be a great pantomimist, but I found I had nothing to say.
Marcel Marceau:	Never get a mime talking. He won't stop.
"Kung Fu" Caine:	When words are no better than silences, one should keep silent.
Leroy Brownlow:	There are times when silence has the loudest voice.
Dave Tyson Gentry:	True friendship comes when silence between two people is comfortable.
Will Durant:	One of the lessons of history is that nothing is often a good thing to do and always a clever thing to say.
Italian Proverb:	Half a brain is enough for him who says little.
Robert Benchley:	Drawing on my fine command of the English language, I said nothing.
Sam Rayburn:	No one has a finer command of the language than the person who keeps his mouth shut.
William Shakespeare:	I do know of these That therefore only are reputed wise For saying nothing.

Rabbi Natan:	If for the wise silence is becoming, how much more for the foolish!
Duran:	One of the chief signs of the wiseman is silence, one of the chief signs of the fool is verboseness.
Proverbs 17:28:	Even a fool, if he keeps silent, is deemed wise.
Martha J. Beckman:	Wise people are not always silent, but they always know when to be.
Thomas E. Dewey:	When you're leading, don't talk.
William Shakespeare:	Give thy thoughts no tongue.
Duran:	Notice that man has two ears but only one tongue, suggesting that his speech ought to be little and his hearing much.
Benjamin Franklin:	Teach your child to hold his tongue; he'll learn fast enough to speak.
James Roosevelt:	My father gave me these hints on speech-making: Be sincere... be brief... be seated.
Susan Stamberg:	The advice that means the most to me right now was not delivered directly to me. It's something I read that Fred Astaire said about his dance routines; "Get it 'til it's perfect, then cut two minutes."
Miguel de Cervantes:	Be brief, for no discourse can please when too long.
Salvador Dali:	I will be so brief I have already finished.

Dean Rusk: One of the best ways to persuade others is with your ears — by listening.

Beirce: Bore: a person who talks when you wish him to listen.

William Shakespeare: Give every man thy ear, but few thy voice.

Swiss Proverb: Speech is silver;
Silence is golden.

Jah: Silence is golden, that's what they say;
So try to be silent three times a day.

Albert Einstein: If A equals success, then the formula is A equals X plus Y plus Z.
X is work. Y is play. Z is keep your mouth shut.

P. L. Stewart: When you are in it up to your ears, keep your mouth shut.

Gregory Ratoff: If you can't keep quiet, shut up!

"Leave It To Beaver"
Wally Cleaver: Look, I've been going to school all my life. You can't get in trouble by keeping your mouth shut.

Sydney Biddle Barrows:
Never say anything on the phone that you wouldn't want your mother to hear at your trial.

Ernest Hemingway: Always do sober what you said you'd do drunk. That will teach you to keep your mouth shut.

Mark Twain:	It is better to keep your mouth shut and appear stupid, than to open it and remove all doubt.
Sir Winston Churchill:	When the eagles are silent, the parrots begin to jabber.
Wilbur Wright:	A parrot talks much but flies little.
Farmer's Almanac:	Actions speak louder than words — but not so often.
Pirkay Avot:	Good deeds are better than wise sayings.
Elie Wiesel:	Words can sometimes, in moments of grace, attain the quality of deeds.
Unknown:	A man of words and not of deeds Is like a garden full of weeds.
Lenny Bruce:	I only said it, man. I didn't do it.
Mother Theresa:	There should be less talk. A preaching point is not a meeting point.
Werner Erhard:	The truth believed is a lie. If you go around preaching the truth, you're lying. The truth can only be experienced.
John Selden:	Preachers say, "Do as I say, not as I do."
Ralph Waldo Emerson:	What you do speaks so loud I cannot hear what you say.
Solon:	Put more trust in nobility of character than in an oath.
Norman Douglas:	Never take a solemn oath. People think you mean it.

Napoleon Bonaparte:	The best way to keep your word is not to give it.
George Burns:	He was the master of deception. By always holding his hand under his jacket, he fooled everyone into thinking that was where he kept his wallet, when all the time it was in his pants pocket.
Pete Seeger:	"Do–so" is more important than "say–so."
David Hockney:	It is very good advice to believe only what an artist does, rather than what he says about his work.
Unknown:	Walk the Talk
R. H. Blyth:	We walk, and our religion is shown (even to the dullest and most insensitive person) in how we walk. Or to put it more accurately, living in this world means choosing, choosing to walk, and the way we choose to walk is infallibly and perfectly expressed in the walk itself. Nothing can disguise it. The walk of an ordinary man and of an enlightened man are as different as that of a snake and a giraffe.
St. Francis of Assisi:	It is no use walking anywhere to preach, unless our walking is our preaching.
Publilius Syrus:	It is no profit to have learned well, if you neglect to do well.
English Saying:	A good example is the best sermon.
Bill Peterson:	Lead us in a few words of silent prayer.

Lawrence C. Coughlin:

Don't talk unless you can improve the silence.

Marcia P. Metzger:

If you can't say anything nice, don't say anything at all.

Hilaire Tattinger:

If you can't say anything — don't.

John Cage:

I have nothing to say and I am saying it.

Meiri:

The fewer the words, the fewer the errors.

Edward Hersey Richards:

A wise old owl sat on an oak,
  The more he saw the less he spoke;
The less he spoke the more he heard;
  Why aren't we like that wise old bird?

~~~*~~~

Chapter Fifteen

A Single Step

"You can stand in the elevator all day, but if you don't press the button... you ain't goin' up," Jah whispered to the crowd as though it were a secret. "Begin a task and you're halfway through.

"If you haven't embarked on the journey to your goals and visions, it's alright to be mad at yourself," again Jah gazed in my direction. "A sense of urgency is necessary to carry out the first step. I've heard some say: 'I'll do that tomorrow.' They won't ever.

"If you don't venture forth now, you probably never will. If nothing else, the internal peace that comes with having attempted the venture makes doing something about aspirations clearly superior than attempting nothing. To me, living with the regret and uncertainty of wondering what I could have done is far worse than falling short of the mark.

"There will be things that you won't want to do blocking your path. Don't stare at them too long," Jah persisted. "I used to use the excuse 'I don't have enough time,' but then I realized that everyone has the same amount every day. We procure time for the things most significant to us, and the only time is now.

"A goal to paddle a thousand miles upstream in life's river is nearly impossible... if it's attempted all in one day. Obviously, at this stage of our evolution, we can't row a thousand miles upstream, which leaves two choices:

> Throw our hands in the air and let the current pull us in the opposite direction as we lean back in our comfortable canoes.

Row the boat, one mile each day for a thousand
days, then hit the beach for a good night's rest.

"We are in command. We can choose either. We can throw or we
can row!

" 'But I've wasted a lot of time already,' some say. Maybe true, so
start now, on the first day of the rest of your life. Start now, at the
youngest chronological age you'll ever be.

"Hate your job?" Jah inquired. "Look through the paper and call
three numbers immediately.

"Not happy with your physique? Do your first workout and learn
about nutrition.

"Always wanted to read Shakespeare? Get thee to a library.

"The secret key to mastering procrastination is to merely begin;
when you do you're half–way through. One doesn't have to plan
everything before beginning," Jah reminded us. "Write the first sentence and the rest of the letter will flow. Tell me, if you were to drive
across Seattle would you wait for all the lights to turn green before
you went?" Jah was looking at me again. "That's just what some of
us are doing. I won't spend *my* life in the parking garage!

"Things don't have to be perfect to set out, but get into position,
get the momentum moving. That will put you in the proper place at
the right time for opportunity to strike.

"W. H. Murray once said, 'This may sound too simple, but is great
in consequence. Until one is committed there is hesitancy, the chance
to draw back, always ineffectiveness. Concerning all acts of initiative
(and creation), there is one elementary truth, the ignorance of which
kills countless ideas and splendid plans: that the moment one definitely commits oneself, then Providence moves too. All sorts of
things occur to help one that would never otherwise have occurred.
A whole stream of events issues from the decision, raising in one's
favour all manner of unforeseen incidents and meetings and material
assistance, which no man could have dreamt would have come his
way.' "

Jah turned my way, pointed at me with his index finger touching
his thumb and motioned with a writing gesture, "Make sure you get
all that, it's powerful.

"Those who have begun will be prepared for opportunity; those who are ready will win."

~~~*~~~

Lao–tzu: The journey of a thousand miles must begin with a single step.

Neil A. Armstrong: That's one small step for a man, one giant leap for mankind.

Ellen DeGeneres: My grandmother, she started walking five miles a day when she was sixty. She's ninety–seven today — and we don't know where the hell she is.

Stephen Wright: Anywhere's in walking distance if you've got the time.

Samuel Johnson: Great works are performed, not by strength, but by perseverance. He that shall walk, with vigor, three hours a day will pass, in seven years, a space equal to the circumference of the globe.

William Lee: The only way to get anywhere is to start from where you are.

English Proverb: One of these days is none of these days.

David Wallechinsky and Amy Wallace: At 99, David Ray of Franklin, Tennessee learned to read. At 92, Paul Spangler completed his fourteenth marathon. At 91, Hulda Crooks climbed Mount Whitney, the highest mountain in the continental United States.

Maurice Chevalier:	If you wait for the perfect moment, when all is safe and assured, it may never arrive. Mountains will not be climbed, races won, or lasting happiness achieved.

Lorenzo Dow:	You can and you can't
	  You shall and you shan't;
	You will and you won't
	  You'll be damned if you do,
	And you'll be damned if you don't.

Jah:	Do it.
Thomas Huxley:	Perhaps the most valuable result of all education is the ability to make yourself do the thing you have to do when it ought to be done, whether you like it or not; it is the first lesson that ought to be learned; and however early a man's training begins, it is probably the last lesson that he learns thoroughly.
Mark Twain:	Do something every day that you don't want to do.
Dale Carnegie:	Do the hard jobs first. The easy jobs will take care of themselves.
George H. Loumer:	Putting off an easy thing makes it hard, putting off a hard one makes it impossible.
Aristotle:	Well begun is half done.
Charles Kettering:	A problem well stated is a problem half solved.
George Balanchine:	If you set out deliberately to make a masterpiece, how will you ever get it finished?

326

Cardinal Newman:	Nothing would be done at all if a man waited until he could do it so well that no one could find fault with it.
John Cage:	If you don't have enough time to accomplish something, consider the work finished once it's begun.
W. Marshall Craig:	It is better to undertake a large task and get it half done than to undertake nothing and get it all done.
François de La Rochefoucauld:	It is praiseworthy to even attempt a great action.
Jordan S. Metzger:	There is never a convenient time to start.
William Shakespeare:	Refrain tonight, and that shall lend a kind of easiness to the next abstinence, and the next, more easy.
Spanish Saying:	Mañana is often the busiest day of the week.
William Shakespeare:	In delay there lies no plenty.
C. Northcote Parkinson:	Delay is the deadliest form of denial.
Huang Po:	You must make the most strenuous efforts. Throughout this life, you can never be certain of living long enough to take another breath.
Hillel:	Say not, "When I have leisure I will study" — perchance thou wilt have no leisure.

John of Salisbury:	He who will not when he may, may not when he will.
Rabbi Tarfon:	It is not thy obligation to complete the task, nevertheless thou art not at liberty to desist therefrom.
George W. Olinger:	Don't wait until you're a man to be great. Be a great boy.
Lily Tomlin:	Why is it we are always hearing about the tragic cases of too much, too soon? What about the rest of us? Too little, too late.
William Shakespeare:	Better three hours too soon than a minute too late.
Yogi Berra:	It gets late early out there.
Robert W. Service:	Ah! the clock is always slow; It is later than you think.
Yogi Berra:	I usually take a two–hour nap, from one o'clock to four.
Benjamin Franklin:	Never leave that till tomorrow which you can do today. Do not squander time, for that is the stuff life is made of.
Aaron Burr:	Never do today what you can put off till tomorrow.
Mark Twain:	Never put off till tomorrow, what you can do the day after tomorrow.

Denis Waitley: Procrastination is the fear of success. People procrastinate because they are afraid of the success that they know will result if they move ahead now. Because success is heavy, carries a responsibility with it, it is much easier to procrastinate and live on the "someday I'll" philosophy.

Benjamin Disraeli: Great men think of opportunity, not time. Time is the excuse of feeble and puzzled spirits.

Graffiti: Time is an illusion perpetrated by the manufacturers of space.

A Packet of Sugar: We are all manufacturers — some make good, others make trouble, and still others make excuses.

Tobias Smollett: There is no time like the present time.

Johann Wolfgang Von Goethe:
One always has time enough, if one will apply it well.

Henry Wadsworth Longfellow:
Trust no Future, howe'er pleasant!
 Let the Past bury its dead!
Act, — act in the living present!
 Heart within, and God o'erhead!

Franklin P. Adams:
And of all glad words of prose or rhyme,
 The gladdest are, "Act while there yet is
 time."

~~~*~~~

Malcolm Forbes: There is never enough time, unless you're serving it.

Charles Buxton:	You will never "find" time for anything. If you want time you must make it.
Stanislaw J. Lec:	People find life entirely too time–consuming.
Juvenal:	The short bloom of our brief and narrow life flies fast away. While we are calling for flowers and wine and women, old age is upon us.

Ernest Dowson:	They are not long, the days of wine and roses;
	  Out of a misty dream
	Our path emerges for a while, then closes
	  Within a dream.

Joseph Conrad:	A man that is born falls into a dream like a man who falls into the sea.
Herbert Prochnow:	If a man wants his dreams to come true, he must wake up.
Stanislaw J. Lec:	I had a dream about reality. It was such a relief to wake up.
P. D. Ouspensky:	What we see appears to be reality, but afterwards we call that very same thing a dream.
Steven Spielberg:	I dream for a living.
Interviewer: Carl Sagan:	Finally, what is a dream? We still don't know — which is amazing when you consider how pervasive dreaming is in the lives of every human being... We simply do not know the answer.

Diogenes:	We are more curious about the meaning of dreams than about things we see when awake.
Dr. Erich Fromm:	Both dreams and myths are important communications from ourselves to ourselves.
P. D. Ouspensky:	I cannot get it into my head, I want to understand: is this a dream or not?
Edgar Allan Poe:	All that we see or seem Is but a dream within a dream.
Chuang–tzu:	Once upon a time, I, Chuang–tzu, dreamt I was a butterfly, fluttering hither and thither, to all intents and purposes a butterfly. I was conscious only of following my fancies as a butterfly, and was unconscious of my individuality as a man. Suddenly, I awaked, and there I lay, myself again. Now I do not know whether I was then a man dreaming I was a butterfly, or whether I am now a butterfly dreaming I am a man.
The Zohar:	On the day of his death, a man feels he has lived but a single day.
Havelock Ellis:	Dreams are real while they last. Can we say more of life?
Chuang–tzu:	While they were asleep, they did not realize that they were dreaming... But when they awoke, they knew. Someday will come a great awakening, when we will know this life was like a dream...
Yiddish Proverb:	The years of a man's life pass like a dream.

Maurice de Saxe (Last Words):
The dream has been short; but it has been fine.

The Buddha:
Thus shall ye think of all this fleeting world:
A star at dawn, a bubble in a stream;
A flash of lightning in a summer cloud,
A flickering lamp, a phantom, and a dream.

John Boyle O'Reilly:
For a dreamer lives forever,
And a toiler dies in a day.

Thomas Jefferson:
My theory has always been, that if we are to dream, the flatteries of hope are as cheap and pleasanter than the gloom of despair.

George Santaya:
There is no cure for birth and death save to enjoy the interval.

Grandma Moses:
I look back on my life like a good day's work, it was done and I am satisfied with it.

The Zohar:
On the day of his death, a man feels he has lived but a single day.

Ellen Goodman:
It has begun to occur to me that life is a stage I'm going through.

Charles Dederich:
Today is the first day of the rest of your life.

George Carlin:
The day after tomorrow is the third day of the rest of your life.

Lorne Elliot:	My teacher told me that today was the first day of the rest of my life. I said, "That explains why I didn't do yesterday's homework!"
Charles F. Kettering:	I am not interested in the past. I am interested in the future, for that is where I expect to spend the rest of my life.

~~~*~~~

John Ciardi:	The day will happen whether or not you get up.
Yogi Berra:	If I didn't wake up, I'd still be sleeping.
Woody Allen:	Eighty percent of success is showing up.
The Talmud:	The sun will set without thy assistance.
Robert Greene:	Time nor tide tarrieth no man.
"The Honeymooners" Ed Norton:	As we say in the sewer, time and tide wait for no man.
Hector Berlioz:	Time is a great teacher, but unfortunately it kills all its pupils.
Henry David Thoreau:	Time is but the stream I go a–fishing in.
Thornton Wilder:	It is only in appearance that time is a river. It is rather a vast landscape and it is the eye of the beholder that moves.
Octavio Paz:	We don't move, today is today, always is today.
Samuel Goldwyn:	We've passed a lot of water since then.

Duke of Wellington:	Always make water when you can.
Heraclitus:	You cannot step twice into the same river, for other waters are continually flowing in.
Gertrude Stein:	Whenever you get there, there's no there there.
Hélène Cixous:	The time, the people, and the individual converge only once.
Macneile Dixon:	The facts of the present won't sit still for a portrait.
Henry Wadsworth Longfellow:	Art is long, and time is fleeting.
Paul Cézanne:	Right now a moment of time is fleeting by!
Ogden Nash:	How confusing the beams from memory's lamp are; One day a bachelor, The next a grampa. What is the secret of the trick? How did I get so old so quick?
"Calvin and Hobbes" Bill Watterson Calvin:	A day can really slip by when you're deliberately avoiding what you're supposed to do.
John Hughes:	Life moves pretty fast; you don't stop and look around every once in a while, you could miss it.
Benjamin Franklin:	Lost time is never found again...

Johann Friedrich von Schiller:
What one refuses in a minute no eternity will return.

William Blake:
If you trap the moment before it's ripe,
  The tears of repentance you'll certainly
      wipe;
But if once you let the ripe moment go
  You can never wipe off the tears of woe.

William Field:
The time is here, and is rapidly approaching.

Robert Greene:
Time is... Time was... Time is past.

Ernest Hemingway:
Time is the least thing we have of.

Rabindranath Tagore:
The butterfly counts not months but moments, and has time enough.

Vera Stravinsky:
When people ask me what I want for my birthday, I always say, "Time, time, time."

William Hazlitt:
As we advance in life, we acquire a keener sense of the value of time.

"Calvin and Hobbes"
Bill Watterson

Calvin:
It's July already! Oh no! Oh no! What happened to June?! Summer vacation is slipping though our fingers like grains of sand! It's going too fast! We've got to hoard our freedom and have more fun! Time rushes on! Help! Help!

Hobbes:
I don't think I want to be here at the end of August.

Calvin:
Aaugh! It's a half–hour later than it was half an hour ago! Run! Run!

Cesare Pavese: We do not remember days, we remember moments.

Robert Grudin: Happiness may well consist primarily of an attitude toward time.

Johann Wolfgang von Goethe:
Since Time is not a person we can overtake when he is gone, let us honor him with mirth and cheerfulness of heart while he is passing.

Ralph Waldo Emerson: This time, like all times, is a very good one, if we but know what to do with it.

Zen Saying: After ecstasy, the laundry.

Charles Dickens: It was the best of times, it was the worst of times.

Art Buchwald: Whether it's the best of times or the worst of times, it's the only time you've got.

Bill Clinton: This is our time, let us embrace it.

Edna St. Vincent Millay:
My candle burns at both ends;
  It will not last the night;
But, ah, my foes, and, oh, my friends —
  It gives a lovely light.

George Bernard Shaw: I rejoice in life for its own sake. Life is no brief candle for me. It is sort of a splendid torch, which I have got hold of for the moment; and I want to make it burn as brightly as possible before handing it on to future generations.

~~~*~~~

Albert Einstein: When a man sits with a pretty girl for an hour, it seems like a minute. But let him sit on a hot stove for a minute — and it's longer than any hour. That's relativity.

William Dean Howells: Some people can stay longer in an hour than others can in a week.

Alfred Joseph Hitchcock:
    ... Suspense takes up an hour.

Ralph Waldo Emerson: A day is a miniature eternity.

Diogenes Laertius: Time is the image of eternity.

Tom Stoppard: Eternity is a terrible thought. I mean, where's it going to end?

Wallace Stevens: Among twenty snowy mountains
        The only moving thing
    Was the eye of the blackbird.

Tibetan poem: In the cold Northern wastes
        There is a mountain
    A thousand miles long
        A thousand miles high

    Once each thousand years
        A small bird
    Flies North
        A small bird flies North
    to sharpen his beak
        on the cold hard stone

    When the mountain
        Is thusly worn down
    One second of Eternity
        Shall have passed.

Albert Einstein:	I have just got a new theory of eternity.
Elias Canetti:	In eternity everything is just beginning.
Max Muller:	How mankind defers from day to day the best it can do and the most beautiful things it can enjoy, without thinking that every day may be the last one, and that lost time is lost eternity.
Unknown:	The only way to live is to accept each minute as an unrepeated miracle, which is exactly what it is — a miracle and unrepeatable.
Thomas Ambrose:	If it just means continual existence, it's not enough. I look at it [cancer] as a wake up call. You can't let your dreams slip.
Henry David Thoreau:	If one advances confidently in the directions of his dreams, and endeavors to live the life which he has imagined, he will meet with a success unexpected in common hours.

~~~*~~~

Dr. Robert H. Schuller:	May I give you, my friend, a sentence now that can change your life? Ready? Don't wait until you're ready.
Johann Wolfgang von Goethe:	If you think you can do it, begin it! Begin and the mind grows heated. Begin, and the task is completed.
John Heywood:	When the sun shineth, make hay.

Singhalese Saying: Eat coconuts while you have teeth.

Arnold Toynbee: The right moment for starting on your next job is not tomorrow or next week.

Jordan S. Metzger: There is never a convenient time to start.

Johann Wolfgang Von Goethe:

> Whatever you can do,
>   Or dream you can, begin it.
> Boldness has genius,
>   Power and magic in it.

Basil King: The bold and mighty powers will come to your aid.

Christian Nestell Bovee:

> We make way for the man who boldly pushes past us.

David Starr Jordan: The world stands aside to let anyone pass who knows where he is going.

Menander: Even God lends a hand to honest boldness.

Aeschylus: When a man's willing and eager, the gods join in.

Cesare Pavese: The only joy in the world is to begin.

Grace Hansen: Don't be afraid your life will end; be afraid that it will never begin.

Seneca: Begin at once to live.

Hasidic Proverb:	There are three types of "doers": If a man says, "I shall do it soon," his character is poor; if he says, "I am ready to do it," his character is average; if he says, "I am doing it," his character is praiseworthy.
George Eliot:	If we want more roses, we must plant more trees!
John F. Kennedy:	The great French Marshall Lyautey once asked his gardener to plant a tree. The gardener objected that the tree was slow growing and would not reach maturity for 100 years. The Marshall replied, "In that case, there is no time to lose; plant it this afternoon!"
Samuel Johnson:	Nothing will ever be attempted if all possible objections must be overcome.
Master Sokei–an:	If you are in a powerful car in the middle of the Gobi Desert, you can step on the gas pedal and go any speed you like, any direction you fancy. But if you are in New York at a busy Broadway crossing, you better look out for the traffic lights.
Unknown:	Throughout history, the most common debilitating human ailment has been cold feet.
Jacob Bronowski:	We have to understand that the world can only be grasped by action, not by contemplation.
William Shakespeare:	Things won are done; joy's soul lies in doing.

Walter Bagehot:	The greatest pleasure in life is doing what people say you cannot do.
Samuel Johnson:	To do nothing is in every man's power.

James Albery:	He slept beneath the moon,
	   He basked beneath the sun;
	He lived a life of going–to–do,
	   And died with nothing done.

Jordan S. Metzger:	You only live a few times.
B. C. Forbes:	To be a nobody, do nothing.
Howe:	The way to be nothing is to do nothing.
Gian–Carlo Menotti:	Hell begins on the day when God grants us a clear vision of all that we might have achieved, of all the gifts which we have wasted, of all that we might have done which we did not do... For me the conception of Hell lies in two words: *Too late.*
Livy:	Better late than never.
Publilius Syrus:	It is better to learn late than never.
Frances Rodman:	It is never too late to mend our ways. The older we grow, the more we need repairs.
Willie "The Lion" Smith:	It's never too late to reach your destination.
George Eliot:	It is never too late to be what you might have been.
Hillel:	And if not now — when?

~~~*~~~

Chapter Sixteen

Not In Our Stars

"**S**it in the barber's chair long enough and you're going to get your hair cut. The fact is, we *are* creating our own reality. Those who eat in the donut shop every day will be rotund — food now, fat later. You set your own buzzer — someday that buzzer is going to go off. Destiny may thrust us into circumstances, from there it's our move. Luck and opportunities are usually near at hand only if we put them in reach through arduous effort and training," started Jah.

"To get the momentum of luck and fate swinging in our favor we must first give it a push ourselves. One of our guests here this evening mastered this notion early in life, which accounted largely toward his extraordinary success. Ben Franklin was launched into the printing business by the Governor of Pennsylvania, when they both lived in Philadelphia. Was it lucky for a very young man to become friends with, then get the opportunity to work with, the Governor? Maybe... but before this all happened Ben worked extremely hard for virtually nothing, mastering the art as an apprentice in his brother's printing shop... ready to take advantage of opportunity. Poised to pounce on providence.

"When we clap our hands, sound comes forth without a moment's deliberation. There is no cleaner illustration of the universal canon of cause and effect," Jah emphatically stated. "Other examples of this truth may take a longer time to come around, yet what goes around does come around, the echo will resound.

"Isaac Bashevis Singer was renowned for his speaking engagements. One time during the question and answer session that followed, a woman asked, 'Could you tell us how you feel about free will verses pre–determinism?' The eminently clever Noble Prize winning writer used these exact words in his heavy Yiddish accent:

> 'I *absolutely* believe in free will. There are fatalists who said everything is destined. Just the same, when you walk with a fatalist on the street, if you cross over the street, and he suddenly realizes that he's crossing a red light, he begins to run *so* quickly... as if he would be a believer in free will.
>
> 'In other words when it comes to our life we all believe in free will. We only try to deny it when it comes to doing some good deeds; then you say: it's destined that this poor man should die from hunger, why should *I* help him?
>
> 'In other words: **We must believe in free will... we have no choice.'** "

~~~*~~~

Ralph Waldo Emerson:
> Shallow men believe in luck. Strong men believe in cause and effect.

Stephen Leacock:
> I am a great believer in luck, and I find the harder I work, the more I have of it.

Jean Cocteau:
> We must believe in luck. For how else can we explain the success of those we don't like.

Jean Ace:
> Time wounds all heels.

Willie Davis:
> If you step on people in this life, you're going to come back as a cockroach.

Earl Wilson:
> Success is just a matter of luck. Ask any failure.

Unknown:
> Good luck is a lazy man's estimate of a worker's success.

Persian Proverb:	Go and wake up your luck.
Benjamin Franklin:	Diligence is the mother of good luck.
William Feather:	Be grateful for luck, but don't depend on it.
Dick Gregory:	If it weren't for bad luck, I wouldn't have had no luck at all!

Ralph Waldo Emerson:

> If you believe in fate, believe in it, at least,
> for your good.

Samuel Valentine Cole:

> Nor fate, nor chance, nor any star
> commands
> Success and failure — naught but your
> own hands.

Kin Hubbard:	Lots of folks confuse bad management with destiny.

Fanny Heaslip Lea:

> It's odd to think we might have been
> Sun, moon and stars unto each other —
> Only, I turned down one little street
> As you went up another.

Henry Wadsworth Longfellow:

> Not in the clamor of the crowded street,
> Not in the shouts and plaudits of the
> throng,
> But in ourselves, are triumph and defeat.

William Shakespeare:	The fault, dear Brutus, is not in our stars, but in ourselves.
Unknown:	Anybody who believes in astrology was probably born under the wrong sign.

Arthur C. Clarke:	The time may come when men control the destinies of the stars.
Albert Einstein:	God does not play dice [with the universe].
Jordan S. Metzger:	The world is too random to be merely random.
Benjamin Disraeli:	We are not creatures of circumstance; we are creators of circumstance.
George Bernard Shaw:	I don't believe in circumstances. The people who get on in this world are the people who get up and look for the circumstances they want and, if they can't find them, make them.
Napoleon Bonaparte:	Circumstances — what are circumstances? I make circumstances.
Jose Ortega Y. Gasset:	I am I plus my circumstances.
Ralph Waldo Emerson:	What you are comes to you.
Francis Bacon:	A wise man will make more opportunities than he finds.
Frederick W. Robertson:	It is not the situation that makes the man, but the man who makes the situation. The slave may be a freeman. The monarch may be slave. Situations are noble or ignoble, as we make them.

"Forrest Gump"
Forrest Gump (Winston Groom):

> I happen to believe we make our own destiny. We have to do the best with what God gave us...

Jah:

> The universe deals us a hand; it's up to us to play it well.

Terence:

> Life is like a game of tables; the chances are not in our power, but the playing is.

Josh Billings:

> As in a game of cards, so in the game of life, we must play what is dealt to us; and the glory consists not so much in winning, as in playing a poor hand well.

Arthur Schopenhauer:

> Fate gives us the hand, and we play the cards.

Francis Bacon:

> It cannot be denied but outward accidents conduce much to fortune: favour, opportunity, death of others, occasion fitting virtue. But chiefly, the mould of a man's fortune is in his own hands.

Rupert Hughes:

> A determined soul will do more with a rusty monkey wrench than a loafer will accomplish with all the tools in a machine shop.

James Allen:

> In all human affairs there are *efforts,* and there are *results,* and the strength of the effort is the measure of the result.

Ralph Waldo Emerson:

> As we are, so we do, and as we do, so is it done to us; we are the builders of our fortunes.

Virgil:	Fortune sides with him who dares.
John Dryden:	Fortune befriends the bold.
Benjamin Franklin:	He that waits upon fortune, is never sure of a dinner.
June Smith:	Few wishes come true by themselves.
Garson Kanin:	Amateurs hope. Professionals work.
Pablo Picasso:	I do not seek, I find.
Bachya ibn Paquda:	Don't rely on If and Perhaps.
Finley Peter Dunne:	Trust everybody, but cut the cards.
Indian Proverb:	Call on God, but row away from the rocks.
Islamic Proverb:	Allah will protect you, but tie up your camel.
Buddy Hackett:	May your tent be filled with oil of myrrh and frankincense. May your camel never tire. May your goat give sweet milk.

The Book Of Koheleth 11:1:
Cast your bread upon the waters, for after many days you will find it.

Zen Saying:	No snowflake falls in an inappropriate place.
Galatians 6:7:	You reap whatever you sow.
Unknown:	You can never tell when you do an act

Just what the result will be;
But with every deed you are sowing a seed,
Though its harvest you may never see.

Unknown:

    Anyone can count the seeds in an apple.
      No one can count the apples in a seed.

Henry Wadsworth Longfellow:

    I breathed a song into the air
      It fell to earth, I know not where...
    And the song, from beginning to end,
      I found again in the heart of a friend.

Edwin Markham:

    There is a destiny that makes us brothers:
      None goes his way alone:
    All that we send into the lives of others
      Comes back into our own.

Hume:

    The universal compensation prevails in all conditions of being and existence.

David Miller:

    You may cheat man–made laws, but you can't escape the eternal law of compensation.

Jim "Bakko" Benton:

    Remember that what you take from the earth, you must give back lest the earth, take something from you that you did not wish to give.

Ralph Waldo Emerson:

    Nature magically suits a man to his fortunes by making them the fruit of his character.

Abigail Van Buren:

    While forbidden fruit is said to taste sweeter, it usually spoils faster.

Henry Miller:

    For every effect there is cause. None of us are well, successful, happy, ill, inefficient, by chance. All of life is under the inexorable rule of cause and effect.

Jordan S. Metzger: Time is merely universal law giving us a temporary reprieve from cause and effect.

Ralph Waldo Emerson:
Skepticism is unbelief in cause and effect.

Albert Einstein: Something deeply hidden had to be behind things.

George Eliot: Our deeds determine us, as much as we determine our deeds.

Jordan S. Metzger: If you don't want to be average, don't do average things often.

~~~*~~~

Henry David Thoreau: If one advances confidently in the direction of his dreams, and endeavors to live the life he has imagined, he will meet with a success unexpected in common hours.

Christian Nestell Bovee:
We make way for the man who boldly pushes past us.

Joe Poyer: Thorough preparation makes its own luck.

Ovid: Let your hook always be cast, in the pool where you least expect it, will be a fish.

Ann Landers: If you want to catch trout, don't fish in a herring barrel.

Gordon Parks:	A lot of people have said to me: "It seems you've always been in the right place at the right time." But what they don't realize is that I was prepared to be there. If luck comes and if you're not ready to take advantage of it, it may just as well not have come.
Benjamin Disraeli:	The secret to success in life is for a man to be ready for his opportunity when it comes.
Abraham Lincoln:	I'll study and get ready and be prepared for my opportunity when it comes.
George Bernard Shaw:	I am the most spontaneous speaker in the world because every word, every gesture, and every retort has been carefully rehearsed.
Mark Twain:	It usually takes me more than three weeks to prepare a good impromptu speech.
Bobby Knight:	The key is not the "will to win"... everybody has that. It is the will to *prepare* to win that is important.
Morton Dean:	From my father: "Always be ready to come off the bench." It was his way of saying, "Be prepared."
Harlan Ellison:	I live by Louis Pasteur's advice that "Chance favors the prepared mind."
Louis Pasteur:	Chance favors only those minds which are prepared.

William Jennings Bryan:
> Destiny is not a matter of chance; it is a matter of choice. It is not a thing to be waited for; it is a thing to be achieved.

Herodotus:
> The destiny of man is in his own soul.

Soyen Shaku:
> When an opportunity comes do not let it pass by, yet always think twice before acting.

Thomas Edison:
> Opportunity is missed by most people because it is dressed in overalls and looks like work.

Elbert Hubbard:
> The actual fact is that, in this day, Opportunity not only knocks at your door, but is playing an anvil chorus on every man's door.

Jah:
> Opportunity won't knock on your door if you've put up a "No Trespassing" sign.

Mark Twain:
> Fortune knocks at every man's door once in a life, but in a good many cases the man is in a neighboring saloon and does not hear her.

~~~*~~~

"The sooner you recognize this the better off you are," Jah added.

Chapter Seventeen

Carry A Pick

"Lend an ear to one of my favorite tales," continued our conductor:

There was an old, God–loving sage, some would have considered him saintly. God cherished him very dearly.

One day there was a flood, and soon the water from a nearby river infiltrated the old man's living room. Before he knew it, water was up to his knees, but he was not afraid, for he believed in God. A short time later, water covered his waist. Fortunately a comrade came by in a canoe crying, 'Hurry up, get in!'

'Don't worry about me,' exclaimed the old man, 'God will take care of me!' After attempting a protest, the friend reluctantly departed.

The water rose fast. When it was up to the old man's neck, two of his students arrived by sailboat, beckoning their mentor to climb aboard. He declined, adamantly announcing, 'The Lord will provide.'

Around about the time the water had ascended to chin level, he spied his best friend straining his way, stroke by stroke, in a small dingy.

'Get in, get in!' begged his buddy.

'No,' said the scholar, 'I'm staying right here. I

have faith that God will look after me.'

After his best friend rowed away, the old man drowned. He went to heaven and was brought to meet his creator.

He cried, 'God, you have always been so good to me, and I have had faith and followed all your commandments. Why didn't you save me?'

'Nincompoop!' said God, 'I sent you three boats!'

"Another fellow," Jah recounted, "kept praying to God that he would win the lottery and take home millions of dollars, thus solving all his problems. He prayed hard and sincerely, so zealously in fact, that eventually God answered him. From on high, the man heard a heavenly voice, 'Meet me halfway,' it thundered, 'buy a ticket!'

"Our prayers are always answered, that is, taking into account a few important parameters:

–They are not always answered right away.

–Sometimes the answer is no.

–And sometimes, as Benjamin Franklin was inspired to articulate, 'God helps them that help themselves.' "

~~~*~~~

Henry Wadsworth Longfellow:
> The heights by great men reached and kept
> Were not attained by sudden flight,
> But they, while their companions slept,
> Were toiling upward in the night.

Benjamin Franklin: Plough deep while sluggards sleep, and you shall have corn to sell and to keep.

Chinese Saying: Be the first in the field, the last to the couch.

Genovese Saying: It is better to wear out one's shoes than one's sheets.

Arthur Brisbane: The dictionary is the only place where success comes before work.

Dr. Robert H. Schuller: Success is spelled W–O–R–K.

Charles O. Finley: Sweat plus sacrifice equals success.

Unknown: How to succeed, if you think it's worth the trouble; Hitch your wagon to a star, put your shoulder to the wheel, keep an ear to the ground and watch the handwriting on the wall.

Abigail Van Buren: If you want a place in the sun, you've got to put up with a few blisters.

Seneca: It is a rough road that leads to the heights of greatness.

Chinese Saying: If you don't scale the mountain, you can't view the plain.

George Eliot: Nothing will give permanent success in any enterprise of life, except native capacity cultivated by honest and persevering effort.

Sir Joshua Reynolds: Excellence is never granted to a man but as a reward of labor.

Andrew V. Mason: If dandelions were hard to grow, they would be welcome on any lawn.

Caryl Haskins: It's funny that we often value what is rare and specialized. What is truly precious is what is common and unspecialized.

David Hume: The greater the obstacle the more glory in overcoming it.

Thomas Paine:
The harder the conflict the more glorious the triumph. What we obtain too cheaply, we esteem too lightly; 'tis dearness only that gives everything its value.

~~~*~~~

Fyodor Mikhailovich Dostoevsky:
A new philosophy, a way of life, is not given for nothing. It has to be paid dearly for and only acquired with much patience and great effort.

Johann Wolfgang von Goethe:
It never occurs to fools that merit and good fortune are closely united.

Confucius:
What the superior man seeks is in himself, but what the small man seeks is in others.

Unknown:
The man who wins is the man who works,
    Who neither labor nor trouble shirks;
Who uses his hands, his head, his eyes;
    The man who wins is the man who tries.

Vallie G. Golden:
I made this important discovery: if I do my work *as if* I really enjoy it, then I do enjoy it to some extent.

Elbert Hubbard:
Folks who never do any more than they are paid for, never get paid for any more than they do.

Frank McKinney:
Th' feller who quits work in th' evenin' like he wuz leavin' a penitentiary never reaches Easy Street.

Anatole France:
His sole concern with work was considering how he might best avoid it.

George Bush:	[I want to] make sure everybody who has a job wants a job.
Interviewer:	Your Holiness, how many people work in the Vatican?
Pope John XXIII:	About half.
Calvin Coolidge:	When a great many people are unable to find work, unemployment results.
Shannon Fife:	The basic cause of failure stems from beginners looking for employment instead of work.
Beverly Sills:	There are no short cuts to any place worth going.
John Updike:	Any activity becomes creative when the doer cares about doing it right, or better.
Henry Wadsworth Longfellow:	It takes less time to do a thing right than it does to explain why you did it wrong.
Vernon Law:	Some people are so busy learning the tricks of the trade that they never learn the trade.
Unknown:	It is easier to admire hard work if you don't do it.
Jerome K. Jerome:	It is impossible to enjoy idling thoroughly unless one has plenty of work to do.
Franklin P. Jones:	One disadvantage of having nothing to do is you can't stop and rest.
Homer:	Too much rest itself becomes a pain.

Henri Frederic Amiel:	The stationary condition is the beginning of the end.
Abraham Lincoln:	Things may come to those who wait, but only the things left by those who hustle.
Thomas A. Edison:	Everything comes to him who hustles while he waits.
Christian Nestell Bovee:	Few minds wear out; more rust out.
Richard Cumberland:	It is better to wear out than to rust out.
George Bernard Shaw:	This is the true joy in life, being used for a purpose recognized by yourself as a mighty one; the being thoroughly worn out before you are thrown on the scrap heap; the being a force of Nature instead of a feverish selfish little clod of ailments and grievances complaining that the world will not devote itself to making you happy.
Fyodor Mikhailovich Dostoevsky:	Originality and the feeling of one's own dignity are achieved only through work and struggle.
Old Chinese Proverb:	Cut your own wood and it will warm you twice.
Sissy Spacek:	When I'm pushing myself, testing myself, that's when I'm happiest. That's when the rewards are greatest.
Garson Kanin:	The best part of one's life is the working part, the creative part. Believe me, I love to succeed... However, the real spiritual and emotional excitement is in the doing.

George Bernard Shaw:	I like a state of continual becoming, with a goal in front and not behind.
Joseph Addison:	The grand essentials to happiness in this life are something to do, someone to love, and something to hope for.
John Cowper Powys:	A certain comfortable security, a certain profound inner peace, a kind of happy numbness, soothes the nerves of the human animal when absorbed in its allotted task.
Thomas Jefferson:	It is neither wealth nor splendor, but tranquility and occupation, which gives happiness.
Ashley Montagu:	It is work, work that one delights in, that is the surest guarantor of happiness.
Dr. Richard C. Cabot:	As a physician, I have had the happiness of seeing work cure many persons.
Rabbi Jonah:	Let no man neglect to work, for idleness will throw a man into depression.
Tennyson:	I must lose myself in action, lest I wither in despair.
Bovee:	Active natures are rarely melancholy. Activity and sadness are incompatible.
J. M. Good:	Happiness consists in activity. Such is the constitution of our nature. It is a running stream, and not a stagnant pool.
Bovee:	The greatest happiness comes from the greatest activity.

R. S. MacArthur:	Activity is God's medicine; the highest genius is willingness and ability to do hard work. Any other conception of genius makes it a doubtful comment if not a dangerous possession.
Walter Lippmann:	Industry is a better horse to ride than genius.
Donald Grant Mitchell:	There is no genius in life like the genius of energy and industry.

Henry Wadsworth Longfellow:
> Genius is infinite painstaking.

Claude Adrien Helvétius:
> Genius is nothing but continued attention.

Thomas A. Edison:	Genius is one percent inspiration and ninety–nine percent perspiration.
Unknown:	Thomas Edison said that genius is one percent inspiration and ninety–nine percent perspiration. I hate to think of anyone that sweaty handling electricity.
Oscar Levant:	There is a thin line between genius and insanity. I have erased this line.
Samuel Goldwyn:	Give me a smart idiot over a stupid genius any day.
Daniel Webster:	It has been said that I owe my success to genius. It is not to genius I attribute my success, but to hard work.
Thomas Edison:	There no substitute for hard work.

George Burns:	Brilliant inventor. His favorite creation was the phonograph. He only invented the light bulb so he could see where to place the needle on the records.
Agatha Christie:	I don't think necessity is the mother of invention — invention, in my opinion, arises directly from idleness, possibly also from laziness. To save oneself trouble.
Mamie Sypert Burns:	Beauty is also to be found in a day's work.
Ralph Waldo Emerson:	To fill the hour, that is happiness.
Barrow:	An hour's industry will do more to produce cheerfulness, suppress evil humors, and retrieve one's affairs than a month's moaning.
Blair:	Industry is not only the instrument of improvement, but the foundation of pleasure... for it is labor only which gives relish to pleasure. It is the indispensable condition of possessing a sound mind in a sound body.
Benjamin Franklin:	Industry need not wish.
B. C. Forbes:	Work now, or wince later.
Sir Joshua Reynolds:	Excellence is never granted to man but as the reward of labor. It argues no small strength of mind to persevere in habits of industry without the pleasure of perceiving those advances, which, like the hands of a clock, whilst they make hourly approaches to their point, yet proceed so slowly as to escape observation.

Simone Weil:	Even if our efforts of attention seem for years to be producing no result, one day a light that is in exact proportion to them will flood the soul.
Solomon Ibn Gabirol:	A sage is wise because he spent more time on oil [on lamps to read by] than others spent on wine.
Charles Dickens:	Father Time is not always a hard parent, and though he tarries for none of his children, often lays his hand lightly on those who have used him well.
Eddie Cantor:	It takes twenty years to make an overnight success.
Henry Ford:	It has been my observation that most people get ahead during the time that others waste.
Benjamin Franklin:	If you were a servant, would you not be ashamed that a good master should catch you idle? Are you then your own master? Be ashamed to catch yourself idle.
A Cafeteria Sign:	Courteous and efficient self–service.
Brian Kiley:	I went into a bookstore and asked the woman behind the counter where the self–help section was. She said, "If I told you that, it would defeat the whole purpose."

~~~*~~~

Ch'en Tu–hsiu:	Man's happiness in life is the result of man's own effort, and is neither the gift of God nor a spontaneous natural product.

362

Benjamin Franklin:	God gives all things to industry.
Addison:	Mankind are more indebted to industry than ingenuity; the gods set up their favors at a price, and industry is the purchaser.
Axel Munthe:	The gods sell all things at a fair price. There is no entrance fee to the starlit hall of light.
Leo Rosten:	God may help those who help themselves, but the courts are rough as hell on shoplifters.

William Cowper:	God moves in a mysterious way
	   His wonders to perform;
	He plants his footsteps in the sea
	   And rides upon the storm.

Danish Saying:	God gives all birds their food, but does not drop it into their nests.
Aesop:	The gods help them that help themselves.
Russian Proverb:	Pray to God, but keep rowing to the shore.
Indian Proverb:	Call on God, but row away from the rocks.
Reverend William Sloane Coffin:	When a man is drowning, it may be better for him to try to swim than to thrash around waiting for divine intervention.
Unknown:	Don't wait for your ship to come in; swim out to it.

Cardinal Francis J. Spellman:
Pray as if everything depended on God, and work as if everything depended upon man.

The Book Of Koheleth 5:3:
For a dream comes through a multitude of business.

Cleveland Amory:
Once, a gushing admirer approached Mr. Pullman and asked him if, in his early days, he ever dreamed of his vast company "with its palaces on wheels scurrying over the face of the earth." Replied Pullman gruffly, "No, I did not. If I had dreamed then, I'd be dreaming still."

Paul Valéry:
The best way to make your dreams come true is to wake up.

James A. Froude:
You cannot dream yourself into a character; you must hammer and forge yourself one.

~~~*~~~

Elbert Hubbard:
Do your work with your whole heart, and you will succeed — there's so little competition.

Indira Gandhi:
My grandfather once told me that there are two kinds of people: those who do the work and those who take the credit. He told me to try to be in the first group; there was less competition there.

Marcia Metzger:
Listen to your mother.

"Calvin and Hobbes"
Bill Watterson

Calvin: I wish I had amazing super powers.

Calvin's Dad: If you work and study real hard for years and years, you could develop the powers you already have.

Calvin: Maybe I can find a radioactive meteorite that mutates me into a living liquid.

Calvin's Dad: Try to find one that mutates you into someone with a work ethic.

Larry Miller: My father had three jobs and went to school at night... If I go to the cleaners and the bank in the same day... I need a nap.

Ashley Montagu: One should labor so hard in youth that everything that one does subsequently is easy by comparison.

Lou Holtz: The man who complains about the way the ball bounces is likely the one who dropped it.

Unknown: The young man who thought the world owed him a living is the old man who blames the world for his failures.

Mark Twain: Don't go around saying the world owes you a living; the world owes you nothing; it was here first.

Bill Clinton: It is time to break the bad habit of expecting something for nothing.

Alexander Pope: Blessed is he who expects nothing, for he shall never be disappointed.

Albanian Proverb: When you have given nothing, ask for nothing.

Bulgarian Saying:	From walking — something; from sitting — nothing.
Unknown:	Men who hang around waiting for something to turn up, should begin with their own sleeves.
Unknown:	He who rolls up his sleeves seldom loses his shirt.
Sidney J. Phillips:	Men are made stronger on realization that the helping hand they need is at the end of their own right arm.
Frank C. Brown:	Many bring rakes, but few shovels.
Hasidic Proverb:	Carry your own lantern, you will endure the dark.
Unknown:	Remember that the faith that moves mountains always carries a pick.
Tom Bodett:	... Of course that and the backhoe I'm gonna dig the foundation with next weekend.
Chinese Proverb:	The man who removes a mountain begins by carrying away small stones.
Dr. Albert Schweitzer:	Any one who proposes to do good must not expect people to roll stones out of his way, but must accept his lot calmly if they even roll a few more upon it.

~~~*~~~

| Don Herold: | Work is the greatest thing in the world, so we should always save some of it for tomorrow. |

| Sir Heneage Ogilvie: | The really idle man gets nowhere, the perpetually busy man does not get much further. |

| Sydney J. Harris: | The time to relax is when you don't have time for it. |

| Wilbur Cross: | Sometimes when I have too many things to do all at once, I sit down and relax and smoke my pipe for an hour and do nothing. |

| Spanish Proverb: | How beautiful it is to do nothing, and then rest afterward. |

"The Many Loves of Dobie Gillis"

| Dobie Gillis: | I don't have anything against work. I just figure, why deprive somebody who really loves it? |

"Peanuts" Charles Schultz

Sally:	Who are those people driving by in those cars?
Charlie Brown:	Those are people going to work...
Sally:	Work?
Charlie Brown:	They used to wait for the school bus like we're doing... Now they have to go to work every day for the rest of their lives...
Sally:	Good grief! Whose idea was that?

| Charlie McCarthy: | Hard work never killed anybody, but why take the chance? |

| James Thurber: | It is better to have loafed and lost than never to have loafed at all. |

Herodotus:	If a man insisted always on being serious, and never allowed himself a bit of fun and relaxation, he would go mad or become unstable.
Dr. Logan Clendening:	Four out of five people are more in need of rest than exercise.
Daniel W. Josselyn:	Rest is not a matter of doing absolutely nothing. *Rest is repair.*
Sir J. Lubbock:	Rest is not idleness, and to lie sometimes on the grass under the trees on a summer's day, listening to the murmur of water, or watching the clouds float across the sky, is by no means a waste of time.
Ralph Waldo Emerson:	The sky is the daily bread of the eyes.
Maria Edgeworth:	All work and no play makes Jack a dull boy, All play and no work makes Jack a mere toy.
Flip Wilson:	You can't expect to hit the jackpot if you don't put a few nickels in the machine.

~~~*~~~

Chapter Eighteen

Not Dead Yet

"**A**re you aware," inquired Jah, "of the especially eye–opening memo, which hung above the fireplace in the Beverly Hills mansion of the late Fred Astaire? Written by the casting director of a performance produced when Fred first auditioned as a young man, the note reads:

> 'Name: Fred Astaire
> 'Comments: Can't act, slightly bald, can dance a little.'

"Another would–be failure was constantly told by his music teacher that he had no voice. His voice broke every time he'd try to hit a high note. His name? Enrico Caruso.

"Terry Bradshaw is in the ninety–ninth percentile — for throwing incomplete passes. Luckily for Terry, he is better known for taking the Pittsburgh Steelers into four Super Bowl victories.

"R. H. Macy folded in seven attempts before 'The World's Largest Store' took off. Walt Disney was bankrupt five times before most of us heard of him. Henry Ford went bankrupt only twice.

"Everyone knows Dr. Seuss, but few know that twenty–eight publishers rejected <u>And To Think That I Saw It On Mulberry Street</u>. English writer John Creasey received seven–hundred and fifty–three rejection slips before he published five–hundred and sixty–four books. Which reminds me, Richard Bach had fifty–three rejections before a publisher finally agreed to print the phenomenal best–seller, <u>Jonathan Livingston Seagull</u>. Most of the first edition copies of <u>Walden</u> were stored in Thoreau's own library. I could write a book on books that were rejected," Jah continued, "but perhaps the saddest lesson is that of John K. Toole, who committed suicide in 1969 after his manuscript for <u>Confederacy of Dunces</u> was turned down by publisher after publisher. His mother, who was more resolute, continued the search and finally found a press to publish the book in 1980. It won a Pulitzer Prize.

"You want to talk music? Giuseppe Verdi's application to study at the Royal and Imperial Conservatory of Milan was rejected by the principal, Francesco Basily, who said that he was, 'overage and certain to prove mediocre.' In 1954, the Grand Ole Opry told Elvis Presley to go back to driving trucks. In 1962, an anonymous record company executive told the Beatles: 'You'll never make it — four groups are out.' He's remained anonymous, but we know John, Paul, George, and Ringo on a first name basis."

Jah was on a roll, "If people don't believe in you, it's none of your concern. Abraham Lincoln's audience was indifferent when he delivered the now esteemed *Gettysburg Address*. Perhaps he'd grown used to it, having: gone broke, been defeated two times in his campaign for a House seat, lost a Senate race twice, survived daily attacks by the press, and been despised by half of the people all of the time.

"In order to hit a home run," Jah quipped, "you have to keep going to bat. Babe Ruth struck out over one thousand thirty times before he made the history books with seven hundred fourteen home runs. Hank Aaron, who beat out 'The Babe' for the all time home run record, struck out over fourteen hundred times. Most of us don't consider either one a failure.

"Thomas Edison was ridiculed for trying some twelve hundred unsuccessful materials for the filament of his famed vision, the incandescent light bulb. 'You have failed twelve hundred times,' said a narrow-minded detractor. 'I have not failed,' countered Edison. 'I have discovered twelve hundred materials that won't work.' By the time he was through, his patents numbered one thousand and ninety-three. And, of course, most of you already know that my friend, Albert Einstein, failed math.

"Wilma Rudolph was a sickly child when she was born in rural Tennessee. She grew up with twenty-two brothers and sisters, and things didn't become any easier for the family when young Wilma was stricken by double pneumonia complicated with scarlet fever then followed by polio. For days she lay near death, and although she did recover, the doctors said she would never walk. Constant care and nurturing from her family enabled her to walk with a brace... and then without one. She soon was able to run, actually joining the track team at school. A scout from Tennessee State offered her a work–aid scholarship. Who would have thought that Wilma, the little girl that the specialists diagnosed as irreparable, would be the same Wilma Rudolph who would anchor the United States Olympic Relay Team in a stunning 'come from behind' victory at Rome, and be the first American woman to take home three Olympic Gold medals?

"How many droves of men and women throughout history have been put down like Fred Astaire, Edison and Einstein, or Wilma Rudolph, but simply neglected to go back to try just one more time? If only they had known success was loitering right around the bend," Jah's words invoked reflection. "When we first tried to walk... we all fell down. Persist. If you want to stop, try changing lanes instead of quitting! Basketball statistics prove that the NBA players with the highest points per game also made the most shots and had the most misses. Like hockey player Wayne Gretzky said, 'You miss one hundred percent of the shots you never take.' Notice that the record books don't record the misses."

Jah's voice, rapidly bombarding us with advice, took on a new urgency as the first signs of a new day were on the horizon. The firmament to the east was beginning to change; the black night blending with the glow of predawn blue. "False ideas of what comprises security and logic, along with jealous people, can seduce us into rationalizing our ambitions, hopes, and desires to dust. At times, we can be a little too 'smart' for our own good; sometimes it's best to let ourselves be dumb enough not to know when something is unachievable, impossible, illogical, insanely preposterous, ludicrous, ridiculous, crazy, absurd, or touched. Why settle? Yogi Berra once snapped, 'It ain't over till it's over.'

"The road to becoming extraordinary is not always one of pleasure in the short run," Jah pointed out, "this cosmic boot camp you call earth is not necessarily easy, but 'the greats' think long term. Most people don't relish a trip to the dentist, but they go, and they thank the man — even pay him, because in the entire context of life seeing the dentist is beneficial. We don't give our kids everything they implore us for, if they eat too much ice cream they'll be unhealthy. God does the same for us, what we get might not be what we'd vote for, but in the long run it is for the good:

The famous Hebrew sage, Rabbi Akiva, once took a journey. He brought with him a donkey to ride on, a rooster so he wouldn't sleep too late, and a torch to light his way at night.

One evening he came to a village, knocking on a door to ask for a night's lodging, he discovered the people there were not so kind and wouldn't let him stay. When he tried the next house, they too refused him. After the third such encounter he gave up, sadly surmising that this community did not take too kindly to strangers. Still of good nature, Rabbi Akiva decided it was for the best, for as he was known to say, 'Whatever God wills is for the good.' If not now, then certainly in the long run he knew that this would be for his own good. Thus he went to the outlying fields of the hamlet to rest for the night.

A mighty gust of wind blew with such intensity that it extinguished his torch; nevertheless Rabbi Akiva remained ardent in his belief that, 'Whatever God wills is for the good.' A short time later a weasel appeared. It ate his rooster. Was the good Rabbi distraught? Of course not, he just said, 'Whatever God wills is for the good.' Finally, a fierce lion came and devoured his donkey. Whereas most people would have considered the loss of their transportation a small catastrophe, Rabbi Akiva was not so troubled. He merely reaffirmed, 'Whatever God wills is for the good.'

Dawn finally came to this seemingly ill–fated night of woes, the wise man made his way back toward the village to buy some breakfast. When he beheld the small village he was astonished — it was in shambles. Bandits had come in the night and looted it!

A crowd amassed around the master, realizing now who he was, so he spoke to the hard–hearted villagers, 'See, everything works out for the good, even inhospitality! If I had lodged with you, the thieves would have robbed me too. If my torch had burned, my rooster crowed, or my donkey brayed; then the robbers would have discovered me even in the fields.' "

Jah stirred further contemplation with an ancient Chinese tale from a twenty–one hundred year old manuscript known as the *Huai Nan Tzu*, which also illustrated the point perfectly:

"Long, long ago a Chinese peasant farmer lived humbly with his wife and his son Liang. His only possession of value was a magnificent horse named Chih–tu. All the farmer's friends and neighbors desired a magnificent horse such as Chih–tu. One day the horse ran away. Liang and his father looked everywhere for Chih–tu, but to no avail. Tired from their searching they returned home, the neighbors having heard the news, came round to express their sympathy. 'That's really bad!' offered the neighbors. But all the farmer replied was, 'You never can tell.'

Every day the old farmer searched the road, looked through the woods, and along the burbling brook, but the horse, Chih–tu, was nowhere to be found. Soon the mid–autumn festival came and went, one moon trailed another and after a time the farmer searched no more. A few days later, the vibration of many hooves woke the farmer early. Chih–tu had returned, and brought with him a small herd of wild horses, each as glorious as Chih–tu himself. The old man and his son got up quickly and opened the gate for all the beautiful horses to trot in. When the neighbors heard of their friend's good fortune they hurried over, exclaiming, 'That's really good!' But the venerable farmer merely stated, 'You never can tell.'

Soon Liang, the farmer's son, took to the task of training the horses, he became a very proficient rider and soon was doing many tricks. One day while showing off with some stunts for his friends, Liang toppled off one of the wild horses and broke his leg. All the neighbors were soon there, having heard the news they said, 'That's really bad!' as they handed him food they had made for him. His father sitting at his bedside whispered, 'You never can tell.' Still the neighbors remarked on his bad luck, for how would the old man harvest his wheat without the help of his son.

Shortly after this, a frivolous war against some northern barbarians was declared by the emperor. The army came through the town forcing the local young men into service. Each able–bodied young man was seized, bound, and taken far away to battle the wild tribes in this desert war. Many of the young men would never return, but Liang couldn't go, he had broken his leg.

Because his son was still disabled and he was too old, the farmer's family was safe from harm. The neighbors soon gathered at the farmer's house, sad and anxious about their own sons who had gone to war. The elder of the village spoke, 'Strange are the ways of fate. Here today, we shall not weep, for we have seen that sorrows many times bring their blessings. Nor yet can our hearts be elated, for we have seen that joys sometimes bring their sorrows.' He turned to the farmer bowing slightly and proclaimed, 'As for which is the good, and which is the bad, you have stated most truly: You never can tell.'

'Yes,' the old farmer humbly agreed, 'you never can tell.' "

~~~*~~~

Antoinette L. Brown: A first failure is often a blessing.

T. H. Huxley: There is the greatest practical benefit in making a few failures early in life.

I Ching:	Difficulty at the beginning works supreme success.
Henry Ward Beecher:	Man's best successes come after their disappointments.
I Ching:	Work on what has been spoiled has supreme success.
Dr. Leon Hammer:	You do better if you have a lot of failures before you go on to success.
Truman Capote:	Failure is the condiment that gives success its flavor.
Robert F. Kennedy:	Only those who dare to fail miserably can achieve greatly.
Norman MacEwan:	Many a man never fails because he never tries.
Bud Wilkinson:	The man who tried his best and failed is superior to the man who never tried.
John F. Kennedy:	The credit belongs to the man who is actually in the arena, whose face is marred by dust and sweat and blood, who knows the great enthusiasms, the great devotions, and spends himself in a worthy cause; who, at best, if he wins, knows the thrills of high achievement, and, if he fails, at least fails daring greatly, so that his place shall never be with those cold and timid souls who know neither victory nor defeat.
H. Gordon–Browne:	It is better to be a has–been than one of the never–wases.

Jerry Martin:	You can either play it safe, or take a chance. If you play it safe, your main interest is in not failing.
John Charles Salak:	Failures are divided into two classes — those who thought and never did, and those who did, and never thought.
Albert Einstein:	I think and think for months and years. Ninety–nine times, the conclusion is false. The hundredth time I am right.
Thomas A. Edison:	There's a way to do it better... find it.
A Packet of Sugar:	If you have tried to do something and failed, you are vastly better off than if you have tried to do nothing and succeeded.
James Joyce:	"A pier," Stephen said. "Yes, a disappointed bridge."
Anne Morrow Lindbergh:	It takes as much courage to have tried and failed as it does to have tried and succeeded.
Theodore Roosevelt:	It is hard to fail, but it is worse never to have tried to succeed.
R. H. Benson:	You will fail sometimes, but not finally.
William Lloyd George:	He's no failure. He's not dead yet.
John Burroughs:	A man can fail many times, but he isn't a failure until he begins to blame somebody else.

William Saroyan:	Good people are good because they've come to wisdom through failure. We get very little wisdom from success, you know.
Albert Einstein:	Show me a man who does not know the meaning of the word 'fail,' and I'll show you a man who ought to buy a dictionary.
Robert Lewis Taylor:	He had read of the keen critical rejection of failures such as Wagner's operas, Lincoln's Gettysburg Address, Walt Whitman's poems, and Christ's Sermon on the Mount, and he was sensibly impressed.
Elder Pedersen:	If at first you don't succeed, you have plenty of company.
Harry F. Banks:	If at first you do succeed, try to hide your astonishment.
William Edward Hickson:	If at first you don't succeed, try, try again.
Jewish Proverb:	Failures are the pillars of success.
Herman Melville:	He who has never failed somewhere, that man cannot be great. Failure is the true test of greatness.
Wilson Mizner:	Failure has gone to his head.
Alex Noble:	Success is a process, a quality of mind and way of being, an outgoing affirmation of life.
Tom Robbins:	Success can eliminate as many options as failure.
Cindy Adams:	Success has made failures of many men.

Fran Lebowitz:	Success didn't spoil me; I've always been insufferable.
Somerset Maugham:	The common idea that success spoils people by making them vain, egotistic, and self–complacent is erroneous. On the contrary, it makes them, for the most part, humble, tolerant and kind. Failure makes people bitter and cruel.

~~~*~~~

J. R. Rogers:	The successful man lengthens his stride when he discovers that the signpost has deceived him; the failure looks for a place to sit down.

Hamilton Wright Mabie:

Don't be afraid of opposition. Remember, a kite rises against, not with the wind.

Frank Leahy:	When the going gets tough, let the tough get going.
Charles De Gaulle:	Faced with crisis, the man of character falls back on himself... Difficulty attracts the man of character because it is in embracing it that he realizes himself.
Albert Einstein:	In the middle of difficulty lies opportunity.
Unknown:	The Chinese word for 'crisis' is composed of two picture–characters... the one meaning 'danger' and the other meaning 'opportunity.'
Henry Kissinger:	Next week there can't be any crisis. My schedule is already full.

Jane Belenky:

I'd give up now, but I don't have the time.

Lt. General Gus Pagonis:

Something goes wrong every minute. What you do is fix it.

Oliver Wendell Holmes:

Trouble creates a capacity to handle it.

M. Scott Peck, M.D.:

It is only because of problems that we grow mentally and spiritually.

David P. Gardner:

We learn simply by the exposure of living. Much that passes for education is not education at all, but ritual. The fact is that we are being educated when we know it least.

Sören Kierkegaard:

Life is not a problem to be solved, but a reality to be experienced.

Jerome Wiesner:

Some problems are just too complicated for rational, logical solutions. They admit of insight, not answers.

Duke Ellington:

A problem is your chance for you to do your best.

Hasidic Proverb:

The man who cannot survive bad times will not see good times.

Dorothy Parker:

... if you can get through the twilight, you'll live through the night.

London Times:

Our lives are like the course of the sun. At the darkest moment there is the promise of daylight.

Corita Kent:	Flowers grow out of dark moments.
Unknown:	Needless we turn to golden repose when yet the grass is green.
Silvio Conte:	This is no time to pull the rug out in the middle of the stream.
J. C. and A. W. Hare:	Half the failures in life arise from pulling in one's horse as he is leaping.
B. C. Forbes:	The thoroughbred goes until he can't go another inch and then—goes the other inch.
Unknown:	All I know is that horses don't bet on people.
H. Ross Perot:	Most people give up just when they're about to achieve success. They give up at the last minute of the game one foot from a winning touchdown.
Thomas Edison:	Many of life's failures are people who did not realize how close they were to success when they gave up.
Dale Carnegie:	Most of the important things in the world have been accomplished by people who have kept on trying when there seemed to be no hope at all.
Lao–tzu:	People usually fail when they are on the verge of success. So give as much care to the end as to the beginning. Then there will be no failure.
James 1:12:	Blessed is the man that endureth temptation: For when he is tried, he shall receive the crown of life.

| Richard M. Nixon: | Only if you have been in the deepest valley can you know how magnificent it is to be on the highest mountain. |

Richard M. Nixon:
Only if you have been in the deepest valley
can you know how magnificent it is to be
on the highest mountain.

Proverb:
Faint is the bliss that never passed through
pain.

German Proverb:
Who has never tasted what is bitter does not
know what is sweet.

Portuguese Saying:
What was hard to bear is sweet to
remember.

Virgil:
Perhaps someday it will be pleasant to
remember even this.

"Saturday Night Live"
Roseanne Roseannadanna (Gilda Radner):
It's always something. If it's not one thing,
it is always another.

~~~*~~~

Marcus Aurelius:
If you are distressed by anything external,
the pain is not due to the thing itself, but to
your estimate of it; and this you have the
power to revoke at any moment.

Nepalese Saying:
It is the mind that wins or loses.

John Patrick:
Pain makes man think.
Thought makes man wise.
Wisdom makes life endurable.

Friedrich Wilhelm Nietzsche:
What does not destroy me makes me strong.

Hubert Horatio Humphrey:

> A fellow that doesn't have any tears doesn't have any heart.

Tom "The Blind Pianist" Sullivan:

> Humans are like tea bags. You don't know how strong you are until you get into hot water.

J. C. Penney:

> I would never have amounted to anything were it not for adversity. I was forced to come up the hard way.

Sydney J. Harris:

> When I hear somebody sigh, "Life is hard," I am always tempted to ask, "Compared to what?"

Menander:

> The school of hard knocks is an accelerated curriculum.

Sal Lederman:

> Usually, we learn more from losing than from winning.

Japanese Saying:

> We learn little from victory, much from defeat.

Epictetus:

> At every occasion in your life, do not forget to commune with yourself, and to ask of yourself how you can profit by it.

Gilbert Keith Chesterton:

> True contentment is the power of getting out of any situation all that there is in it.

Bernie S. Siegel, M.D.:

> Diseases can be our spiritual flat tires — disruptions in our lives that seem to be disasters at the time, but end by redirecting our lives in a meaningful way.

M. Scott Peck, M.D.:	Through this healing process, the very things that had caused him agony, became the things that brought him wisdom.
Jordan S. Metzger:	Wisdom is found wherever absurdity is, you just have to be able to see it.
William James:	Our very infirmities help us unexpectedly.
Charles Darwin:	If I had not been so great an invalid, I should not have done so much work as I have accomplished.
Harry Emerson Fosdick:	That is life, to have your A string snap and finish on three strings.
Boxcar Bertha:	Nobody ever said it was gonna be easy, baby!
Laotian Saying:	If you like things easy, you'll have difficulties; if you like problems, you'll succeed.
Henry Kissinger:	Each success only buys an admission ticket to a more difficult problem.

~~~*~~~

Unknown:	Trouble is often the lever in God's hands to raise us up to heaven.
Mother Teresa:	I know God will not give me anything I can't handle. I just wish that He didn't trust me so much.
Dr. Robert H. Schuller:	Failure doesn't mean God has abandoned you; it does mean he has a better idea.

Daniel Boone:	What fretted you so much was really the means of Providence for our salvation. But for the storm, we should have run into the very jaws of our enemies.
Ralph Waldo Emerson:	The years teach us much the days never knew.
Sören Kierkegaard:	Life can only be understood backward, but it must be lived forward.
Edgar Watson Howe:	Few men progress, except as they are pushed by events.
Epictetus:	Learn to wish that everything should come to pass exactly as it does. I am always content with that which happens, for I think that which God chooses is better than what I choose.
Isaiah 55:8–9:	My thoughts are not your thoughts Nor are My ways your ways — declares the Lord. But as the heavens are high above the earth, So are My ways high above your ways And My plans above your plans.
Joseph Heller:	Nothing succeeds as planned.
Homer:	Zeus does not bring all men's plans to fulfillment.
Fred Hoyle:	There is a coherent plan in the universe, though I don't know what it's a plan for.
Ellease Southerland:	God has plans which mortals don't understand... We do not understand the mysteries of God.

Irish Proverb:	If God shuts one door, he opens another.
Andy Rooney:	The closing of a door can bring blessed privacy and comfort — the opening, terror. Conversely, the closing of a door can be a sad and final thing — the opening a wonderfully joyous moment.
Alexander Graham Bell:	
	When one door closes, another opens, but we often look so long and so regretfully upon the closed door that we do not see the one which has opened for us.
Tom Stoppard:	Every exit is an entry somewhere else.
Ralph Waldo Emerson:	For everything you have missed you have gained something else.
Jordan S. Metzger:	Go one way, and you're bound to miss the other.
Dr. Leon Hammer:	Grief for what one gives up is replaced by joy for the new life one embraces.
Yogi Berra:	When you arrive at a fork in the road, take it.
Michael Curtiz:	Now ride off in all directions.
Sir Boyle Roche:	A man could not be in two places at the same time unless he were a bird.
Judge Amado Guerrero:	
	In no way is it possible for a person to be in two places at the same time, especially if there is a great distance in between.

Gore Vidal:	One is sorry one could not have taken both branches of the road. But we were not allotted multiple selves.
Isak Dinesen:	God made the world round so we would never be able to see too far down the road.
Mark Twain:	Your road is everything that a road ought to be... And yet you will not stay in it half a mile, for the reason that little, seductive, mysterious roads are always branching out from it on either hand, and as these curve sharply also and hide what is beyond, you cannot resist the temptation to desert your own chosen road and explore them.
Robert Frost:	Two roads diverged in a wood, and I — I took the one less traveled by, And that has made all the difference.
David Miller:	All advantages are attended with disadvantages.
W. Clement Stone:	To every disadvantage there is a corresponding advantage.
Jewish Proverb:	Nothing is so bad that no good may come of it.
George Herbert:	Sometimes the best gain is to lose.
Jeff "Zazz" Zaslow:	Remember that not getting what you want is sometimes a stroke of luck.
Saint Therese:	More tears are shed over answered prayers than unanswered ones.
Oscar Wilde: Whistler:	I wish I had said that! You will, Oscar, you will.

Tony Schwartz:	If it works, copy it.
Oscar Wilde:	When the gods wish to punish us they answer our prayers.
Winston Churchill:	If this is a blessing, it is certainly *very* well disguised.
Kitty O'Neill Collins:	What I'm looking for is a blessing that's *not* in disguise.
Henry Ford:	I believe God is managing affairs and that He doesn't need any advice from me.
George Santayana:	Fanatics are those people who know what they are doing is what God would be doing, if He only had all the facts.
C. S. Lewis:	There are two kinds of people: Those who say to God, "Thy will be done," and those to whom God says, "All right, then, have it your way."
Andrei D. Sakharov:	Whatever else God prompts you to get. He won't suggest anything useless.
B. W. M. Young:	In God's economy, nothing is wasted. Through failure, we learn a lesson in humility, which is probably needed, painful though it is.
Albert Einstein:	God may be subtle, but He isn't mean.
Lou Gossett, Jr.:	The Lord may not come when you want him, but he's always going to be there on time.

Harry Emerson Fosdick:

God is not a cosmic bellboy for whom we can press a button to get things done.

~~~*~~~

Confucius:

Our greatest glory is not in never failing, but in rising every time we fall.

Japanese Proverb:

Fall seven times, stand up eight.

Haitian Saying:

A stumble is not a fall.

English Proverb:

A stumble may prevent a fall.

Edmund Cooke:

You are beaten to earth?
   Well, well, what's that?
Come up with a smiling face,
   It's nothing against you to fall down flat
But to lie there — that's disgrace.

William James:

To him who has a hold on vaster and more permanent realities, the hourly vicissitudes of his personal destiny seem relatively insignificant things.

Carl Jung:

Nobody, as long as he moves about among the chaotic currents of life, is without trouble.

Mickey Spillane:

Freud's stupid. I didn't like Jung or Adler, either. I go along with Samuel Goldwyn, he said: anybody who has to see a psychiatrist ought to have his head examined.

Ashley Montagu:

Most psychiatrists need to have their heads examined.

Dr. Murray Weisenfeld: A runner once came to me and told me that he was in a fifty–five mile race, and at thirty–five miles he began to get foot cramps. He asked me what he should do. I told him to see a psychiatrist.

The Midrash: If you do not run so far, the way back will be shorter.

"Ziggy" Tom Wilson: My first psychiatrist said I was paranoid, but I wanted second opinion because I think he was out to get me.

Truman Capote: In California everyone goes to a therapist, is a therapist, or is a therapist going to a therapist.

~~~*~~~

Henry Wadsworth Longfellow:
Trouble is the next best thing to enjoyment; there is no fate in the world so horrible as to have no share in either its joy or sorrows.

Richard Lewis: I have problems flown in fresh daily wherever I am.

Calvin Coolidge: Never go out to meet trouble. If you will just sit still, nine times out of ten someone will intercept it before it reaches you.

American Proverb: Never trouble trouble, till trouble troubles you.

Matthew 6:34: So do not worry about tomorrow, for tomorrow will bring worries of its own. Today's trouble is enough for today.

Henry Ward Beecher:	Troubles, like babies, grow larger by nursing.
B. C. Forbes:	You have no idea how big the other fellow's troubles are.
Lao–tzu:	Trouble is easily stopped before it commences.
John McEnroe:	This taught me a lesson, but I'm not sure what it is.
Vernon Law:	Experience is a hard teacher because she gives the test first, the lesson afterward.
Elbert Hubbard:	A failure is a man who has blundered and then is not able to cash in on the experience.
George Bernard Shaw:	We learn from experience, that men never learn anything from experience.
Aldous Huxley:	Experience is not what happens to a man. It is what a man does with what happens to him.
Michael McGuire:	I like to collect experiences the way other people like to collect coins and stamps.
Franklin P. Jones:	Anybody who profits from the experience of others probably writes biographies.
Walter Pater:	Not the fruit of experience, but experience itself, is the end.
Clarence Day:	Information's pretty thin stuff unless mixed with experience.
Elie Wiesel:	Not to transmit an experience is to betray it.

Unknown:	Good judgement comes from experience. Experience comes from bad judgement.
Bob Packwood:	Judgments comes from experience, and great judgment comes from bad experience.
Oscar Wilde:	Experience is the name everyone gives to their mistakes.
Earl Wilson:	Experience is what enables you to recognize a mistake when you make it again.
Lewis Thomas:	Mistakes are the very base of human thought... feeding the structure like root nodules. If we were not provided with the knack of being wrong, we could never get anything useful done.
Mel Brooks:	As long as the world keeps turning and spinning, we're gonna be dizzy, and we're gonna make mistakes.
David M. Burns, M.D.:	Assert your right to make a few mistakes. If people can't accept your imperfections, that's their fault.
Mark Twain:	Always acknowledge a fault frankly. This will throw those in authority off their guard and give you an opportunity to commit more.
James Joyce:	Mistakes are the portals of discovery.
Ed Land:	A mistake is an event, the full benefit of which has not yet been turned to your advantage.

George Bernard Shaw:	The man who has never made a mistake will never make anything else.
Bishop W. C. Magee:	The man who makes no mistakes does not usually make anything.
Jerry Lewis:	Only the man who does nothing makes no mistakes.
Fiorello LaGuardia:	When I make a mistake, it's a beaut.
George Bernard Shaw:	A life spent in making mistakes is not only more honorable, but more useful, than a life spent in doing nothing.
Plutarch:	To make no mistakes is not in the power of man; but from their errors and mistakes the wise and good learn wisdom for the future.
Lee Iacocca:	Mistakes are part of life; you can't avoid them. All you can hope is that they won't be too expensive, and that you don't make the same mistake twice.
Chuck Berry:	Don't let the same dog bite you twice.
Confucius:	A man who knows he has committed a mistake and doesn't correct it is committing another mistake.
Jonas Salk:	Life is an error–making and an error–correcting process.
Yogi Berra:	We made too many wrong mistakes.
Sir Humphrey Davy:	I have learned more from my mistakes than from my successes.

Aesop: Better be wise by the misfortunes of others than by your own.

Publilius Syrus: Learn to see in another's calamity the ills which you should avoid.

H. G. Bohn: Wise men learn by other men's mistakes, fools by their own.

William Bolitho: The really important thing is to profit from your losses. That requires intelligence; and it makes the difference between a man of sense and a fool.

Dale Carnegie: The difference between a successful person and a failure often lies in the fact that the successful man will profit by his mistakes and try again in a different way.

James Gordon Bennett: I have made mistakes, but I have never made the mistake of claiming that I never made one.

Yogi Berra: ... How can I get mad at myself?

Jordan S. Metzger: If you find a mistake in my book, consider that I put it there for a reason. We print something for everyone, including those who are always searching for mistakes.

Thomas Carlyle: It will be noticed that some omissions will also appear in this edition.

Ralph Waldo Emerson: Every artist was first an amateur.

George Moore: It does not matter how badly you paint, so long as you don't paint badly like other people.

Edgar Degas:	Painting is easy when you don't know how, but very difficult when you do.
Samuel Goldwyn:	When it comes to ruining a painting, he's an artist.
Isaac Bashevis Singer:	Every creator painfully experiences the chasm between his inner vision and its ultimate expression.
André Gide:	Art is a collaboration between God and the artist, and the less the artist does the better.
Fred Astaire:	The higher up you go, the more mistakes you're allowed. Right at the top, if you make enough of them, it's considered to be your style.
"All in the Family" Archie Bunker:	God don't make no mistakes — that's how He got to be God.
William Blake:	If the fool would persist in his folly he would become wise.
Henry C. Link:	While one person hesitates because he feels inferior, The other is busy making mistakes and becoming superior.
M. L. Woods:	We're wasting precious time by believing we aren't as good as we are.
Jack Nicholson:	The whole thing is to keep working and pretty soon they'll think you're good.

Robert Benchley:	It took me fifteen years to discover that I had no talent for writing, but I couldn't give it up because by that time I was too famous.
Ernest Hemingway:	Writing is something that you never do as well as it can be done.
Richard Bach:	A professional writer is an amateur who didn't quit.
Eddie Cantor:	It takes twenty years to make an overnight success.
Jack Kerouac:	Walking on water wasn't built in a day.

Corollaries To Murphy's Law:

> Everything will take longer than you think it will.
> Nothing is as easy as it looks.

Unknown:	Play the game long enough to control it.
Unknown:	Diamonds are coal that went through pressure.
Japanese Saying:	Difficulties make you a jewel.
Christopher Morley:	Big shots are only little shots who keep shooting.
Valentine Monnier:	I'm not a big deal yet, but I will be.

~~~*~~~

George Ohsawa:

[Opposites rely on each]... other in order to exist. Without day there can be no such thing as night, and only after we have experienced sickness can we appreciate how wonderful it is to be healthy.

Bertolt Brecht:

What happens to the hole when the cheese is gone?

Tao Te Ching:

We shape clay into a pot, but it is the emptiness inside that holds whatever we want.

"Kung Fu"
Master Po:

The threads that make up our human nature are two–ended. There is no capacity for feeling pride without an equal capacity for feeling shame. One cannot feel joy unless one can also feel despair.

W. Clement Stone:

To every disadvantage there is a corresponding advantage.

Elbert Hubbard:

The cheerful loser is the winner.

James A. Michener:

Character consists of what you do on the third and fourth tries.

Abraham Lincoln:

Ability may get you to the top, but it takes character to keep you there.

Roy Eisenhart:

The easiest thing in sport is to win when you're good. The next easiest is to lose when you're not any good. The hardest is to lose when you're good. That's the test of character.

Richard M. Nixon:

You've got to learn to survive a defeat, that's when you develop character.

Don Herold: Many people have character who have nothing else.

German Motto: When wealth is lost, nothing is lost; when health is lost, something is lost; when character is lost, all is lost.

Miguel de Cervantes: He who loses wealth loses much; he who loses a friend loses more; but he that loses his courage loses all.

Hubert Horatio Humphrey:
Oh, my friend, it isn't what they take away from you that counts — it's what you do with what you have left.

Albert Einstein: Try not to become a man of success, but rather try to become a man of value.

Charles F. Kettering: Keep on going and the chances are that you will stumble on something, perhaps when you are least expecting it. I have never heard of anyone stumbling on something sitting down.

~~~*~~~

Conrad Hilton: Successful people keep moving. They make mistakes, but they don't quit.

William James: The fatigue gets worse up to a certain point, when, gradually or suddenly, it passes away and we are fresher then before!

French Proverb: One may go a long way after one is tired.

Galatians 6:9: So let us not grow weary in doing what is right, for we will reap at harvest time, if we do not give up.

Jack Dempsey:	I can't get hurt. I am going to keep going, no matter what happens.
Marilyn Vos Savant:	It has been my observation that being beaten is often a temporary condition. Giving up is what makes it permanent.
Hubert Horatio Humphrey:	Never give up and never give in.
Sir Winston Churchill:	Never give in. Never give in. Never give in.
Peter Arno:	Well, back to the old drawing board.
Dr. Robert H. Schuller:	To really succeed in life, all you have to do is, number one: get started; and number two: never quit.
Stephen Leacock:	If at first you don't succeed, quit, quit at once.
"Peanuts" Charles Schultz Spike (Snoopy's brother):	I've decided to spend the rest of my life looking for 'The Big Rock Candy Mountain.' I didn't find it today, but maybe I'll find it tomorrow... If you really want something in this life, you have to be determined! If I don't find it tomorrow. I think I'll quit looking...
David Zucker:	Quit now, you'll never make it. If you disregard this advice, you'll be halfway there.
Virginia Hutchinson:	Quitters never win. Winners never quit.

Mike Ditka:	You're never a loser until you quit trying.
Elbert Hubbard:	Genius is only the power of making continuous efforts. The line between failure and success is so fine that we scarcely know when we pass it: so fine that we are often on the line and do not know it. How many a man has thrown up his hands at a time when a little more effort, a little more patience, would have achieved success. As the tide goes clear out, so it comes clear in. In business sometimes, prospects may seem darkest when really they are on the turn. A little more persistence, a little more effort, and what seemed hopeless failure may turn to glorious success. There is no failure except in no longer trying. There is no defeat except from within, no really insurmountable barrier save our own inherent weakness of purpose.
Franklin D. Roosevelt:	When you get to the end of your rope, tie a knot and hang on.
Unknown:	When you have reached the end of your rope there is only one thing left to do, start climbing.
Woody Hayes:	It isn't the size of the dog in the fight, but the size of the fight in the dog that counts.

~~~*~~~

Yiddish Proverb:	In time, even a bear can be taught to dance.
Jewish Proverb:	Time can transform everything.
Norman Cousins:	Infinity converts the possible into the inevitable.

Jewish Proverb: Quiet waters wash down cliffs.

Titus Lucretius Carus (Lucretius):
> The drops of rain make a hole in the stone, not by violence, but by oft falling.

Benjamin Franklin: Little Strokes fell great Oaks.

Jamaican Saying: A little ax can cut down a big tree.

William Shakespeare: Many strokes, though with little axe,
> Hew down and fell the hardest–timber'd oak.

Plato: Never discourage anyone who continually makes progress, no matter how slow.

Napoleon: Victory belongs to the most persevering.

Goethe: Austere perseverance, harsh and continuous, may be employed by the least of us, and rarely fails of its purpose, for its silent power grows irreversibly greater with time.

I Ching: Perseverance brings good fortune.

Henry Wadsworth Longfellow:
> Perseverance is a great element of success. If you only knock long enough and loud enough at the gate, you are sure to wake up somebody.

Woody Hayes: Paralyze resistance with persistence.

Calvin Coolidge:	Nothing in the world can take the place of persistence. Talent will not; nothing is more common than unsuccessful men with talent. Genius will not; unrewarded genius is almost a proverb. Education alone will not; the world is full of educated derelicts. Persistence and determination alone are omnipotent.
Zig Ziglar:	Failure is often the line of least persistence.
Josh Billings:	Consider the postage stamp: its usefulness consists in the ability to stick to one thing till it gets there.
The Book Of Koheleth 7:8:	The patient in spirit is better than the proud in spirit.
Benjamin Franklin:	Genius is nothing but a greater aptitude for patience.
Darryl F. Zanuck:	I decided to become a genius.
Benjamin Franklin:	He that can have patience can have what he will.
Howard Wise:	Great artists and great scientists share many of the same qualities: tenacity, courage, and imagination.
Louis Pasteur:	Let me tell you the secret that has led to my goal. My strength lies solely in my tenacity.
A Fortune Cookie:	You will conquer all obstacles and achieve success.

Abraham Lincoln:	Always bear in mind that your one resolution to succeed is more important than any one thing.
Richard M. Nixon:	A man is not finished when he is defeated. He is finished when he quits.
Count Basie:	I'll be here until they take me away.
Yogi Berra:	It ain't over till it's over.
"Animal House" John Belushi:	Over? Did you say over? Nothing is over until we decide it is.
Ruth Gordon:	I think there is one smashing rule — never face the facts.

~~~*~~~

Chapter Nineteen

Sign Of Wisdom

"Leading Thoreau's proverbial 'lives of quiet desperation,' many people go through life miserably secure," Jah's voice resounded. "With a standard of material comforts unequaled in history, we live with a luxury not afforded even to royalty of old; yet stability brings only stagnancy, not happiness. Some say living with sensations of dissatisfaction and misery is better than feeling nothing, but I say it is infinitely more clever and gratifying to experience happiness than to focus on what we lack.

"I find it no mystery when folks awake into the depressing despondency of a mid–life crisis, questioning whether they have spent their lives in what Henry Miller eloquently described as:

> 'The rigmarole which we call everyday life, and
> which is not life, but a trance–like suspension above
> the great stream of life.'

"There is such a thing as being miserably comfortable," Jah reiterated, as he circled the seated crowd like a youngster serious about the game of duck, duck, goose. "Is melancholy easier to feel than elation? Those who want to be happy can be, the less wise spend their time sweltering in sorrow."

"Flying above the clouds, there... is always sunshine," Jah spoke. "Be with the happy. Break out of the molded life. Love lifelong things — revise the mind to fresh ones. Relish reading, studying, walking, smelling, swimming, seeing, really staring. Then close your eyes and remember how much there is to hear."

~~~*~~~

Old Irish Saying: Continual cheerfulness is a sign of wisdom.

Ralph Waldo Emerson: To make the knowledgeable, you must have the cheerfulness of wisdom. Goodness smiles to the last.

Sidonie Gabrielle Colette:
Be happy. It is a way of being wise.

Cicero: There is no fool who is happy, and no wise man who is not.

Erich Fromm: Happiness is proof of partial or total success in the art of living.

John W. Gardner: Storybook happiness involves every form of pleasant thumb–twiddling; true happiness involves the full use of one's powers and talents.

George Carlin: That's the trouble with "Have a nice day!" It puts all the pressure on you.

Yun–men: Every day is a good day.

William McDougall: The richer, the more highly developed, the more completely unified or integrated is the personality, the more capable it is of sustained happiness, in spite of intercurrent pains of all sorts.

Seng–T'San: The Great Way is not difficult for those who have no preferences. When love and hate are both absent, everything becomes clear and undisguised. Make the smallest distinction, however, and heaven and earth are set infinitely apart.

Aristotle:	Suffering becomes beautiful when any one bears great calamity with cheerfulness, not through insensibility, but through greatness of mind.
Joseph Addison:	Cheerfulness keeps up a kind of daylight in the mind, and fills it with a steady and perpetual serenity.
Thomas Paine:	I love the man that can smile in trouble, that can gather strength from distress, and grow brave by reflection.
Benjamin Disraeli:	Despair is the conclusion of fools.
Ren and Stimpy:	Happy, Happy, Joy, Joy!
Fannie Hurst:	It takes a clever man to turn cynic, and a wise man to be clever enough not to.
Robert Redford:	I've always had a very low regard for cynicism; I think it is the beginning of dying.
H. L. Mencken:	A cynic is a man who, when he smells flowers, looks around for a coffin.
Oscar Wilde:	A cynic is a man who knows the price of everything and the value of nothing.
Edgar A. Shoaff:	A cynic is a person searching for an honest man, with a stolen lantern.
Norman Cousins:	Cynicism is intellectual treason.

Sam Walter Foss:	Then why should I sit in the scorner's seat, Or hurl the cynic's ban? — Let me live in my house by the side of the road And be a friend to man.

Ralph Waldo Emerson:	Life is too short to waste
	   In critic peep or cynic bark,
	Quarrel or reprimand:
	   'Twill soon be dark...

Henry David Thoreau:	The mass of men lead lives of quiet desperation and go to the grave with the song still in them.
Henry Miller:	Most men have a tendency to imprison themselves — without the help of authorities.

<div align="center">~~~*~~~</div>

The Talmud:	When a wise man is angry he is no longer wise.
Alfred Adler:	We must interpret a bad temper as a sign of inferiority.
Samurai Proverb:	The angry man will defeat himself in battle as well as in life.
Malcolm Muggeridge:	Bad humor is an evasion of reality; good humor is an acceptance of it.
Wavy Gravy:	If you don't have a sense of humor — it just isn't funny.
Timothy Leary:	You have to remember, the truth is funny.

George Bernard Shaw:	When a thing is funny, search it for a hidden truth.
Jean de La Bruyere:	Life is tragedy for those who feel, and a comedy for those who think.
John Churton Collins:	Half the mistakes in life arise from feeling where we ought to think, and thinking where we ought to feel.
Henry Miller:	To the person who thinks with his head, life is a comedy. To those who think with their feelings, or work through their feelings, life is a tragedy.
Unknown:	Time and thinking tame the strongest grief.

~~~*~~~

W. H. Auden:	Among those whom I like, I can find no common denominator; but among those whom I love, I can: all of them make me laugh.
Raymond Hitchcock:	A man isn't poor if he can still laugh.
German Saying:	People show their character by what they laugh at.
Unknown:	An optimist laughs to forget, a pessimist forgets to laugh.
Geechy Guy:	My eyes were bothering me, so I went to an optimist. He said, "Don't worry, you'll be fine."
Walter Winchell:	Optimist: a man who gets treed by a lion, but enjoys the scenery.

James Branch Cabell:	The optimist proclaims that we live in the best of all possible worlds; and the pessimist fears this is true.
Winston Churchill:	An optimist sees an opportunity in every calamity; a pessimist sees a calamity in every opportunity.
Frederick Langbridge:	Two men look out through the same bars: One sees the mud, and one the stars.
Masahide:	Barn's burnt down — now I can see the moon.
Dr. Albert Schweitzer:	An optimist is a person who sees a green light everywhere, while the pessimist sees only the red stop light... But the truly wise person is color–blind.
McLandburgh Wilson:	'Twixt optimist and pessimist The difference is droll; The optimist sees the doughnut But the pessimist sees the hole.
Norman Cousins:	Optimism doesn't wait on facts. It deals with prospects. Pessimism is a waste of time.
Jordan S. Metzger:	Opt for optimism.
Irving Kristol:	Even if we can't be happy, we must be cheerful.
Isaac Bashevis Singer:	I'm a pessimist with cheerfulness. It's a riddle even to me, but this is how I am.

Unknown:	A pessimist is one who feels bad when he feels good, for fear he'll feel worse when he feels better.
Quentin Crisp:	A pessimist is someone who, if he is in the bath, will not get out to answer the telephone.
Norman Cousins:	No one really knows enough to be a pessimist.
Ansel Adams:	They know the cost of everything, but the value of nothing.
Alexander Pope:	All looks yellow to a jaundiced eye.
Charles Eliot:	Do not expect the world to look bright, if you habitually wear gray–brown glasses.

Henry Wadsworth Longfellow:

> Be still, sad heart! and cease repining,
>   Behind the clouds is the sun still shining;
> Thy fate is the common fate of all,
>   Into each life some rain must fall,
> Some days must be dark and dreary.

D. O. Flynn:	A pessimist sees only the dark side of the clouds, and mopes; a philosopher sees both sides and shrugs; an optimist doesn't see the clouds at all — he's walking on them.
Gerald Ford:	We see nothing but increasingly brighter clouds every month.
W. Burton Baldry:	Every cloud has a silver lining — but that is small consolation when you cannot see through the cloud.

Helen Keller:	Keep your face to the sunshine and you cannot see the shadow.
Dwight D. Eisenhower:	Pessimism never won any battle.
Elbert Hubbard:	Positive anything is better than negative nothing.
John Ray:	Misery loves company.
Henry David Thoreau:	If misery loves company, misery has company enough.
Hubert Horatio Humphrey:	Happiness is contagious, just exactly like being miserable. People have to believe that they can do better.
W. W. Ziege:	Nothing can stop the man with the right mental attitude from achieving his goal; nothing on earth can help the man with the wrong mental attitude.
Benjamin Franklin:	The discontented man finds no easy chair.
Frank Irving Fletcher:	No man can deliver the goods if his heart is heavier than the load.
Eldridge Cleaver:	You're either part of the solution or part of the problem.
Benjamin Franklin:	Two dry sticks will burn a green one.
Oliver C. Wilson:	What poison is to food, self–pity is to life.
Cornelius Ryan:	The mathematics of self–pity can be raised to infinity.

Abe Martin:	Being an optimist after you've got everything you want doesn't count.
Golda Meir:	It's a sad world. A very sad world. But I'm an optimist.
Sir Winston Churchill:	I am an optimist. It does not seem too much use being anything else.
Orison Swett Marden:	Nothing else will give such a tremendous return in happiness and efficiency as the cultivation of a cheerful, hopeful philosophy, the habituating ourselves to looking on the bright side — for there *are* two sides to everything.
Thomas Edison:	My philosophy of life: ... looking on the bright side of everything.

~~~*~~~

John Masefield:	The days that make us happy make us wise.
Scottish Proverb:	Better be happy than wise.
Jordan S. Metzger:	If you are not happy, you are not wise.
Solomon Ibn Gabirol:	The wise are pleased when they discover truths; fools are pleased when they discover falsehoods.
Jah:	Only you know what you don't know — only you don't know — you know it.
Ralph Waldo Emerson:	We are wiser than we know.
Jordan S. Metzger:	I know more than you think I do, but less than I think I do; or maybe it's the other way around, I don't know.

John Wooden:	It's what you learn after you know it all that counts.
Harry S. Truman:	The only things worth learning are the things you learn after you know it all.
Ezra Pound:	At seventy, I realized that instead of being a lunatic, I was a moron.
Jordan S. Metzger:	My brother told me I was eccentric. I agreed, saying that perhaps I was the world's first eclectic eccentric. My grandfather, overhearing, snapped, "You're not eccentric, you gotta be rich to be eccentric. You're crazy!"
Marcel Pagnol:	The most difficult secret for a man to keep is the opinion he has of himself.
Lord Chesterfield:	Be wiser than other people, if you can, but do not tell them so.
William Butler Yeats:	Think like a wise man, but communicate in the language of the people.
Alvin "Junior" Samples:	I'd rather be wise and act dumb than be dumb and act wise.
Benjamin Franklin:	Proclaim not all thou knowest, all thou owest, all thou hast, nor all thou can'st.
L. B. Mayer:	Be smart, but never show it.
Lorraine Hansberry:	The thing that makes you exceptional, if you are at all, is inevitably that which must also make you lonely.

Solomon Ibn Gabirol: The beginning of wisdom is to desire it.

V. S. Prichett: The mark of genius is an incessant activity of the mind. Genius is a spiritual greed.

Maimonides: If I do not acquire ideals when young, when will I? Not when I am old.

John Lyly: There is no fool like an old fool.

Wilson Mizner: A fellow who is always declaring he's no fool usually has his suspicions.

Elbert Hubbard: Every man is a damn fool for at least five minutes every day. Wisdom consists in not exceeding that limit.

Alistair Sim: It was revealed to me many years ago, with conclusive certainty, that I was a fool and that I had always been a fool. Since then I have been as happy as any man has a right to be.

Albert Einstein: Before God we are all equally wise — and equally foolish.

Sayings of the Fathers 3:5: The man who thinks wisdom is greater than virtue will lose his wisdom.

Margaret Fuller: If you have knowledge, let others light their candles at it.

Ralph Waldo Emerson: The wise, through excess of wisdom, is made a fool.

Czech Saying: Wisdom is easy to carry but difficult to gather.

Abraham Ibn Ezra:	Wisdom is to the soul as food is to the body.
John Locke:	A sound mind in a sound body is a short, but full, description of a happy state in this world.
Maimonides:	The purpose of maintaining the body in good health is to (make it possible for you to) acquire wisdom.
Ralph Waldo Emerson:	Health is the condition of wisdom, and the sign is cheerfulness — an open and noble temper.
Will Durant:	Knowledge is power, but only wisdom is liberty.
Unknown:	Philosophy is the road to knowledge, and knowledge is the road to freedom.
Jewish Proverb:	Thought is a universe of freedom.
Fulton J. Sheen:	Freedom is the right to do what you ought to do.
Epictetus:	The man who masters himself is free.
William Shakespeare:	No one is free who is not master of himself.

~~~*~~~

After(words)

Words Into Wisdom

The wisdom which a wise man tries to communicate always sounds foolish. Words do not express thoughts very well. They always become a little different immediately they are expressed, a little distorted, a little foolish.

Hermann Hesse

Jah responded before anyone else could speak, "This reminds me of a Rabbi I knew:

He once boarded an airliner, leaving behind his congregation and traditional garb. Looking forward to a bit of peace and serenity, he took his seat on the plane next to a scholarly looking gentleman.

When the seat belt sign 'dinged' off, as if on cue, the academician leaned over and nudged the Rabbi in the arm inquiring, 'What do you do in the real world my friend?'

'I'm a Rabbi,' he answered, being as brief as possible, hopeful that the man would go back to his business and allow him some repose.

But no such luck, 'Oh *really*, I'm a nuclear physicist, but I've always considered myself a bit of a theologian as well. I try to keep abreast on religion now and then,' the man pushed on enthusiastically.

'That's good,' quipped my friend, trying to keep

415

the conversation to a polite minimum.

'Yes, I think so. I mean, I read the Bible once in a while, but I've got it all figured out anyway. It all just boils down to one thing: Do Unto Others.'

'Well,' retorted the Rabbi, 'it does, but it doesn't; I suppose that's the essence, but there's more to it than that. By the way, I'll bet you didn't know that I consider myself an amateur nuclear physicist.'

'*Really*, you don't say,' returned the scientist.

'Sure,' reasoned the Rabbi, 'in fact, I subscribe to Scientific American and read an article or two from it each month, and of course I always watch Carl Sagan on television. And you know, I figure nuclear physics is simple too... I mean doesn't it all just really boil down to: Twinkle Twinkle Little Star?'

With that the wise old man left the rocket–scientist wide–eyed... reclined into his chair, and concealing his smile with his hat, closed his eyes."

Jah proceeded, "Plainly you can't learn everything from words. I'm told that Einstein onetime expressed that the difference between the concept and the word for it, is like the difference between your overcoat and the ticket the hat–check girl gives you. While words do their best, we've sometimes got to discover things ourselves.

"Quotations are magical though, representing our best attempts, at putting words into wisdom."

~~~*~~~

Ludwig Wittgenstein: Everything that can be thought at all can be thought clearly. Everything that can be said at all can be said clearly. But not everything that can be thought can be said.

Antoine De Saint–Exupéry:

How should men know what is coming to pass within them, when there are no words to grasp it?

416

Jules Renard:	How describe the delicate thing that happens when a brilliant insect alights on a flower? Words, with their weight, fall upon the picture like birds of prey.
Tom Robbins:	Using words to describe magic is like using a screwdriver to cut roast beef.
Steve Martin:	Those French have a different word for everything!
Lewis Carroll:	What's the French for fiddle–de–dee?
James Thurber:	You could look it up.
Steven Wright:	What's another word for 'thesaurus'?
Zöe Akins:	The Greeks had a word for it.
William Carlos Williams:	
	I don't know what they're saying (and I don't care, I can talk my own language).
Steve Martin:	You never appreciate your language until you go to a foreign country that doesn't have the *courtesy* to speak English.
"Sonny Spoon" Sonny Spoon:	If you speak three languages, you are trilingual. If you speak two languages, you're bilingual. If you speak one language, you're American.
"Batman" Batman:	You must always try to keep abreast of other tongues.

Christopher Morley:	Life is a foreign language: all men mispronounce it.
Joseph Conrad:	Words, as is well known, are great foes of reality.
Tao Te Ching:	The tao that can be told is not the eternal Tao. The name that can be named is not the eternal Name.
Chris O'Leary:	I've always thought there should be a shorter word for monosyllabic.
Joyce Cary:	The concept, the label, is perpetually hiding from us all the nature of the real.
Niels Bohr:	When it comes to atoms, language can be used only as poetry.
Antoine De Saint–Exupéry:	More wisdom is latent in things-as-they-are, than in all the words men use.
Chuang–Tzu:	The purpose of a fish trap is to catch fish, and when the fish are caught, the trap is forgotten. The purpose of a rabbit snare is to catch rabbits. When the rabbits are caught, the snare is forgotten. The purpose of words is to convey ideas. When the ideas are grasped, the words are forgotten. Where can I find a man who has forgotten words? He is the one I would like to talk to.
Nathaniel Hawthorne:	Articulate words are a harsh clamor and dissonance. When man arrives at his highest perfection, he will again be dumb!

Jim Benton: Oh well.

Maha Sthavira Sangharakshita:
Having failed to distinguish thoughts from things, we then fail to distinguish words from thoughts. We think that if we can label a thing, we have understood it.

Ancient Saying: A painting of a rice cake does not satisfy hunger.

Howard Ogden: Symbols are just symbols; the thing's the thing.

Alfred Korzybski: The map is not the territory.

~~~*~~~

Charles Simmons: A proverb is much light condensed in one flash.

William Gilmore Simms:
The proverb answers where the sermon fails.

Miguel de Cervantes: Proverbs are short sentences drawn from long experience.

Samuel Johnson: He is a benefactor of mankind who contracts the great rules of life into short sentences, that may easily be impressed on the memory, and so recur habitually to the mind.

Henry David Thoreau: Whatever sentence will bear to be read twice, we may be sure was thought twice.

Quentin Crisp: My function in life was to render clear what was already blindingly conspicuous.

Friedrich Wilhelm Nietzsche:

It is my ambition to say in ten sentences what other men say in whole books.

George Bernard Shaw: My method is to take utmost trouble to find the right thing to say, and then to say it with the utmost levity.

Melville Landon: Levity is the soul of wit.

William Shakespeare: Brevity is the soul of wit.

Judith Viorst: Brevity may be the soul of wit, but not when someone's saying "I love you".

Jewish Proverb: Words should be weighed, not counted.

Joseph A. Califano Jr.: Writing things clearly does not necessarily mean writing them short.

Sophocles: A short saying oft contains much wisdom.

Samuel Butler: Summaries that contain most things are always shortest themselves.

Baltasar Gracian: Good things, when short, are twice as good.

Winston Churchill: The short words are the best, the old words are the best of all.

James Russell Lowell: Though old the thought and oft expressed,
'Tis his at last who says it best.

Dale Carnegie: The ideas I stand for are not mine. I borrowed them from Socrates. I swiped them from Chesterfield. I stole them from Jesus. And I put them in a book. If you don't like their rules, whose would you use?

Marshall McLuhan:	A successful book cannot afford to be more than ten percent new.
David H. Comins:	People will accept your idea more readily if you tell them Benjamin Franklin said it first.
Saul Steinberg:	People who see a drawing in the *New Yorker* will think automatically that it's funny because it is a cartoon. If they see it in a museum, they think it is artistic; and if they find it in a fortune cookie, they think it is a prediction.
Franklin P. Jones:	Originality is the art of concealing your source.
Mark Twain:	Adam was the only man who, when he said a good thing, knew that nobody had said it before him.
André Gide:	Everything has been said before, but, since nobody listens, we have to keep going back and beginning all over again.
The Book of Koheleth 1:9:	That which has been will be, and that which has been done, will be done; and there is nothing new beneath the sun.
Ben Wattenberg:	There is nothing so powerful as an old idea whose time has come again.
George Orwell:	Sometimes the first duty of intelligent men is the restatement of the obvious.
Henry David Thoreau:	What the first philosopher taught, the last will have to repeat.

Blaise Pascal: All the good maxims already exist in the world; we just fail to apply them.

Chretien Malesherbes: A new maxim is often a brilliant error.

Luc de Clapiers Vauvenargues:
Few maxims are true in every respect.

Stanislaw J. Lec: Proverbs contradict each other.

Russian Saying: There is no proverb without a grain of truth.

Icelandic Saying: All old sayings have something in them.

George Santayana: Almost every wise saying has an opposite one, no less wise, to balance it.

Elias Canetti: The great writers of aphorisms read as if they had all known each other well.

Jorge Luis Borges: Writing is nothing more than a guided dream.

Michel Eyquem De Montaigne:
I quote others only the better to express myself.

George Bernard Shaw: I often quote myself. It adds spice to my conversation.

Ralph Waldo Emerson: I hate quotations.

Marlene Dietrich: I love them because it is a joy to find thoughts one might have, beautifully expressed with much authority, by someone recognizedly wiser than oneself.

Dorothy Parker: I might repeat to myself, slowly and soothingly, a list of quotations beautiful from minds profound — if I can remember any of the damn things.

Simeon Strunsky: Famous remarks are very seldom quoted correctly.

Pirkay Avot: Whoever quotes a thing in the name of him that said it, brings deliverance into the world.

The Talmud: Who is wise? He who learns from all men.

Philip James Baily: The worst men often give the best advice.

Maimonides: Just as a small burning tree may set a bigger tree on fire, so may a young pupil sharpen the mind of a teacher, and by means of questions stimulate him toward glorious wisdom.

Walloon Saying: A tree falls the way it leans.

Woodrow Wilson: I not only use all the brains I have, but all that I can borrow.

Rabbi Nathan: To be in the company of a wise man is like going into a perfumery; you may buy nothing, but the scent will cling to you for a day.

Henry Wadsworth Longfellow:

> Lives of great men all remind us
>   We can make our lives sublime,
> And, departing, leave behind us
>   Footprints on the sands of time —
>
> Footprints, that perhaps another,
>   Sailing o'er life's solemn main,
> A forlorn and shipwrecked brother,
>   Seeing, shall take heart again.

The Mathnawi:

> These are our works, these works our souls
> display;
> Behold our works when we have passed
> away.

Stanislaw J. Lec:

> Value your words. Each one may be your
> last.

Jean Rostand:

> Certain brief sentences are peerless in their
> ability to give one the feeling that nothing
> remains to be said.

~~~*~~~

I awoke at the rising sun, the shimmering sapphire still clutched in my hand. The last thing I recall, Jah was whispering something into my ear, a phrase from the ancient, timeless Talmud:

> "Who is wise?
> He who learns from all men."

Then, suddenly, passing his hand slowly in front of my face, downward from forehead to chin, like a hypnotist at a stage show, he sternly commanded...

>   ... *"REMEMBER!!"*

And with the echo of Jah's phrase fading into the firmament, my eyes were opened.

John Heywood: All is well that ends well.

Ethel Barrymore: That's all there is, there isn't any more.

Porky Pig: *Th–Th–Th–Th–Th–That's All Folks!!*

         Until we meet again!

            Jah

Friendly Reader-

I invite you to personalize your copy of <u>Lightning Fast Enlightenment</u>. Add your own thoughts and favorite sayings, or copy sections and post them for inspiration. People have also used this book:

      ~In speeches or personal journals.

      ~In classes or meetings, as a basis for dialogue and debate.

      ~In clarifying values and discussing different philosophies of life.

      ~As a meditation tool, the book's concepts and sayings are ideal.

      ~To read aloud; around the campfire at sleep-away camps, or to those we love and want to grow with us.

Counselors and therapists find this is a quick way to give clients a basic platform of knowledge from which to grow.

The Mission of This Book

I want to distribute copies to as many underprivileged young people as I can, at little or no cost. If we can influence them to make seven different decisions in the course of their lives, based on the philosophies of the great thinkers quoted herein, we will have accomplished some small good in changing our world. Twenty percent, or more, of the profits from <u>Lightning Fast Enlightenment</u> go to distributing free copies. If you would like to donate or help with this effort I would love to hear from you.

If you know of someone who really needs the ideas in this book, but can't afford a copy — write me with the story and I'll see what I can do.

Speaking Engagements

Jordan S. Metzger is available to speak on the many subjects in <u>Lightning Fast Enlightenment</u>, including:

-Why The Wise are Happy
-Thought Sculptures Destiny
-Flexibility vs. Planning
-Life is Short — Time is Fleeting
-Doubt vs. Faith
-Say Little — Do Much
-No Procrastination
-Brotherhood — One World
-Optimism vs. Pessimism
-Being Centered
-Savoring the Moment
-Living in the Here & Now

-Full Circle to Enlightenment
-Habits & Tradition
-Reality Is But Isn't
-Smile — Laugh at life
-Cause & Effect
-Troubles — Pain
-Regret & Worry
-No Fear
-More Risks
-Kindness
-Freedom

-Death
-Humility
-Healing
-Hard Work
-Persistence
-First Failures
-Free Will
-Money
-Love
-Hate

You may book him through:

Profound Press™
21 Seward Street,
Saratoga Springs, NY 12866
or
www.profoundpress.com
or

Call: Toll free **1-(888)-777-4065**

Book Orders

Lightning Fast Enlightenment is a great present for any one who is feeling down.

It's easy to order copies of <u>Lightning Fast Enlightenment</u> for friends, classes, or clients, just follow the directions below:

Use our Toll free hotline: 1-(888)-777-4065
For telephone orders and more information or
Outside of the USA, call: 1-(518)-584-0900
or
On-Line orders: www.profoundpress.com
or
Use the form below for mail orders:

Price: Each copy is only $18.95 plus shipping, call for special rates on bulk orders of 7 or more.

Domestic Shipping: $3.00 + $1.00 for each additional book. Please call for immediate delivery, international rates, and bulk orders.

Sales Tax, California residents only: Please add 7.75% sales tax.

Payment

Number of Copies ordered: _____ X $18.95 =

Sub Total: _____+
CA Tax, 7.75% (If applicable): _____+
Shipping (See above): _____=

TOTAL DUE: _____

<u>Please indicate payment method:</u>
____Check Enclosed ____Money Order Enclosed ____Visa
____MasterCard
Card Number: _____
Name on card: _____
Expires on: _____
Mailing Address: _____
_____
Phone Number: _____

Mail orders to: Profound Press, 21 Seward Street, Saratoga Springs, NY 12866

Don't Be A Stranger

Stop by and chat. We would like to know how this book has effected you. We're interested in your responses, comments, and experiences. Contact us by mail, or visit Jah at our Web Site:

www.profoundpress.com

~~~*~~~

Remember: "A person needs a book to pick up, when he needs a book to pick him up."

Jordan S. Metzger

~~~*~~~